The Wake of ⌐

The Miss Firecracker Contest

The Lucky Spot

Abundance

BETH HENLEY

$\mathcal{F}$OUR PLAYS

The Wake of Jamey Foster

The Miss Firecracker Contest

The Lucky Spot

Abundance

HEINEMANN/METHUEN

Heinemann Educational Books, Inc.
361 Hanover Street
Portsmouth, NH 03801-3959
Offices and agents throughout the world

Methuen Ltd.
Michelin House
81 Fulham Road
London SWI GRB

Library of Congress Cataloging-in-Publication Data

Henley, Beth.
    [Plays. Selections]
    Beth Henley: four plays.
      p.   cm.
    Contents: The wake of Jamey Foster—The Miss Firecracker contest
    —The lucky spot—Abundance.
    ISBN 0-435-08612-X
    I. Title. II. Title: Four plays.
  PS3558.E4962A6   1992   92-4075
  812.54—dc20   CIP

Cover photo © 1992 by Rocky Schenck
Series design and cover by Jenny Jensen Greenleaf
Printed in the United States of America
92 93 94 95 96   10 9 8 7 6 5 4 3 2 1

CONTENTS

❖

INTRODUCTION

❖

BETH HENLEY:
STRAIGHT FROM THE HEART

When *Crimes of the Heart* opened at the Manhattan Theatre Club in New York in 1981, Beth Henley became the first woman to win the Pulitzer Prize in twenty-eight years.

And the world of playwrighting opened up for women.

Since that time, Beth Henley has continued to delight, surprise, and engage us with qualities that remain rare and remarkable, and, thus, will always be instantly recognizable, applauded, and cherished: an original mind, a mastery of craft, and a vibrant passion and relentless empathy for the human condition.

She denies being a poet, but her language is poetic. It is her heritage.

Born in Jackson, Mississippi, Beth Henley grew up watching her mother, Lydy Caldwell, star in many of the productions produced by the Jackson Community Theatre. She helped her mother learn her lines and loved attending the rehearsals. What better way to learn about writing than going over an accomplished master's work, repeatedly. What better way to learn how plays are put together than by sitting endlessly and patiently through years of rehearsals. These lessons were invaluable. By the time she got to college, she knew a lot more about the theatre than she was probably aware of.

Perhaps not since Northwestern University with Mike Nichols, Barbara Harris, et al, in attendance, has such a gifted group of artists landed in a collegiate setting as when Oscar winner Kathy Bates, Emmy winner Powers Boothe, Tony winner Judith Ivey, and Pulitzer Prize winner Beth Henley all attended Southern Methodist University. It was fellow playwright Frederick Bailey who later entered Beth's play *Crimes of the Heart* in the Louisville Play Contest, after his own play, *Bridgehead,* won the very first contest that the Actor's Theatre in Louisville ever had. Fellow classmate, Sharon Ullrick, first gave *Crimes of the Heart* to her agent, who turned it over to Gilbert Parker at William Morris, who has been Beth's agent ever since.

Who else was at Southern Methodist University then? Playwrights and actors, Jim McGrath and Jim McLure. Beth Henley collaborated with Mark Hardwick on *his* first musical.

It was also at Southern Methodist University that Beth Henley found Belita Moreno, who has the distinction of having had a part created specifically for her in every single play in this book: Katty in *The Wake of Jamey Foster,* Popeye in *The Miss Firecracker Contest,* Lacey in *The Lucky Spot,* Macon in *Abundance.*

These are, by the way, the same people you find around her dining room table Thanksgiving and Christmas.

Beth Henley fell in love with the theatre the first time she saw Chekhov. The impression took, for if she is to be compared to anyone, it is to him.

Her plays are classical in construction, in that they are centered around a problem that will eventually be resolved, but the crisis will take us into the hearts and souls, history and dilemmas, paradoxes, and confusions of the characters as they bicker, blunder, stumble, embrace, and fight their way toward resolutions and dignity.

What is utterly appealing is her dead-on refusal to make the people in her plays look any better (or any worse) than people do in real life. And if Beth Henley is anything, she is a realist. A romantic sees the world as they would like it to appear. A realist calls it like they see it. And anyway, what is required in any writer's work, is to sustain a tone, a point of view, to make us believe.

There is no mistaking Carnelle's need for acceptance in *Firecracker,* or Marshael's grief and rage in *The Wake,* or Cassidy, Sue Jack, and Reed's needs for new beginnings in *The Lucky Spot.*

We shudder at their mishaps and embrace their resolutions because we have been there. We identify. We, too, are trying to get it right, to make sense of our lives. We don't have to have made frog clothes to feel like Popeye. We know what it's like to need to win a contest, to capture respect. We've seen death and been angry at the ones who died in spite of whether it was self-imposed, accidental or one of those acts of God. We've been spurned by lovers and fought with all our underhanded souls with every trick in the book to get the despicable, loathsome, onery, subhuman slugs back again. And again.

And if we have lived long enough, we have started out with hopes and dreams, perhaps only to get what we never had the insight to fear.

Abundance. What a triumph of writing. Four people's twenty-year life span given to us in two epic-filled hours. What a monumental tour de force for actors and audience. What an endless plethora of treasured challenges. Frank Rich called *Abundance* Beth Henley's "most provocative play." It is. It is profoundly moving. It is thickly, masterfully textured, the layers brilliantly constructed, mesmerizingly unfolding, culminating in a heart-breakingly human epic. It is extraordinarily ambitious and it is distinctly successful; the text meets its challenges.

Beth Henley is as daring and challenging in what she asks of herself as a writer, as she is discriminating and rigorous in protecting herself as an artist. Moreover, she is supportive of other artists. When my son, Caley, decided to try playwrighting at Oxford, he called Beth on the telephone. "How do you write a play?" he asked. "Well," she said, "just take two characters and get them in an argument...."

CAMILLA CARR
Santa Monica, California
November 24, 1991

THE WAKE OF JAMEY FOSTER

World Premiere at Hartford Stage Company, Hartford, Connecticut.

THE WAKE OF JAMEY FOSTER was presented on Broadway by FDM Productions, Francois De Menil/Harris Maslansky, Elliot Martin, Ulu Grosbard, Nan Pearlman and Warner Theatre Productions Inc. at the Eugene O'Neill Theatre, in New York City, on October 14, 1982. It was directed by Ulu Grosbard; the setting was by Santo Loquasto; costumes were by Jennifer von Mayrhauser; lighting was by Jennifer Tipton; sound was by David Rapkin; and the associate producer was Arla Manson. The cast, in order of appearance, was as follows:

MARSHAEL FOSTER ....Susan Kingsley
LEON DARNELL ....Stephen Tobolowsky
KATTY FOSTER ....Belita Moreno
WAYNE FOSTER ....Anthony Heald
COLLARD DARNELL ....Patricia Richardson
PIXROSE WILSON ....Holly Hunter
BROCKER SLADE ....Brad Sullivan

SYNOPSIS OF SCENES

The action of the play takes place throughout Marshael Foster's house and yard in Canton, Mississippi.

ACT I

Scene 1: Morning
Scene 2: Supper Time

ACT II

Scene 1: Late that night
Scene 2: Throughout the night
Scene 3: The following morning

"FOR MAYPOE AND CHARLIE"

THE CAST

MARSHAEL FOSTER, 33, Jamey's widow
LEON DARNELL, 25, Marshael's brother
KATTY FOSTER, 29, Wayne's wife
WAYNE FOSTER, 29, Jamey's brother; Katty's husband
COLLARD DARNELL, 30, Marshael's sister
PIXROSE WILSON, 17, Leon's friend; an orphan
BROCKER SLADE, 53, Marshael's friend

THE SETTING

The entire action of the play takes place at Marshael Foster's house. The rooms that are visible are: the parlor; the front hall with stairs leading to the upstairs hall; Marshael's bedroom; and an outside area along the right side of the house. The house is an old rambling country home that is in distinct disrepair with faded drapes, peeling paint, old furniture, worn out rugs, etc. Throughtout the house books, papers, journals, etc. are scattered about, as evidence of Jamey's excessive though incomplete historical research. In the front hall there is a grandfather clock, a love seat, and a card table with chair that has been temporarily set out for the occasion. There is a front door Up Center. There is also a door that leads to the parlor. The furniture in the parlor has been rearranged to leave a vacant space for the expected

3

coffin. Several funeral wreaths and flower arrangements surround this area. The second door in the front hall, which is Stage Left, is a dining room door that leads to the rest of the downstairs. Upstairs the hallway has one exit leading to Marshael's bedroom. The bedroom is by far the most cluttered room in the house. There is a bed, a vanity with stool, a chaise lounge, a table with a world globe, a sewing machine, a dress dummy, a clothes rack with pink and gold drill team outfits on it in different stages of completion, and several boxes of household improvement items that are stacked against the wall. There is also a closet, a door leading to the bathroom, an Upstage window, and a balcony Stage Right. The Upstage window looks out onto the front yard. The balcony looks over the side yard. In the outside area there is a tree that grows at least as high as the balcony.

THE TIME

Spring

ACT I

Scene 1

*The lights go up on stage. It is morning. Upstairs,
Marshael Foster, 33, is sitting on her bed. She is
thin with shoulder length, curly hair and deep set
haunted eyes. She wears a black dress. Marshael pulls
a chocolate Easter rabbit out of an Easter basket and
bites off the top of its ears. She has another bite,
then rises, picks up a ladies' magazine and drops
back down onto her bed. She lies glancing through
the magazine; gnawing on the ears of the chocolate
rabbit.*

KATTY'S VOICE. (*Offstage.*) Go on and set them in there
with the other flowers. (*Leon Darnell, 25, enters the front
hall from the dining room. Leon is tall and gangly. He wears
a white shirt and a dark skinny tie with black Sunday pants
that are a bit high-waisted. He carries two large flower arrangements that he is swinging haphazardly about.*)
LEON. Where?! (*Katty Foster, 29, follows him into the
room carrying a small arrangement of flowers in a basket.*

5

Katty is pretty in a baby-doll-matron sort of way. She is still wearing a beehive hairdo that was popular when she was in college.)

KATTY. I'll arrange them myself. You just set them down there. In the parlor.

LEON. (*As he moves into the parlor.*) All right! Fine. 'Cause my angel is arriving today!

KATTY. (*Setting her basket down.*) These'll look real nice right out here on the card table by the memorial book—don't you think?

LEON. (*Swinging the baskets of flowers around the parlor.*) 'Cause she's riding in to see me.

KATTY. Do you think that we should serve the mourners any refreshments?

LEON. Riding in on the Greyhound express!

KATTY. Do you suppose just assorted beverages will do? I don't know what's called for—I've never done all this before—Oh no, Leon; not there! We have to leave some room. (*She moves the flowers away from the area reserved for the coffin.*)

LEON. Well, look, I'm going. I gotta get those soda bottles cashed in—got a car load.

KATTY. Oh, wait, Leon! Has anyone heard further from your sister, Collard?

LEON. Due in yesterday; that's the latest. Ah! (*He steps on a large tack and sits down to pull it out of his shoe.*)

KATTY. (*Arranging the flowers.*) Oh, mercy, I hope she's all right. Heavens knows, she should be used to driving up and down the highways of this state. But life is so full of unknown horror—

LEON. (*Pulling out a tack with a pocket knife.*) Collard's coming, she said she's coming—She always comes home when anybody dies. Wow! Look at the size of that tack!

KATTY. Why, here, let me throw that thing away! Where'd it come from, anyway?

LEON. (*Pondering his shoe.*) It's Pixrose I'm anxious on.

KATTY. Why, she's not due in till twelve noon? (*About*

the tack.) Maybe it dropped out of one of these folding chairs.

LEON. It's just—It's just I love her so much! I do. I love her. Oh, and she loves me too. She does. Is my hair looking funny down in front where Margarite Roper yanked out that handful?

KATTY. It could stand a comb.

LEON. (*Pulling out his comb.*) See, we're exactly alike. Pixrose and me. We're exactly the same. Both of us enjoy public transportation and both of us have bumps right here on our heads. (*Showing her.*) Look! We do! We do!

WAYNE'S VOICE. (*Offstage.*) Katty! Katty! Katherine! (*Wayne Foster appears on the upstairs landing, as Katty and Leon move into the front hall. Wayne, 29, is an attractive man with cold, nervous eyes.*)

KATTY. (*Overlapping.*) What?! Yes, darling! What?!

WAYNE. (*Running on.*) My cuff links—the silver ones with the monograms. Did you forget to pack them?

KATTY. Why, I hope not. Did you check your little jewel case.

WAYNE. I've checked everything—all the luggage! Look, here, my cuff are totally undone!

KATTY. Well, now, I'll go take a look myself.

WAYNE. And nobody's doing a thing about Marshael's children. She's supposed to be getting them dressed! One's got gum all stuck in it's ears and hair—

KATTY. Oh, dear, Leon, quick, you bring me those scissors from in there. (*Leon goes to get scissors from the parlor. As she straightens his collar.*) Now just hush down, Honey Lamb. Why we're all gonna do every little bitty thing we can do to unburden poor, old Papa Sweet Potato.

LEON. (*Slinging the scissors.*) Here, catch!

WAYNE. My God!

KATTY. (*Overlapping.*) Leon!

WAYNE. And just what is he doing inviting strange house quests over, as if we don't have misery enough to deal with?!

KATTY. She's not a house guest, Angel Cake, she's a homeless refugee.

LEON. She's my girl!

WAYNE. I don't care what she is. I need my time of grief. I need my solitude. God.

KATTY. I know. Of couse, you do. It's awful. But try to be charitable, darling. Two entire wings of that orphanage were destroyed, and it seems Leon is the only obliging friend that child has.

WAYNE. Friend?! Ha! He hardly knows her.

LEON. Hardly know her?! Ha! Why, I've kissed her!

KATTY. Oh, please, now, honey, go on and force yourself to eat some breakfast. It'll do you good. I'll go up and check on those children and find your cuff links for you. (*On her way upstairs.*) I know I packed them. They gotta be there. (*She exits down the upstairs hall.*)

LEON. (*Turning back to face Wayne.*) And guess what? We both hate Dr. Peppers and Orange Crushes are our favorite beverage. Both of us.

WAYNE. Forget it, Leon. I'm sorry. I'm on the edge here. You understand. It's been a blow.

LEON. Yeah. I'm lucky. I never had a brother. Well, gotta go cash in them bottles.

WAYNE. Leon, would you wait here a minute?

LEON. What is it?

WAYNE. I just wanted to know what all went on with Marshael yesterday afternoon over at the funeral parlor? I mean what all did she decide on?

LEON. Well, not much. 'Cept she said for me to handle it, and so I did. I handled it all.

WAYNE. You mean, she left the arrangements entirely in your hands? She let you settle on everything—all by yourself?

LEON—Yeah. 'Cept for the coffin. She pointed at it and said, "That's the one." Then she tells me she needs to get home and dye up some Easter eggs; so I'm supposed to handle it all. And I did too. Precisely that.

WAYNE. Well, I certainly would have hoped that the

details and arrangements of my only brother's funeral would have concerned his wife more than coloring up a batch of goddamn Easter eggs! (*Upstairs, Marshael puts down the bunny, leaves the bedroom and exits up the hall.*)

LEON. Now look here, Willie Wayne, I handled it all. Picked out a nice cheerful suit for Jamey to be wearing here today. Took down a dress shirt and matching tie. Why, I even signed him up for a shave, shampooing and manicure. He's gonna look his best.

WAYNE. It's just I—I want it done proper. He's my brother. I want things done with class and dignity and respect.

LEON. Well, I'm the one you want in charge then. See, I ordered this memorial book here and a solid blanket of roses for the coffin. Why, tommorrow we've got us a limousine being escorted by a policeman on a motorcycle. I even got us black arm bands to pass out and black veils for the ladies I got the works! No need to worry, Willie Wayne. No need at all.

COLLARD'S VOICE. (*Offstage*) Hello! Wooh! Hey, I made it! I'm home! How's Mashy?! (*The front door flies open and Collard Darnell enters in a muddy red evening gown and a pair of men's cowboy boots that are several sizes too large. She carries a large straw bag. Her hair is wild and her face is dirty. She is thirty years old.*)

LEON. (*Overlapping.*) Collard! You?! Collard Greens! Collard Greens!!

COLLARD. (*Overlapping as she hugs him.*) Leon! Baby boy! Baby boy!

LEON. I told you she'd make it! I told ya!

COLLARD. (*Stopping.*) Well, hi ya, Willie Wayne! Let's see, car exploded; suitcase stolen; and shoes stuck in the Memphis mud. It's funny, Willie Wayne, but I always know just what you're gonna say even before you open your mouth.

WAYNE. I wasn't gonna say anything, Collard. Nothing you do surprises me much less your lack of concern for your bereaved sister. Excuse me, but I've got to go see if I can

9

force some breakfast down this lump in my throat. (*He exits out the dining room door.*)

COLLARD. How do people get like that? How the hell do they do it?

LEON. Must be born to it.

COLLARD. I suppose he's not even gonna acknowledge the Get Well Soon card I sent t'Jamey. Pompous little pig. Shit. Well, home again, home again, jigady jig. (*Pause.*) So Jamey's really dead?

LEON. Looks like it.

COLLARD. How's Marshy taking it?

LEON. Seems t'be doing all right.

COLLARD. Well, shit. So how'd it happen? Willie Wayne's giving me this song and dance about some sorta head injury. Didn't sound all that serious when I got the call last Sunday.

LEON. Well, I guess it was pretty serious cause by Wednesday noon he's dead.

COLLARD. Jesus.

LEON. Seems that head injury he'd acquired caused him to have a stroke Tuesday evening, paralyzing one half of his entire body. Then Wednesday 'bout noon time . . .

COLLARD. (*Finding her cigarettes.*) Lord. So how'd he get this head injury? He run into some wood post?

LEON. No, he's kicked in the head by a cow.

COLLARD. He's what?!

LEON. Right out in the field over by Cambden on Highway 17. I suppose he'd had quite a load t'drink.

COLLARD. Out boozing in a field and gets kicked in the head by a cow. What the hell was he doing out there?

LEON. Chasing cows, I guess.

COLLARD. Holy Church of the Lord. You got a light?

LEON. (*Moving into the parlor.*) In here. There are matches galore right here in this dish—

COLLARD. (*Entering the parlor.*) What's all this? What's happening here? What's all the crap? Jesus!

LEON. They're setting up for the exhibition of the body—for the wake.

COLLARD. A wake? Here? In this house? Aren't they going to use a funeral home like most decent, civilized folks?

LEON. Jamey's mother wanted it here. She says that's how it's been done for generations in her family up in north Mississippi 'round Tubler.

COLLARD. God. Poor Marshy. She must be going to pieces 'bout now.

LEON. Well, I'm seeing that she's gonna have some close personal relatives and friends t'help t'get her through this long and desolate night.

COLLARD. (*Looking around slowly at the flowers.*) Close relatives? Swell, like Willie Wayne and his bee-hive wife.

LEON. Well, yeah, there's them and there's you and also I've called in Mr. Brocker Slade.

COLLARD. Who's he?

LEON. Close personal friend of Marshael's. He built her them new red kitchen chairs. You'll like him for sure. He's done it all. Everything. He's eaten certified dog meat in China and he's got tattoos up and down his arms and legs both.

COLLARD. (*Still dazed by all the flowers.*) Sounds remarkable t'me.

LEON. Oh, he's absolutely your style of person. I told him to please come over and help stand guard over the body here tonight. Just by chance peculiar things start t'happening.

COLLARD. (*With a shudder.*) Well, I'll just bet our Mama and Daddy are rolling over in their sweet graves right about now at the thought of those North Mississippi dirt farmers bringing a rotting old carcass right into our very home.

LEON. Well, it ain't our home anymore.

COLLARD. No, not since Jamey Foster took it over lock, stock, and barrel with his dusty books and pamphlets and idiotic papers. Imagine, we used to play dominoes right down here on this torn up rug.

LEON. You and me live other places now.

COLLARD. Oh, I know it. It's these bright flowers here giving me the jumping jitters. They make the whole place look morbid and scary. Now look here, I'm practically on the verge of tears.

LEON. Why, Collard. Collard Greens, what's wrong? I'll save ya.

COLLARD. (*Crying.*) Oh, it's nothing. Just I—I really could have been here earlier to help Marshy out with things —I told her I'd be here, but it's my Easter vacation, you know, and I didn't want t'spend the time watching some man die in a hospital. Shit. I already tried doing that with Daddy.

LEON. Well, nobody was for sure he'd die. Nobody guessed it.

COLLARD. (*Wiping her eyes with her red skirt.*) But even after I knew he was already dead, I went on up t'Memphis for a wild party. That's why I didn't make it home yesterday. I'm a shit. A hopeless shit! Oh, but you should see the car G.W. Porter lent me t'get down here in—a beautiful, white, Cadillac convertible.

LEON. No kidding?

COLLARD. Go on and take a look at it. It's parked out there in the street. See it?

LEON. Wow!! A cloud! Why, it looks just like a big, fat white cloud! Can I—Could I go out—

COLLARD. No, you can't! Don't even touch it! I can't afford t'get it all smudged up.

LEON. But I could sit in it, couldn't I? Just sit in it. I mean, when my girl comes—My girl! Oh, brother, I gotta go get those bottles turned on in. (*Racing to the front hall.*)

COLLARD. What girl? What bottles? What're you talking? (*She follows him into the front hall.*)

LEON. My girl, Pixrose, she's arriving at twelve noon. I gotta get those empty bottles turned on in so I can afford t'get her a precious remembrance.

COLLARD. (*In the front hall.*) Jesus, are you back t'gathering up those goddam coke bottles?! What happened to your paper route?

LEON. Why, Collard Greens, you're not up to date. I have

12

me a permanent full time job now. Them bottles are strictly sideline. Well, I gotta run, Marshael wants me back before they arrive with—well, with the body. See ya!

COLLARD. Yeah. (*Leon exits slamming the door, Katty enters through the upstairs hallway. She carries the cufflinks.*)

KATTY. Wayne?! Baby, I found your silver—(*Spotting Collard as she comes down the stairs.*) Why, Collard! Honey, when did you arrive? We were so anxious for your safety— Why, my you're—all dressed in red.

COLLARD. It's the only stitch I got, Katty. Rest a my clothes was filched up in Memphis.

KATTY. Filched? How utterly astounding. How astounding. What were you doing up in Memphis?

COLLARD. (*Uncomfortable.*) Oh, on a visit.

KATTY. Well, I just don't know what you're gonna wear. The people will be arriving from ten this morning on. Do you think you could find something of Marshael's that might be suitable? You see, the only clothes I brought are strictly organized. I mean, I'm wearing this outfit all day today, and then tomorrow I'm wearing my navy blue suit with my navy pumps and my navy dress hat with the white piping.

COLLARD. Forget it Katty, I'll manage.

KATTY. But, of course now, if you feel you could fit into my navy outfit, I suppose you could wear it today. I mean, you're welcome to try it.

COLLARD. (*Going into the parlor.*) It's all right.

KATTY. (*Following her.*) I could wash and iron it out tonight so I could still wear it tomorrow morning for the funeral. That is if Marshael has all the cleaning apparatus that I'll be needing.

COLLARD. Look, Katty, I don't want to wear your navy suit. I don't like navy. It reminds me too much of blue.

KATTY. Well, pardon me, I'm sure. I was just trying to be gracious. (*Pause.*) We're all overwrought. (*Pause.*) Reverand Rigby says sudden violent deaths are the most difficult to deal with. (*Pause.*) So, how's your job going?

COLLARD. Swell, I'm on vacation from it.

KATTY. Oh, right. How stupid of me. How could you be taking school portraits of the children when they're all out for their Easter holidays.

COLLARD. It'd be hard.

KATTY. (*Laughing.*) Oh, it would be. I tell you. I've always envied your job. How you get to travel all over the state—going to all the public and parochial schools—taking pictures of those precious children—thinking up amusing tricks to make them smile—driving in a company car—seeing the world.

COLLARD. Right.

KATTY. Oh, by the by, Mother Foster asked me to see if I could implore you to take some memorial pictures for her of, well, of Jamey. Since you're the professional in the family, we thought you could do them really nicely.

COLLARD. Well, I didn't bring my photographic equipment home with me—

KATTY. Oh, that's alright. We've got a camera right here that's got a flash attachment for the indoors and everything. You could take the shots as soon as the body arrives—before we open up the room for all the mourners.

COLLARD. I'm sorry, Katty. I—I just don't like t'look at dead people. Look, I gotta go change. I'm tired. I gotta lie down.

KATTY. Oh, Collard, wait! Wayne and I are staying in your old room. (*Collard stops.*) We moved James Jr. in with his sisters. Course the children are all going over to your Aunt Muffin's for tonight. That way they won't have to be here with the wake and all going on. It might could frighten little children.

COLLARD. It might could.

KATTY. Anyway, this friend of Leon's coming in and she's gonna stay up in the children's room. That means you'll be sleeping with Marshael in her room for tonight. I'm sure she can use the company.

COLLARD. Fine.

KATTY. (*Trying to grab hold of Collard's straw bag.*) Here, let me help you with your bag? You look tired.

COLLARD. I got it.

KATTY. No, really—I'll get it—

COLLARD. Katty—(*A few things fall from the bag, among them a small pink sack.*)

KATTY. Oh, mercy, here—some things dropped out. Here you go. Just call me butter fingers.

COLLARD. (*About the sack.*) Oh, well, that's for you anyway, if you want it.

KATTY. For me? How thoughtful. (*She opens the sack.*) Why, look, it's a pair of spring booties with sweet, little yellow ribbons.

COLLARD. I saw 'em in a store window. I thought with the baby coming in the winter—maybe it'd be able to wear 'em by next spring.

KATTY. (*Shaken.*) Oh, well, thank you, Collard. But I lost the baby. It's not gonna be coming. I don't know what t'do with the present I—I guess I'll just give it back t'you.

COLLARD. Katty.

KATTY. I gotta go see to Marshael's kids. I gotta go get 'em ready. (*She exits down the upstairs hall.*)

COLLARD. Katty—(*Slinging the booties back in her bag.*) Jesus! (*She takes a deep breath and opens the door to Marshael's room.*) Marshy? (*She is intensely relieved to find no one is there. She takes a moment to notice the rack of marching costumes, sighs, then drops her bag down and sinks onto the bed. There is a knock at the front door. Collard pulls a boot off and slings it against the wall. A second knock is heard. Collard slings off her other boot. After a third knock Wayne enters from the dining room carrying a cloth napkin and a half eaten piece of toast.*)

WAYNE. What's wrong around here? Doesn't anyone have the good manners to open a door? Must I do it all? Everything?! (*He opens the door. Pixrose Wilson, 17, stands on the other side holding a small torn up suitcase. Pixrose wears red stockings and a long sleeved dress. She has sunken eyes, long, stringy hair and white, white skin.*) Hello. Oh. Won't you come in.

PIXROSE. Much obliged.

WAYNE. I'm Wayne Foster, the, ah, brother of the deceased.

PIXROSE. I'm Pixrose Wilson from the Sacred Heart Orphonage Asylum.

WAYNE. Yes, well, we're glad to have you, Prissrose.

PIXROSE. It's Pix. Like fix.

WAYNE. Oh, of course, Pix. Here, let me take your luggage for you.

PIXROSE. Thank you, sir. That's very obliging.

WAYNE. Well, why don't you come into the parlor and take a seat. (*They start into the parlor.*) I don't believe Leon was expecting you till about twelve noon.

PIXROSE. Well, I started early and got myself a ride on back of a milk truck. That way I was able to save my bus fare in it's entirety.

WAYNE. That's very economical of you. They do say "A penny saved is a penny earned."

PIXROSE. Is this where they're gonna be setting down the body?

WAYNE. Why, yes. I, ah, hope you don't find it too upsetting.

PIXROSE. What's that?

WAYNE. A, well, a body. The presence of a body in the house.

PIXROSE. (*With a silght, slight shrug.*) It won't be going nowhere.

WAYNE. Well, ah, it is regrettable, Pixrose, that your, ah, stay falls at what is a time of grave personal tragedy for our family. I do hope that you'll be able to bear with us through our grief. Won't you have a seat? (*Pause.*) Leon should be returning any minute. Probably very soon. He'll be back. Would you like some breakfast?

PIXROSE. No, sir.

WAYNE. How about some coffee?

16

PIXROSE. I appreciate it, sir, but I don't believe I'm feeling thirsty.

WAYNE. Hmm. Well, we were all very distressed to hear about the fire over at the orphanage. It appears the damage was quite extensive.

PIXROSE. Yes. It's a terrible crime—arson.

WAYNE. Arson? Was it actually arson?

PIXROSE. Oh, no doubt in my mind.

WAYNE. Arson. How loathesome, inflicting misery and terror on a group of helpless children.

PIXROSE. Well, fortunately, I was able to drop some of the small infants out from the windows and down into the azalea bushes below.

WAYNE. It must have been quite a terrifying episode for you.

PIXROSE. Why, it certainly was. Particularly as I've been afflicted by fire most of my entire life.

WAYNE. How do you mean?

PIXROSE. Well it started out my mama hating the house we lived in. She used t'say it was trashy. She'd sit around in the dark holding lit matches—always threatening to burn this trashy house down—and one day she did it. She lit up the dining room curtains, loosing flames over the entire house and charcoaling herself to death as a final result.

WAYNE. My God.

PIXROSE. It's a terrible crime, arson. Caused me t'get burns all over the lower parts of my body.

WAYNE. (Rubbing his forehead.) That's horrible.

PIXROSE. (Pulling at her stockings.) Well, I can cover up the scars by wearing these leg stockings.

WAYNE. I see.

PIXROSE. I just wish my arms hadn't caught on fire in that automobile explosion. I used t'like to look at 'em. But, of course, my daddy, he died an instantaneous death, and my brother, Franky suffered permanent brain damage; so I guess I was just lucky t'be flung burning from outta the car. That explosion was also diagnosed as deliberate arson.

17

WAYNE. I don't feel well. My nose——

PIXROSE. Arson . . . It's a terrible, terrible crime.

WAYNE. Excuse me. I'm bleeding. I apologize. (*About his nose.*) This damnable business. How disturbing. This is extreme. (*The phone begins ringing, as he runs out of the room bringing the napkin up to his massively bloody nose. Upstairs Collard throws a pillow over her head. As he exits out the dining room.*) I can't get it now—I can't do everything! My nose . . . it's—It's sickening. (*The phone stops ringing. Pixrose goes to look at the drops of blood that have fallen from Wayne's nose. Marshael appears on the upstairs landing. Pixrose gently presses the drops of blood into the carpet with the toe of her shoe then goes to sit down on the sofa. Marshael goes into her bedroom. Collard turns to see her.*)

MARSHAEL. Collard! Coll, you're home! You're here! You're home!

COLLARD. (*Overlapping as she jumps out of bed.*) Marshy! Marshy! Marsh! Are you doing all right? How are you doing?

MARSHAEL. (*Opening her mouth.*) Look—look, here—canker sores! All over my mouth! I'm in pain; I'm not kidding: I'm about to die! Do you see 'em? They're all purple and swollen

COLLARD. God. Well—Well, get yourself some salt water and start t'gargling. That looks awful!

MARSHAEL. Oh, hell, I've been gargling my mouth raw, but just to no avail. Well, so you're looking awfully fine. I see ya came dressed for the occasion.

COLLARD. (*Uncomfortable.*) Yeah, well, I gotta borrow something a somebody's. (*Getting up to get a cigarette.*) Hey. I'm sorry I'm late. I don't mean t'keep relentlessly letting everyone down. Some unavoidable circumstances.

MARSHAEL. Doesn't matter.

COLLARD. Now that I'm here I'll try to help out. What needs to be done?

MARSHAEL. Nothing.

COLLARD. I could order some flowers or call up a church or something.

MARSHAEL. It's all taken care of.

COLLARD. Well, I'll try not to screw things up. (*About the costumes on the clothes rack.*) God, what the hell's all this?

MARSHAEL. Oh, my costumes. I'm making the marching dresses for all of next year's Prancing' Ponies.

COLLARD. Jesus, they're still using those same awful colors. And look, they've still got the same tacky tassels and vests to go with 'em. Praise God, I always had sense enough to stay out of that fascist organization. How many of these ya gotta make?

MARSHAEL. Oh, this is only the beginning you see right here. I've got about twenty more t'cut out.

COLLARD. Well, you're mighty industrious.

MARSHAEL. You're telling me (*Kicking a sealed box.*) Look, here, I've even taken to selling household improvement ornaments.

COLLARD. What're they?

MARSHAEL. Oh, you know; things like wall light fixtures and decorative place mats—salt and pepper shakers shaped like crocodiles. A load of junk.

COLLARD. When'd you start doing all this?

MARSHAEL. Been at it a long while. Gotta keep busy. I, ah, can show you the catalogue if you want—(*She gets catalogue.*)

COLLARD. No, that's all right. I don't use place mats.

MARSHAEL. Oh . . . Sure.

COLLARD. (*Pause.*) So. Well. Gosh. I'm sorry.

MARSHAEL. Yeah. Well. Heck.

COLLARD. He was a real smart man. I know he would have been able to publish his work in time. He was just so awfully young.

MARSHAEL. You think? Nah. he's thirty-five. He'd put on plenty of weight and started losing his hair. He'd even developed this sorta rash all over his knuckles. He'd always get nervous and start t'rubbing it. He wasn't that young. Everyone's saying he died so young. He wasn't really. He'd changed alot.

COLLARD. Well, I didn't mean to imply he was a spring chicken or anything.

MARSHAEL. No. (*Pause.*)Oh, do you hear those birds chirping outside.

COLLARD. Yeah.

MARSHAEL. They're right out my window. They've made a nest down there on the ledge. Go on and look. (*Collard goes to the window.*) See it. I saw some eggs in their nest. They were speckled.

COLLARD. Oh . . . I see it. Yes. Your very own bird's nest. (*Katty comes down the hall and knocks at Marshael's door. She carries a blue satin ribbon.*)

KATTY. Marshael, honey?

MARSHAEL. Yes?

KATTY. (*Entering the bedroom.*) Hi. Listen, Mr. Mommett called from the funeral home. He said the hearst is on its way. They should be arriving any minute.

MARSHAEL. All right.

KATTY. I'll go downstairs to greet them.

MARSHAEL. That's good.

KATTY. Oh, one more thing. Do you mind me twisting Cherry Lee's braids up into a bun on top of her head? She said she likes the way it looks.

MARSHAEL. No, I appreciate it, Katty. It's real nice of you.

KATTY. Good. Then I'll go on and put the bow in it. Bye bye now. (*Katty exits. Collard starts to pull at her hair.*)

COLLARD. (*In a whisper.*) God. Rip out my soul.

MARSHAEL. What?

COLLARD. Tear out my heart with jagged glass.

MARSHAEL. What—

COLLARD. Oooh, I just gave Katty baby booties—for her new baby.

MARSHAEL. Oh, God, no one told you? She lost the baby about three weeks ago. It makes her third miscarriage.

COLLARD. It does?

MARSHAEL. She keeps going out to that fertility clinic, but it never seems to work out for her.

COLLARD. I could die.

MARSHAEL. Oh, it's not your fault. You didn't know. I should have called you.

COLLARD. But you know, the funny thing is, Marshy . . . I sensed it. For some reason I sensed she'd lost it. But I just gave her the booties anyway.

MARSHAEL. Why would you do that?

COLLARD. I don't know. I'm a black sheep. A black, black soul. (*A car is heard pulling up.*)

MARSHAEL. (*Rushing out onto the balcony.*) God, that's probably them. Oh, it is! I don't believe it! Look at that horrible black car. This whole thing's a joke! I could just about eat fire! So this is how he finally returns to the house. It's so humiliating. So cheap.

COLLARD. (*Overlapping.*) What are you saying? Marshy, what's wrong?

MARSHAEL. Oh, he'd abandoned me. Four months ago. Abandonment.

COLLARD. He did? But you never said. You never called me. I wish you'd call me.

MARSHAEL. Well, I just kept thinking if the blood ever dried he'd be back home. Foolish notion. I got over it. Filed for divorce not two weeks ago. Now he pulls this little stunt. Thinks he can leave it all in my lap to sort out and make right. Well, as you can see, I've got mixed emotions about the entire event.

COLLARD. I don't wonder you do. (*Leon enters from the dining room below.*)

LEON. Pixrose? Pixrose! I heard you'd arrived! They told me you'd arrived!

PIXROSE. I have, Leon! I'm here! Right here!

MARSHAEL. (*Hanging over the balcony railing.*) Look, there it comes—the box he's in. They're lifting it out of the car.

COLLARD. My God, they are!

LEON. (*Finding her in the parlor.*) Why, you've finally arrived.

PIXROSE. I know—I have. (*They stare at each other.*)

COLLARD. I hope they're careful. It looks awfully flimsy.

MARSHAEL. It oughta be. It was the cheapest pinebox they had. (*Lights fade to blackout. End of scene.*)

ACT I

Scene 2

It is evening. The door to the parlor is closed. Pixrose's suitcase has been removed. A cheap pine lift-lid coffin has been set up inside the room. The upper half of the lid has been removed from the case and left leaning against a nearby wall. Thus part of the corpse is visible. It wears a bright orange and yellow plaid jacket.

Marshael sits on the stairway in the front hall drinking a glass of gin and eating jelly beans that she carries in her dress pocket. After a moment, she throws a jellybean at the umbrella stand. It lands inside. She tries two more jellybeans that miss. She pauses a moment—looks at the closed parlor door and throws a jellybean at it. She goes back to drinking her gin.

Leon enters from the dining room L., carrying a plate and some silverware.

LEON. How ya doing?

MARSHAEL. Fine.

LEON. I brought out your food for you. You didn't touch nothing on your whole plate.

MARSHAEL. I'm not hungry.

LEON. I know, but ya need t'try and eat something. I swear, I haven't seen ya eat or sleep for three days now. Your eyes are blood red.

MARSHAEL. I feel fresh.

LEON. Just try some of your ham. It's awfully good. Annie Hart sent it over. Go on have a bite. Try it. You're gonna like it. (*A pause as he looks at her waiting for her to eat.*)

MARSHAEL. I can't eat with you watching over me. Go on back to the kitchen and finish your supper. Go on now, Leon. I'll eat it.

LEON. All right. (*He starts to leave, then stops.*) Hey, Marshael?

MARSHAEL. What?

LEON. Do you like Pixrose?

MARSHAEL. She's a real nice girl. Go on now, Leon. I'm gonna eat this ham. (*He exits. She waits a moment then begins messing the food around on her plate. Collard enters from the front door. She has changed into one of Leon's shirts and a pair of rolled up jeans. She has washed her face, but her hair is still a mess.*)

COLLARD. Hi.

MARSHAEL. Hi. Get the kids off okay?

COLLARD. Oh, sure. Aunt Muffin had frozen coca colas waiting for them and she's letting them watch TV till ten o'clock.

MARSHAEL. That's good.

COLLARD. (*Getting a cigarette from the carton that she has brought in with her.*) Oh shit, you know I forgot t'ask Aunt Muffin if I could borrow something of hers for the funeral. Jesus, I'm so unreliable it's almost perfect.

MARSHAEL. Oh, well. Never matters. We'll make do. So did the children really enjoy the ride over in the convertible?

COLLARD. Sure. I'll say. Lucy had a sack full of rocks she kept throwing out at cows as we passed by. She said she hates cows now and she wants to kill them all! I love that child. She reminds me of me.

MARSHAEL. Well, I hope she didn't hurt any of the poor animals.

COLLARD. Oh, no. Missed 'em by a mile. She just had to blow off steam, that's all. Don't blame her for that. Some miserable day, huh?

MARSHAEL. Sure was.

COLLARD. Lordy, Lord.

MARSHAEL. Katty kept going around pretending like we were giving some sort of ghastly tea party. "Here's a coaster and a fresh napkin for your drink. Do you need some more ice cubes? Oh, by the by, the deceased is residing in the parlor."

COLLARD. He's the one in the yellow plaid coat.

MARSHAEL. Agony, agony, agony.

COLLARD. Course now, Katty is a Windsor form North East Jackson. That makes her real quality folk.

MARSHAEL. Did you see the way Willie Wayne started tap dancing around when her daddy and uncles arrived to pay their respects?

COLLARD. I expected him to start passing out his business cards at any moment.

MARSHAEL. The thing I love about Willie Wayne is I can just totally despise him.

COLLARD. She's got him monogramed from top to toe—wearing those three piece business suits—

MARSHAEL. Don't forget his genuine cow leather brief-case—

COLLARD. He's moving up at the bank—

MARSHAEL. He ain't trash no more!

COLLARD. Speaking of trash—

MARSHAEL. Who?

COLLARD. Mother Foster and her humpbacked brother!

MARSHAEL. Please! If I hear the tale about—

COLLARD. What?

MARSHAEL. How she was just like her brother, Wilbur, had a hump growing in her back—but she prayed to God and He straightened up her back and at the same time made all her dandruff disappear.

COLLARD. Oh, no!

MARSHAEL. Yes!

COLLARD. What are you drinking?

MARSHAEL. Gin.

COLLARD. Where's the bottle? (*Suddenly a loud commotion is heard coming from the kitchen off L. Smoke comes pouring in from the kitchen. As she exits R.*) What the hell is that? What's all this smoke? (*Marshael takes a sip of her drink, Wayne enters in an uproar from U.C.*)

WAYNE. She's a firebug, a menace, a pyromaniac lunatic! (*Katty follows him into the room.*)

KATTY. Hush up! Hush up!

WAYNE. I don't wonder she's a third degree burn victim!

KATTY. Will you please hush up!

MARSHAEL. What happened?

KATTY. Nothing. Little grease fire in the kitchen.

WAYNE. I haven't even finished my dinner. That smoke'll never clear!

KATTY. (*Calling off L.*) Just bring your plates on in here! We'll eat in here! The dining room table's already set for tomorrow's buffet! (*Pixrose and Leon enter carrying their supper plates.*)

WAYNE. And she stays out of the parlor! There's flammable material in there. She stays away from it!

PIXROSE. I'm so sorry. I'm so sorry. I'm so sorry.

LEON. (*Overlapping.*) It's nobody's fault. That rag just burst into flames. Why it's no more your fault—(*Katty exits to the kitchen. Collard enters with the bottle of gin and two red kitchen chairs.*)

PIXROSE. (*Overlapping; to Wayne and Marshael.*) I'll pay for all the damages. Here, you can have my grandmama's garnet brooch. It's a priceless brooch. See—(*While trying to show the brooch, she manages to drop her plate and break*) it.) Oh, no! Oh, no!! Now my super plate is shattered! Look at the pieces! It's broken for life!

MARSHAEL. It's an old plate, Pixrose. For Heaven's sake! It doesn't even matter—

WAYNE. That girl is a menace! A total menace!

PIXROSE. (*Overlapping, as she tries to pick up the pieces.*) OH, oh, oh, oh, oh—

LEON. (*Overlapping.*) Look, here, you're making Pixrose unhappy! You're making her cry!! Don't cry!

PIXROSE. I'm just picking up the pieces. I've never been in people's homes.

COLLARD. Here, sit down, Pixrose. Sit down. Have some gin. Take a swallow.

WAYNE. Will somebody sit her down before she tears this place apart!? What's this I'm stepping on?! Looks like jelly beans! It's jelly beans! Oooh!! What next?! What next?!!

(*Wayne scrapes jelly beans off his shoes as Katty enters from the dining room with a tray of supper plates, glasses, etc.*)

KATTY. Here, everyone. We'll just finish our supper in here. We'll have a nice quiet supper in here. Oh, was there another accident?! For Heaven's sake!

MARSHAEL. It's all right, Katty—It's nothing at all. Just a stupid plate!

KATTY. Fine then. Just fine. Wayne, why don't you come sit down over here and finish your supper. (*Leon throws the broken pieces into a garbage can with a loud crash. There is a long moment of silence.*) I heard a very interesting piece of information this afternoon. (*Leon surreptitiously throws an English pea at Wayne. Wayne looks around.*) Mattey Bowen informed me that when you're buying canned stewed tomatoes the cheapest brand is actually preferable to the most expensive. (*Leon throws another pea at Wayne.*) You see, those cheaper brands move off the shelves at a much faster rate, and, therefore, they're the fresher product. (*Leon throws a third pea.*)

WAYNE. Are you throwing food at me? (*Leon throwing*

a pea at him.) He's throwing food at me! (*Leon slings a pea.*) Look at this! English peas! (*Leon is now openly throwing peas.*)

KATTY. Leon, really!

WAYNE. You'd better stop that! He'd better stop that! I mean it, by God!

COLLARD. For Heavens sake, Willie Wayne, it's just vegetables!

WAYNE. I don't care! I won't have it! This is a serious night! Give me that plate!

KATTY. (*Overlapping.*) Leon, please!

COLLARD. (*Overlapping.*) I don't believe he's having a conniption fit about a few vegetables!

WAYNE. I'll jerk you bald headed, boy! Give me that plate!

LEON. (*Throwing the rest of his food in Wayness's face.*) Here! I'm finished anyway. I cleaned my plate!

WAYNE. (*Taking the plate.*) What a brainless imbecile! I'm surprised they don't send him off to the moon!

LEON. He's always disliked me, ever since I was alive.

WAYNE. It's no surprise to me that you've never held down a job—have to live in a shack—

KATTY. Hush, now, honey—

WAYNE. Goes around picking up trash just for the fun of it. It near t'killed him when they brought out those no deposit bottles—cut his income clean in half. Isn't that so, Leon?

KATTY. Hush up, now, Wayne, darling. Leon has himself a permanent job now. Don't you dear?

COLLARD. Well, now, that's just wonderful.

WAYNE. First I've heard of it.

COLLARD. So, what do you do?

LEON. I work over at the chicken factory. I'm a turkey jerker.

COLLARD. A what?

LEON. A turkey jerker. They send them old turkey carcasses by on this conveyor belt, and I jerk out the turkey innards and put 'em in a sack. Have me an apron I wear and everything.

WAYNE. Classic! That is too classic! Suit the man to the job, that's what I always say! Make a turkey jerker out of a jerky turkey! Classic! (*Leon is hurt.*)

COLLARD. Oh, cute, Willie Wayne. You've always been so cute. Remember how cute Willie Wayne used to be when we'd wrap him up in white surgical bandages—make him into a mummy and roll him down the hill? He made the best damn mummy!

PIXROSE. How could he breathe?

WAYNE. For a girl who flunked out of Co-lin College you're awfully smart. Course everyone knows Collard is a real live genius. Her and her high IQ.

MARSHAEL.	COLLARD.	KATTY.
Just, please, don't start—	Yes, we all have beautiful histories —Don't we now?	Now, if we can't say something nice, let's not say anything at all.

MARSHAEL. Owww!!!

LEON. What?

MARSHAEL. I bit down on that damn sore in the side of my mouth.

KATTY. Anyway, we've got all sorts of pressing issues to debate. For instance, we've got to make a decision about who all is going to ride out to the graveyard tomorrow in the limousine.

COLLARD. What limousine?   LEON. I hired it. (*The phone begins to ring.*)

KATTY. I'm sorry to have to bring it up, but Mother Foster is very concerned about it.

KATTY. Will you be a papa sweet potato and get that?

WAYNE. All right.

LEON. Why does she talk to him in that funny voice? (*Collard shrugs. Wayne answers the phone.*)

WAYNE. Hello . . . Hi, mama, what's going on?

KATTY. (*Overlapping.*) Now Mother Foster and you and Wayne and I are supposed to all ride out in the limousine, but Mother Foster sincerely desires for James Jr. to ride along with us.

LEON. I'm going to get those Rice Krispie bars out from the kitchen. (*He exits U.C.*)

KATTY. (*Running on.*) She feels although he is the youngest of the children, he is the only son and Jamey's namesake. (*Collard gets up and pours some more gin.*) Of course, I don't mind where I ride. It makes no never mind to me. But Mother Foster just thought— (*To Wayne.*) Who was that, darling?

WAYNE. Mother Foster.

KATTY. What'd she want?

WAYNE. Ah, well, it seems that, ah, Uncle Wilbur split some gravy on his good suit; so, ah, he'll need to get something of Jamey's to wear tomorrow. Mama says they're close to the same size in a lot of ways.

KATTY. Well, I'll pick something out for him. Marshael's been real busy.

WAYNE. She, ah, said she'd prefer the blue-pin-striped suit. I don't know which one she means.

MARSHAEL. Well, it's okay. I know which one it is.

WAYNE. (*Uncomfortable.*) And she mentioned something about you picking out a few suits for Uncle Wilbur to take on back up to Tubler with him tomorrow; seeing as, well, as you won't have much future use for them.

MARSHAEL. Whatever she wants. I've no objections.

WAYNE. She's a very practical old bird.

COLLARD. Sure and there's some silverware in the sideboard and coffee in the cupboard while she's at it!

WAYNE. Look, don't make fun of my mama.

COLLARD. Why not?

WAYNE. It's just too easy to poke fun at a poor, old farm woman who had to move down here and sell mattresses just so her two small boys could eat. (*Collard makes like she's crying.*) Oh, sure, she's just some red necky hick to you! But what makes y'all so high and mighty? Just 'cause your father was some drunken lawyer. You never learned a damn thing!

Why just look at the way this funeral is being run. I've never stood and witnessed such a tawdry affair in all my born days. (*Leon enters with a plate of Rice Krispie bars.*)

LEON. Who sent the Rice Krispie bars? They sure are good!

WAYNE. Why look at him!! He's got Jamey wearing a plaid sports jacket, for Christ's sake! It's—it's a mockery to decorum!

LEON. You don't like that jacket? I thought it was cheerful.

WAYNE. A red nose is cheerful! And that coffin in there! It is a disgrace! You may as well of sent off for a mail order job, or just picked up a couple of orange crates over behind the A & P! What could have possessed you, Marshael? What in the world could have possibly possessed you?

COLLARD. Well, what with all the insurance and savings and trust funds Jamey left her—

WAYNE. I'm not talking about that! Why the way you've refused to go in that room all day long shows me how ashamed you are of the way Jamey's been laid out on display —looking like some penniless clown in a box.

MARSHAEL. (*Rising to her feet.*) Willie Wayne, I'm getting awfully tired of listening to you talk—I'm getting awfully sick and tired of listening to one white man talk!

KATTY. Reverend Rigby says we all have to learn to face our own finiteness—

MARSHAEL. I mean all this sudden deep show of concern and respect when you never even liked Jamey! You never even cared for him at all. It made you happy watching him struggle and fail!

WAYNE. It never did—

MARSHAEL. I remember clearly how you gloated with joy last Christmas Eve giving us that colored TV set when all we could to give y'all was a double book of Life Savers! You never wanted him to succeed! You never wanted him to make good!

WAYNE. I never wanted! Hey, listen, Missy, you're the one who saddled him with those three children and that job he despised. You're the reason he never got his damn Master's degree.

30

MARSHAEL. Don't you talk to me about his Master's degree! You could have lent him the money. When I came to you—

WAYNE. I wanted to talk to him, not to you. It was a business arrangement! I needed to talk to him!

MARSHAEL. You needed to humiliate him! You needed to make him beg and plead and give up his pride!

WAYNE. What pride? You destroyed any pride he ever had! Why, by the time you were finished with him he was nothing but a broken alcoholic slob!

MARSHAEL. What the hell do you know about anything?

WAYNE. I know about you sneaking his incompleted manuscript off to that New York publisher and them telling him it was superficial and sophomoric and what were some of those other adjectives they used?

COLLARD. How 'bout noxious, putrid, stinking, balless, rotten, lousy junk? And I never even read it!

MARSHAEL. I had to see. I needed to see.

WAYNE. (*Continuing after a monent's pause.*) I don't blame him for walking out on you, after you showed him that letter! I don't blame him for that at all!! It was cruel and vicious and mean!

MARSHAEL. (*Continuing.*) I couldn't let us keep on lying and hoping. It was like slow poison! I never wanted him to leave. I didn't mean for him to leave.

WAYNE. Besides, I wanted him to have that TV set! I didn't care what he gave to us. We enjoyed those Life Savers. We did. (*There is a tense pause.*)

KATTY. Look, I—I brought my Sunday school pamphlets with me and my Bible and my Bible dictionary. Whatever you'd like to use.

MARSHAEL. I'm going upstairs. I'm tired. I'm going upstairs. I've gotta polish Lucy's shoes. I'm going upstairs. (*She goes up the stairs and walks into her bedroom.*)

WAYNE. (*After a moment.*) Anyway, he must have left her some money; some insurance.

COLLARD. Not a dog's dime.

PIXROSE. It says on this tag Mrs. R.K. Miller sent the Rice Krispie bars.

LEON. Are they your favorite dessert?

PIXROSE. So far.

LEON. They're mine too.

PIXROSE. It doesn't mean anything. 'Cept we like 'em.

WAYNE. (*About Marshael's plate.*) Look at this; she just messed the food around on her plate. She's thirty three years old and she's still messing the food around on her plate.

LEON. Pixrose is gonna be a dog bather when she graduates from high school. They've already got her placed at a dog hospital and everything.

KATTY. Well, how nice for you.

WAYNE. He was my brother. Of course you love him. She needs professional help.

LEON. Maybe I'll be moving up to Jackson and become her assistant or something.

PIXROSE. It's not that easy a job.

LEON. But I could do it. I could! I know I could! (*Pixrose gets up to leave the room.*) Where are you going?

PIXROSE. To watch the moon. (*Leon rises to go with her.*) By myself. (*Leon stops in his tracks, as Pixrose turns and leaves out the door.*)

LEON. I've loved her ever since we first met at Monkey Island.

KATTY. (*To Leon, who is on his way out.*) Where are you going?

LEON. To watch her watch the moon. (*He exits.*)

WAYNE. It's funny how, even after she showed him that rejection letter, he never stopped belittling my job at the bank.

KATTY. (*After a moment of silence.*) My. What a night. (*Pause.*) Well, the silences are all right too. Here, let me just clear these plates. (*She exits U.C. with some dishes.*)

WAYNE. (*About the gin.*) Do you mind?

COLLARD Never.

WAYNE. (*Pouring himself a glass.*) You know, even without combing your hair, you're still very pretty. (*Collard looks at him. There is a knock at the front door.*) Who do you think—

COLLARD. I don't know. (*Wayne opens the door for Brocker Slade. Brocker Slade, 53, enters holding a beat up hat in his hands and wearing a ten year old brown suit that he seems to be breaking out of. He carries two wooden spoons in his coat pocket. Brocker is big, tired, and worn out. Yet sometimes when he smiles, he will look like a confused child.*)
WAYNE. Yes?
BROCKER. Evening, I'm Brocker Slade. I hear you're having a wake.
WAYNE. Oh, yes, well, please do come in. I'm Wayne Foster, the younger brother of the deceased. And, ah, this is Collard Darnell. She's the sister to the widow.
BROCKER. Mighty pleased to make your acquaintence.
COLLARD. (*Immediately attracted.*) Likewise, I'm certain.
WAYNE. Perhaps you'd, ah, like to pay your respects?
BROCKER. Oh . . . yeah.
COLLARD Here, I'll show Mr. Slade to the parlor. I've yet to pay my own respects.
WAYNE. Why don't you then—
COLLARD. (*Taking her ham sandwich and drink with her.*) This way, Mr. Slade.
BROCKER. Brocker's fine.
COLLARD. Brocker then. (*They go into the parlor. Trying to avoid looking at the coffin.*) He's over there.
BROCKER. I see. (*Collard moves away from the coffin and eats a bite of her sandwich. In the hallway Wayne's drinking gin. Upstairs Marshael spins the world globe around. She stops it with her finger.*) So you're Marshael's sister?
COLLARD. Right. I don't live in this part of the state any longer. Generally, I just get back home for deaths; and Christmas occasionally.
BROCKER. Oh.
COLLARD. I don't like to affiliate myself with the rest of of this menagerie (*Upstairs Marshael looks at her violin. Katty enters the front hall from U.C.*)
KATTY. (*As she stacks the dishes onto a tray.*) Where's Collard?

WAYNE. In the parlor

KATTY. Oh, really? Well, at least she finally decided to go in!

WAYNE. Ah well, some visitor's in there with her—a Mr. Slade.

KATTY. No! Not that horrible man whose pigs all exploded.

WAYNE. (*Totally in the dark.*) I don't know.

KATTY. That old man who painted Marshael's kitchen chairs red. Terrible man—He told little Lucy she was an animal. She cried all day because of it.

WAYNE. (*In an annoyed whisper.*) Talk a little louder, why don't you?

KATTY. I'm sorry—But he's a barbarian, an absolute barbarian. (*She exits U.C. with the tray.*)

WAYNE. (*Whispering after her.*) Twat.

BROCKER. (*Staring at the corpse.*) Wonder why she married him? I do. I often wonder why.

COLLARD. Did you know him?

BROCKER. Met him when I moved here 'bout two years ago. Saw him off and on; here and there.

COLLARD. What'd did you think of him?

BROCKER. He appeared to me to be a miserable, bewildered man.

COLLARD. I never liked him. He had a genius IQ and all the promise in the world, but he was a lazy coward with no guts and never finished a thing he'd start. He lied to himself and to everyone else.

BROCKER. Still he had that woman.

COLLARD. Oh, he deluged her with gifts and things when they were young. Bought her barbecued chicken every Saturday night. And he could tell stories and paint up dreams real pretty. She was sincerely mad for him. (*Setting her drink down.*) Oh, hell, I may as well have one last look at the son of a bitch. (*She moves up to the coffin carrying her ham sandwich. Totally amazed.*) God. When did he get so fat? He's downright fat.

BROCKER. Beats the hell out of me.

COLLARD. And his glasses. They've got him wearing his glasses. Oh— (*A piece of her ham falls onto the corpse.*)
BROCKER. Watch out here. (*Picking up the ham slowly, and offering it to her.*) You dropped some ham.
COLLARD. I don't want it.
BROCKER. (*After a moment of indecision.*) Ah, hell. (*He eats it. Katty enters U.C. with a dish rag.*)
KATTY. Wasn't it sweet of Uncle Ben and Uncle Walter to make the trip up from Jackson?
WAYNE. Yeah.
KATTY. (*Wiping up crumbs.*) Uncle Ben likes you alot. He said you were very poised. His opinion means a lot at the bank. Better move that glass, the napkin's soaked through and through.
WAYNE. Stop acting like my mother.
KATTY. What?
WAYNE. You remind me of my mother.
KATTY. (*Hurt.*) Oh. (*She goes back to cleaning.*)
COLLARD. Well, shit.
BROCKER. Huh?
COLLARD. If this fool can get through dying, anyone should be able to do it. I mean, look, here—he's doing it right. No questions asked. Shit, so what's the big deal?
BROCKER. I'd like t'know. (*Leon racing into the front hall.*)
LEON. Hi! Where's Brocker? Is he here? I saw his dog out back—
WAYNE. He's in the parlor.
LEON. Great! I'll go get Marshy—(*He starts up the stairs.*)
BROCKER. Think we've been in here long enough?
COLLARD. Sure. (*She goes to get her glass.*)
KATTY. (*Quietly to Wayne.*) If we only could have a child. You'd see I had so much to give.
LEON. (*Knocking at Marshael's bedroom door.*) Marshy. Hey, Marshael—
MARSHAEL. (*Still holding her violin.*) Yeah?
LEON. (*Opening her door.*) Come on downstairs. There's

35

someone here to see you.

MARSHAEL. Leon, I'm done in here—

LEON. Please, I know you'll be glad to see him. It'll ease your mind.

MARSHAEL. Who is it? (*Downstairs, Collard and Brocker move into the front hall.*)

LEON. You'll see; come on; please—

MARSHAEL. (*Moving to the upstairs landing.*) It better not be—(*Spotting Brocker.*) Brocker Slade.

BROCKER. Hi M. It's good to see you.

MARSHAEL. Well, I guess, you don't mind coming here tracking mud all over my feelings.

LEON. What's wrong?

BROCKER. Look, I came here for the wake. I hope to be of some meager help.

MARSHAEL. Help?

KATTY. She's upset 'cause he let her children eat Gravy Train. He told little Lucy she was an animal.

BROCKER. For God's sake, lady, she is an animal! The kid's a mammal!

KATTY. See! He's crazy!

MARSHAEL. (*Coming down the stairs.*) Look, Brocker, there is no reason to concern yourself with my vulgar travail; so just take that flea bitten mongrel of yours and get off a my place.

BROCKER. Hey, now, M. I'm telling ya I'm sorry about that night but frankly—

MARSHAEL. Go home, Brocker! I'm telling you to go home!

BROCKER. No ma'am, I'm staying here tonight. I'll sleep in a ditch; but I'm not leaving here, not till the last dog is dead. (*Pixrose enters U.C. with a pie.*)

PIXROSE. Marshael, a lady just brought over this pie for you. She says it's bluebarry.

MARSHAEL. What lady?

PIXROSE. A yellow haired lady.

MARSHAEL. (*Standing on the middle of the stairs.*) Give me that pie.

WAYNE. Don't give her the pie.

MARSHAEL. It's my pie. Bring it here.

KATTY. Look, I'll just take the pie—

MARSHAEL. Don't you dare take that pie!

WAYNE. Won't you please just—let me take the pie.

MARSHAEL. Give me that Godamn blueberry pie!! (*Pixrose takes the pie to Marshael.*)

WAYNE. Go on and give her the pie.

MARSHAEL. (*Tearing off the card.*) "With deepest love and condolence, Esmerelda Rowland." She sent me one of her pies.

COLLARD. Who's Esmerelda Rowland?

WAYNE. Ssshush up.

MARSHAEL. (*Walking up and down the stairs.*) She actually went and sent me one of her pies. Course they must be pretty good. Jamey got awfully fat eating them. Why, he must of put on twenty-five pounds in just four months they were living together.

COLLARD. Jamey was living with another woman?

MARSHAEL. You didn't know? Why it's been noised all over Madison County—Jamey Foster and his twenty-two year old, twice divorced, yellow haired, sweet shop baker!

COLLARD. I never heard.

MARSHAEL. (*Still pacing.*) Oh, sure, she was right out there in the field with him on the fatal night of his demise. So, who wants some pie? Who wants a big piece of blueberry pie? It's Jamey's favorite kind! It oughta be really good!

WAYNE. Come on, now, put the pie down.

MARSHAEL. (*Running to the top of the staircase.*) You'd better eat some. You'd better it all! I mean it now—

WAYNE. Come on, now, and give it to me—Marshael, just calm down and hand me that pie.

KATTY. Your nervous system's just all shocked—

MARSHAEL. (*Screaming as she waves the pie back and forth and over her head.*) Ooooooh!! Oooooooohhh!!

PIXROSE. (*Overlapping.*) She's gonna smash it.

COLLARD. (*Overlapping.*)

KATTY. It's all so trying. Why, Reverend Rigby always says—

37

the scream.) No, she's not— BROCKER. (*Overlapping.*) Oh, Lord, she's hot as a fire-cracker now!

MARSHAEL. (*Throwing the pie from the upstairs landing down to the floor below.*) You shitty pie!!

COLLARD. She did it! WAYNE. All over the rug!

PIXROSE. She sure did! KATTY. Look at that mess!

MARSHAEL. (*Totally still.*) I don't know how I'm gonna get through this night.

LEON. I never seen her scream out like that.

MARSHAEL. I can't imagine ever seeing the morning. (*The lights fade to blackout.*)

END OF ACT ONE.

ACT II

Scene 1

The setting is the same. The blueberry pie has been cleaned up. Marshael and Pixrose are upstairs in the bedroom. Marshael is working on one of the drill team costumes that is on the dress dummy. She wears the same black dress that she wore throughout Act one. Pixrose is dressed in a long cotton nightgown. She is polishing a small black patent leather shoe. Downstairs, Wayne is sitting at the card table that has been cleared. He is studying a camera and its flash attachment. He is also drinking gin. Leon is pacing back and forth in the front hall. From time to time he glances into the parlor to look at the casket that has now been closed.

LEON. (*After several moments of pacing.*) We just stand here? Is that all there is to it? This is it? This is a wake?
WAYNE. That's right.
LEON. Well, then I gotta go get me a drumstick! (*He exits U.R.C.*)
PIXROSE. Marshael, I've finished the first coat on Lucy's shoe. I'm gonna set it down here by Jamey Jr.'s and do the other one while it dries. (*She puts the shoe down on a sheet of newspaper and starts on the second one.*)
MARSHAEL. You're a big help. I appreciate it. (*The phone rings. Marshael starts.*) God, I hate it when that phone rings. It scares me. (*She picks up the phone.*) Hello? . . . Well,

39

how're you doing? How're your sisters? . . . Well, that's good
. . . What? . . . Why sure I remember the cut-out bunny you
made at school—It's green, right? . . . Well, I don't know,
Jamey, Jr., maybe you could—just give it to someone else . . .
Sure . . . No, Daddy wouldn't mind . . . No, honey, he wouldn't
mind a bit. I'm sure . . . Well, that's a good idea. I know
Uncle Leon would just love it. It's an awfully fine bunny . . .
Alright then, you sleep tight and don't let the bedbugs bite.
I love you, boy. Bye, bye. (*She puts down the phone.*) My little
boy's calling. He's only six. Gee. Thank God he's not crying
or anything. That's the worst thing for me, watching my
children cry.

PIXROSE. That's exactly how I feel about my brother,
Franky. I can't bear t'watch him cry.

MARSHAEL. Oh, I didn't know you had a brother.

PIXROSE. Well, he's out at Ellisville.

MARSHAEL. Oh. I'm sorry.

PIXROSE. He does all right. They've got him wearing this
football helmet all day and all night just in case he starts
banging his head into walls. Seems he's got some sorta brain
damage.

MARSHAEL. Do you see him much?

PIXROSE. Once a year 'bout Christmas time I'll visit him
and take him his gift—soap on a rope. He loves the soap on
a rope to wear in the shower. But other than my brother,
Franky, I have nobody.

MARSHAEL. Well . . . how do you feel about Leon?

PIXROSE. I don't know. He's probably just in love with love,
and he's something of a misfit. Still we did kiss each other at
Monkey Island. No, it will never, never be.

MARSHAEL. Why do you say that?

PIXROSE. (*Putting the shoe down to dry.*) I'd just rather
keep him like a jewel in my mind. That way I will always
have him. (*Picking up the violin.*) My, this is a fine looking
instrument. Do you play it?

MARSHAEL. Sort of. Jamey always left the house when I
started to play it though. He said it sounded screechy. (*Pixrose*

picks up the bow and plays a weird array of notes.)
PIXROSE. Sounds lovely t'me. (*Katty enters into the up-stairs hall. She is wearing a pink robe and fluffy slippers. She leans over the bannister and whispers down to Wayne.*)
KATTY. Psst, Papa Sweet Potato? Honey Pie? I've laid out all your night clothes for you, if you decide you want to retire.
WAYNE. (*Looking up at her.*) Why do you talk to me in that funny voice?
KATTY. (*Stung.*) I don't know. I just do. Excuse me, I've got to go and floss my teeth.
WAYNE. You sure do keep yourself clean. (*Katty hears this last jab as she exits down the hallway. Wayne goes back to drinking his gin.*)
MARSHAEL. (*After staring at the closet.*) Oh, well . . . Lord. I'd better go on and get those suits out for Uncle Wilbur while I'm thinking about it, leastwise I'll never do it. (*She opens closet and gets his suits out.*) There. Here it is. His blue pin-striped suit. I liked it best, and here I am holding it, but somehow I don't feel a tear in this world. It's like a hole's been shot through me, and all my insides have been blown out somewhere else.
PIXROSE. Well, I know from my own experience that it ain't ever gonna be worth it feeling all that love for somebody.
MARSHAEL. (*She gets a brush and starts brushing the suit.*) Feeling love for somebody? I just wish I knew what I felt for Jamey. First one thing, I guess, and then another, I sure wish I knew. It haunts me not to know.
PIXROSE. Well . . . was he nice?
MARSHAEL. (*Continues to brush suit.*) He could be, I suppose . . . He did things different. I remember one time he brought this huge, ugly, fat boy home with him about supper time. Jamey whispered that he'd found the fat boy crying in the road 'cause his only pet bird had flown away and could I please fix blueberry muffins for dessert. He kissed my fingers when I said I would. (*Cross to hall door—hang up suit.*) He had dreams though. And it's hard being involved with a man

whose dreams don't get fulfilled.

PIXROSE. What dreams did he have?

MARSHAEL. Oh, he wanted to be a great world-wide historian. He used to have all sorts of startling revolutionary ideas about the development of mankind that he kept trying to write into books and theories.

PIXROSE. Well, he must a been a real smart man.

MARSHAEL. Oh, he was. And fun too. Why the way he laughed was so big and so strong—like the world was going to crack open and there's be beautiful treasures all inside. We sometimes played this game where we'd spin this globe around. (*Spin.*) Saying like, "We're gonna go . . . there!" (*She yells out the name of the country her finger actually lands on.*) Or, "We're taking a banana boat (*spin.*) to . . . here!" (*She looks down and reads the name.*) Then we'd imagine how it would be when we arrived. (*Sits on chest.*) It was a fun game, but we stopped playing after he had to take that awful job in real estate. (*She spins the globe around and around. She stops the globe with her finger and says the name of the country it lands on.*) I was afraid to ask him for anything. I never wanted him to know how scared I was. I just kept on telling him how, until all his theories were finished and started selling, that real estate was fine with me.

PIXROSE. And real estate's when you sell other people's homes for 'em?

MARSHAEL. Right. Except he didn't sell much of anything. I wanted so badly for things to be right for us. My parents fought all the time when I was little. Yelling and crying in the night. I wanted a different kind of life; but it didn't work out.

PIXROSE. He started yelling at you?

MARSHAEL. Oh, all the time. Stupid things like, "This mayonnaise jar is too damn small! Don't you know you save more money with the large economy size!" Slam! Break the jar! It was ridiculous.

PIXROSE. You musta cried a lot.

MARSHAEL. Oh, yeah. It seemed the harder I tried the less

he cared. The more he blamed me and the children for his dreams not coming true, I thought maybe it would help, if we just knew one way or the other about his work. That's why I sent it off to the publisher. When he found out, he was gone. Went off to live with that fat yellow-haired woman. And now he's really gone. He's out of the whole deal; and I don't even know what we felt for each other. Stupid. Lord. My mouth aches. (*Collard runs into the outside area R., carrying two bottles of gin.*)

COLLARD. (*Calling off R.*) Hey! Hey, last one here's a rotten egg! You're a rotten egg, Brocker! A goddamn rotten egg! Marshy! Marshy!

MARSHAEL. (*Going out onto the balcony.*) What? Don't shout.

COLLARD. Look! We got it! We got a load of gin! Here, I'll throw ya up a bottle.

MARSHAEL. No!

COLLARD. (*Swinging the bottles around and around in a circle.*) You ready?! Get ready!!

MARSHAEL. Stop! Don't be stupid, Collard! It's gonna break!!

COLLARD. Right! (*She stops swinging the bottles.*) Don't be stupid. That's kind of hard for me, huh? What with my low IQ—my bovine mind!

MARSHAEL. Oh, please! Look, just come on up here.

COLLARD. Why? You don't need things from me. You handle it all yourself.

MARSHAEL. Oh, please, I can't tonight. My mouth hurts.

COLLARD. That's right! Don't talk to me! Just run off carrying the world on your lonely shoulders.

MARSHAEL. Look, Collard, don't you talk to me about running off! You're the one who ran off and left me to keep care of Mama the six months she was sick, and then later, when Daddy was dying, you were here just long enough to upset everyone, then you ran off again!

COLLARD. He didn't wanna see me! He didn't need my help and neither did you! Nobody asked me to stay, 'cause I'm just too stupid! Just too damn stupid to live!

MARSHAEL. Shut up saying you're stupid! I'm so sick of that excuse I could wretch up blood! Ooh!!! (*She goes back inside.*)

PIXROSE. What's wrong with Collard?

MARSHAEL. She thinks she's stupid. She took some idiotic test twenty years ago that said she was dumb, and she believed them; so I guess she must be dumb. I don't know. My eyes ache. I'm gonna go put a cold rag over them. (*She exits into the bathroom. Brocker enters, D.R. carrying a bottle of whiskey. He is shaken.*)

BROCKER. Where the hell were you going to, a fire?

COLLARD. I only wish.

BROCKER. You hit something in the road, you know?

COLLARD. When?

BROCKER. That's what that large thud was that bumped us five feet out of our bucket seats.

COLLARD. It was probably just some old armadillo or coon crossing the road.

BROCKER. Well, there's blood and fur all stuck to your front fender!

COLLARD. It's okay; I never liked having solid colored cars.

BROCKER. Well, you don't.

COLLARD. Have a drink, Brocker. Clam yourself down. What's the matter with you? Don't you like plowing up the fields, raising some hell, dancing with glee?

BROCKER. Look, love, I don't need crazy. I've had crazy. I'm an old man.

COLLARD. You look mighty appealing to me (*Moving in on him.*) I don't think much of men, ya understand, I just can't live without 'em.

BROCKER. Honey . . .

COLLARD. Look, I just want somebody who's fun and crazy and mean as me.

BROCKER. Well, I'm none of those.

COLLARD. What's the matter, Brocker, honey . . . you gonna leave me forever unravished?

BROCKER. Look, it's just I — I like Marshael. I mean, God help my feeble soul, but — I do.

COLLARD. Oh, Marshael. Right, Marshael. Well, that's all right then. 'Course she's nothing like me. She doesn't caress death and danger with open legs. (*She takes a long, slow slug of gin.*)

BROCKER. (*Not accusing.*) Are you really this tough?

COLLARD. No, darling, I'm pretending to be tough. But if you pretend really hard, it amounts to about the same thing. Here, now, I'll call your lady love out for you. Marshael! Hey! Come on out here! An old troll wants to woo you! (*Pixrose goes out on the balcony as Collard exits.*)

PIXROSE. What is it? Marshael's putting water on her eyes.

BROCKER. It's not a thing. Sorry for the disturbance. Go back to sleep.

PIXROSE. Hey, listen, you need to dip that skinny black dog of yours. He's practically more flea than dog.

BROCKER. I don't own that old junk yard dog. It's not my dog. I never feed it. I got no idea how it even stays alive— chews on the same damn piece of wood all winter long. It's not my dog. I got no use for it! (*Marshael comes out of the bathroom with a washcloth.*)

MARSHAEL. (*Moving out to the balcony.*) Who's that? Is that Brocker? Is that Brocker Slade?

PIXROSE. (*Moving out of the way.*) It is.

MARSHAEL. You lily-livered man! When I needed you where were you? I'm sick of betrayal! Sick!

BROCKER. Look, I'm sorry, M. I'm sorry about last Tuesday night, but I'm a fifty-three years old jackass, and I hadn't even kissed a woman in close on to two years—

MARSHAEL. You're no good, Brocker! No damn good! I don't even like laying my eyes on you.

BROCKER. God, M., honey, you're breaking my heart. I'm about ready to run jump into the Big Black River.

MARSHAEL. Well, don't forget to hang a heavy stone

around your scrawny old neck.

BROCKER. Lordy, lord, is there no redemption in your heart?

MARSHAEL. It's in mighty short supply.

BROCKER. What do you want from Me? What?

MARSHAEL. (*It comes to her.*) Triumph! It's a feeling I'm sadly lacking. Give me some triumph: some glory: some exaltation!

BROCKER. So what do you want me to do? Climb up the side of the house and carry you up to the moon on a cloud?!

MARSHAEL. Yes! Try it! At least you can try it!

BROCKER. I'd break my scrawny old neck!

MARSHAEL. Then why don't you use some ingenuity!

BROCKER. Ingenuity?! Hell! Here goes — (*He makes a feeble attempt to climb up the side of the house and falls back down to the ground.*)

MARSHAEL. You call this ingenuity?!

PIXROSE. He might make it, he might.

MARSHAEL. No, he won't, he'll never — ow!

BROCKER. What's wrong?

MARSHAEL. My mouth! Those sores!

BROCKER. Christ! Oh, my back!

MARSHAEL. You stupid old fool! Oh, I'm through with it! Through with it all! (*Marshael leaves the balcony and slams into the bathroom. Pixrose looks out on the ledge as Brocker gathers himself together.*)

PIXROSE. Hey, there's a bird's nest out here. It has little blue speckled eggs in it waiting to be born.

BROCKER. I'm falling on my butt for a woman with sores in her mouth. Hell, I think I'm gonna go 'round and kick that stupid dog till he dies! (*Brocker hobbles off as Collard enters the front door. The lights in the front hall are dim. Collard is brooding: her shoulders are slumped. She carries a bottle of gin under each arm.*)

COLLARD. (*To Wayne.*) Hello.

WAYNE. Hey, Collard. Say, could you come take a look at this camera? Have I got this on right? (*She walks over to the table. He hands her the camera.*)

COLLARD. Hmm. Sure, it's right. It's perfect. Now all you do is look through here and click this button and you'll have a pretty picture.

WAYNE. Thanks.

COLLARD. (*Setting a bottle of gin down on his table.*) Here's your gin.

WAYNE. Thanks, Charlotte.

COLLARD. Huh?

WAYNE. Charlotte. That's your name isn't it? I like it better than Collard. Charlotte. (*As he lifts her chin wth his fingers.*) It suits a certain side of you. Charlotte.

COLLARD. What are you doing?

WAYNE. Huh?

COLLARD. Lifting my chin up like that—you're making me feel like some sort of goddamn horse—I'm not a horse!

WAYNE. (*As he backs her against the red chair.*) You are a horse! A goddamn horse! Come here—come here—

CLOOARD. (*Overlapping.*) Oh, so you do like your women dirty?

WAYNE. (*Grabbing her.*) I like you—I like you—Charlotte! Oh, Charlotte!! (*They manage to knock a chair over as Katty appears on the upstairs landing. She is winding a clock.*)

KATTY. (*Coming down the stairs.*) What's this? Wayne? What's going on here?! Excuse me, please, but what's going on?! (*Leon enters U.R.C. with a plate of chicken.*)

LEON. You know, that green dish detergent really does feel softer on your hands . . . What's going on?

COLLARD. (*After a tense moment.*) Oh, Willie Wayne was just giving me extremely good chance at nothing.

KATTY. It is becoming more and more painfully apparent that you have no affection or regard for me, whatsoever!

WAYNE. Go on up to our room, Katty. We'll talk up there.

KATTY. Just because my daddy gave you a decent job there's no reason to resent me! (*Marshael comes out of the bathroom upstairs.*)

MARSHAEL. Who's fighting? (*Pixrose shrugs her shoulders.*

Marshael goes and opens the bedroom door.)

WAYNE. We'll discuss it all in our room—

KATTY. Just because I lose those babies is no reason to treat me viciously—No reason at all! You know I can't help it!

WAYNE. You're crazy now, Katty—Totally crazy!

KATTY. And I'm nothing like that redneck mother of yours! I wouldn't be caught dead wearing those broad, bright-colored stripes! Especially if I was as fat as she is!!

WAYNE. Go to our room, Katty! Now!

KATTY. I won't! I won't! I won't! (*Katty starts up stairs and rushes past Marshael into the bedroom.*)

MARSHAEL. Katty—(*Marshael follows her into the bedroom.*)

KATTY. (*Runs to bathroom.*) She should be wearing dark clothes with vertical stripes!! (*Katty slams the bathroom door shut and locks it. As she continues yelling she bangs her fists on the door.*) Everyone knows that!! Everyone!!!! Everyone but that stupid, fat, old redneck! (*Brocker opens the front door—shuts it—looks around at everyone.*)

BROCKER. (*Gesturing with his whiskey bottle.*) What'd I miss? (*The lights fade to Blackout.*)

END OF SCENE

ACT II

Scene 2

The lights go up on the bedroom. Three large Easter baskets are out around the room. Most of the candy from these baskets has been devoured. Pixrose is pulling through the green grass in one of the baskets look-

ing for more candy. Marshael is fooling with her violin and drinking gin. She still wears the black dress but has taken off her shoes and stockings. Collard is pounding on bathroom door.

PIXROSE. Look, here's another marshmallow chicken—who wants it?

MARSHAEL. I'll take it!

COLLARD. How long you think she's gonna stay in there? All night or what? Katty?! Hey, Katty!

KATTY'S VOICE. *(She speaks from inside the bathroom.)* Look, please, I'll be out soon. Really.

COLLARD. When? You've been in there over an hour and a half already. Now, when?

KATTY'S VOICE. Soon. I—I just can't come out now.

COLLARD. For Christ's sake, why not?

KATTY'S VOICE. I don't know. I'm too ashamed. I can't forget it. My life has ended. I can't forget it.

COLLARD. *(Turning back to Marshael and Pixrose.)* So what am I supposed to do, go down to East Peace Street and throw myself in front of cars or what?! Oh, shit! I'm just leaving then. Going back up the Natchez Trace and stop stirring up trouble for everyone here. What'd I do with G.W.'s boots? Where the hell are those stupid boots?

MARSHAEL. Oh, damn it, Collard.

PIXROSE. Oh, Collard, wait. Here, wait. Hey, Katty? Katty? This is me, Pixrose Wilson. And, well, I'm really sorry you're feeling so badly upset. But you just need to, ah—come on out a the bathroom.

KATTY'S VOICE. I just can't face it. I can't. Why, none of y'all have suffered the cruel humiliation I have. None of y'all.

PIXROSE. Oh, sure. We've all had cruel, sad, unbearable things happen to us in this life.

COLLARD. ׀ No kidding.

PIXROSE. Look, here's one just happened recently to me. It's when Laurie Crussy said she would set the Sacred Heart Orphanage Asylum on fire, if I wouldn't give to her my grandmama's garnet brooch which is my only cherished possession.

COLLARD. What?

MARSHAEL. Really?

PIXROSE. That's right and she did it too. Burned down two entire wings 'cause she knows how fiercely and dreadfully afraid I am of fires.

COLLARD. My God! That's awful! Did you tell someone? Did you report that little monster?

PIXROSE. Well, 'course I did, but old Sister Daniel said I told lies out of jealousy over Laurie's pink, satin skin. Now I know my skin is ugly, but it wasn't a lie. (*Moment of stunned silence.*) So Collard? What about you? Do you have one?

COLLARD. Yeah. Well . . . the one that keeps coming to my mind is about Daddy.

KATTY'S VOICE. What? I can't hear it?

COLLARD. (*Moving to the bathroom door.*) Daddy—our daddy—how I used to be his favorite. We'd always talk and discuss life and politics. He wanted me to come join his firm —be a lawyer with him. Then when I was twelve we took these stupid IQ tests. Mine, well, mine said I was below average; ninety-two or something.

KATTY'S VOICE. But Collard, honey, those tests aren't accurate. You should have taken it again.

COLLARD. I did. Twice more! It got lower each time! I ended up with an eighty-three. That's twenty-one points lower than Leon, for Christ's sake! Twenty-one points below Leon!! Oh, God! I was nothing in his eyes from then on! Just dumb and stupid and nothing! So, Katty, you coming out now?

KATTY'S VOICE. I don't know. I'm starting to feel better. Oh, I don't know.

MARSHAEL. Hey, Katty—I went to see Jamey Tuesday afternoon over at the hospital and Esmeralda was there. She was all dressed up in a flowered dress and a flowered hat. I didn't look very good; so I thought, "Well, I'll just say, Hello, and leave." But Jamey, he kept talking to me and making conversation and all the time he was holding Esmeralda's hand, or putting his arm around her waist to give it a squeeze. He said, "Hey, Marshael, why don't you try one of those delicious caramel pecan balls Essey brought? You could stand some weight on those saggy bones." It fiercely hurt me and my pride—like I wasn't even a woman.

KATTY. (*Coming out of the bathroom.*) Oh, Marshael, honey, you are a woman. A beautiful woman. Don't let anyone tell you different from that.

MARSHAEL. Oh, Katty. Katty. (*Then realizing.*) Katty!! You're out of the bathroom!!

COLLARD. Praise God! You're out!

PIXROSE. Bravo! (*Pixrose showers Katty with a handful of eggs in silver foil, as the lights go down in the bedroom and come up in the front hall below. Wayne is sitting on the stairs drinking and fooling with the camera. Brocker is sitting at the card table drinking the last of his whiskey. His sleeves are rolled up. You can see his tattoos. Leon is sitting, looking at a deck of dirty cards.*)

LEON. Wow! Great! Great! Hey, look Willie Wayne! Brocker's got a deck of playing cards with pictures of necked women on 'em! Well, well, some of 'em are wearing like aprons or tropical flowers, or looks like garden hoses—just take a look! They're spectacular!

WAYNE. Then *you* keep them. I'm gonna go and get those photographs taken for Mama. (*He goes into the living room.*)

LEON. Think he's still upset about his wife?

BROCKER. Who knows? He left his bottle though. I'll grab it while he's gone. (*He jumps up to get the bottle. The bones in his body crackle.*)

LEON. Gosh! Will you listen to all them bones cracking away under your skin!

BROCKER. Well, Christ. I'm an old man. What the hell do you expect?

LEON. Shoot. Yeah. So what's it like being old?

BROCKER. Pure D-shit. That's what. The highs are never

as high. The lows get lower. Hangovers'll last ya ten days. Your back aches; your butt hurts; you can't smell spring . . . Hey, how 'bout a game of Bid Whist?! (*Wayne returns.*)

WAYNE. I'll do it later. I'll get to it later, that's all. It's too dark in there now. Where's my gin?

BROCKER. (*Brocker holds up the bottle.*) Here.

WAYNE. Oh. Well, go ahead. Have a drink. Sure, help yourself. So, Mr. Slade, what's all this about pigs? I hear you, ah, raise pigs.

BROCKER. (*As he shuffles the cards and proceeds to deal out four hands.*) Right. That's right. I came down here for that distinct purpose. Came down here with a wild-haired, big-thighed woman—she's the one who supposedly knew all about this hog raising business. I was just backing her with my cash and affection, but, by the by, she runs off and leaves me holding the fuckin' bag. Seems we had some sort of run-in over a dog I'd kicked. She leaves me out in that old shack saddled with twenty-seven hogs. Only three of which remain, a good fifteen of 'em having exploded, the other nine got loose or died mysteriously. Hey, do you play Bid Whist?

WAYNE. Poorly.

BROCKER. Have a seat. Now we've got this one extra hand to deal with . . . hell, I'll just bid 'em both. No problem. (*They start picking their cards up.*)

WAYNE. So what about these hogs exploding? Was it a munitions accident, or what?

BROCKER. Hell no. They just got bigger and fatter, and, of course, they were eating like pigs, and one day their bellies would be dragging along the ground, and the next day their skin would be all stretched out and they'd explode and die.

WAYNE. Jesus. Amazing. This man's amazing.

BROCKER. Well, before it was all over I discovered a good many of 'em had these deformed damn butt holes and that was the major cause of it all. I mean, it certainly was the crux of it. Hey, Leon! Your bid, boy! Your bid! (*The lights black out downstairs and go up on the women in the bedroom.*)

KATTY. (*Pulling at her hair with glee.*) Oh, it's so awful!

It's too horrible! You won't think I'm sweet anymore!

COLLARD. We don't care! We don't care!

PIXROSE. No, we don't care! Tell us!

KATTY. Oh, all right. See, I was always rich, you know, and people always hated me for it. And one Easter Sunday I was walking to church with my maid, Lizzie Pearl. Well, I was all dressed to kill for in my white ruffled dress and my white Easter bonnet and carrying my white parasol. Well, we had to pass by the Dooleys' house, and the Dooleys were always known as white trash, and that bunch really despised me. Well, Harry and Virginia Dooley came up and shoved me down into a huge mudhole, spoiling my entire Easter outfit! I cired, I tell you, I cried!

COLLARD. For God's sake, Katty! This is supposed to be a story about the cruelest thing *you've* ever done, not that's been *done to you!*

KATTY. I haven't finished yet! Will you let me finish! See later on in the day, when the Dooleys were all in for their dinner, Lizzie Pearl and I sneaked back over to their back yard and yanked the chirping heads off of every one of their colored Easter chicks—We murdered them *all* with our bare hands! Those brats cried for weeks! I swear it was weeks!

COLLARD. Great! Katty, that's rotten. That is really rotten!

PIXROSE. (*Overlapping.*) Yes, that's cruel, Katty! That's very cruel!

KATTY. I know, that's why I told it. Who's got one now? Collard, I bet you've got one. I bet you do.

COLLARD. Oh, yeah—I've slept with married men, I've slept with priests, I've stolen from stores, I've killed animals in the road, lied and cheated just to win at a game of cards.

PIXROSE. Oh, but what I did was worse than that.

COLLARD. Yeah?

PIXROSE. See, after I was burned and had to be in bandages, I bandaged up all my dolls, put methiolade on the bandages and kept 'em down in the cellar. I kept 'em wearing slings and using crutches and some of 'em were even blind. See, just 'cause I was scarred, I wanted them to be too. It was not fair.

MARSHAEL. Well, listen to this one. After Jamey'd had that stroke and the left half of his body'd gotten paralyzed, I went into see him, and he asked me to bring him some of his papers from home. I told him he'd have to hobble home on his good side and get them himself 'cause I'd just sold our car t'pay for these ridiculous hospital bills. That's the last night I ever saw Jamey. He'd always made me feel so ashamed for being stronger and for getting our house and feeding the kids. Well, now he was gonna be weaker and more dependent than ever and I just wanted him t'pay for it.

KATTY. Oh, Marshael, I know Jamey was grateful to you for all the help you gave him.

MARSHAEL. No, he hated me for it. 'Cause when I left he said to me, "Fine, then when I die you just stick me in a pine box. Don't you dare go making five hundred drill team suits so that you can bury me in something nice, 'cause I won't be taking any more favors from you."

COLLARD. If Jamey didn't want your damn favors, he shouldn't of taken them.

MARSHAEL. No, 'cause after his work never came to anything again and again, we both got to resenting each other so bad. It seemed like the house and the children became mine and something else was his. It wasn't always awful but somehow it got to be. I don't know when it changed. I don't know when we changed. But I still remember the first time he said he loved me 'cause we were lying under the purple trees. (*The lights slowly fade out in the bedroom then go up immediately in the hall below. The men are all drunk. Brocker is playing the spoons. Leon is making loud, weird sounds. Wayne is singing a sad song.*)

LEON. OOH AHHH BREAKAAAAA!!!

BROCKER. (*Overlapping.*) Yes sir! Let the good times roll!

LEON. BREAKAAAWOOSHAA!!! Whoo! Sometimes I just like to make noises. Stimulates the old brain.

WAYNE. (*Coming out of some sort of stupor.*) You know,

people just get deader and deader each day they live!

LEON. (*Impressed.*) Wow. He's right. He's absolutely correct.

WAYNE. See I too can say sensitive, provocative things. Sir Jamey is not the only one among us with a brain which is what my dear Mama would have us all believe.

BROCKER. My dear old Mamee!

WAYNE. Get this. Get this! I'm pulling in fifty-five thousand bucks a year. Fifty-five thousand, and she's telling me how Jamey's the smart one, the creative one, the special one; and I'm just good in arithmetic! Just good in arithmetic, too classic! And now—now she wants me to take some farewell pictures of Saint Jamey so she can build him up a goddamn shrine! Well, screw her pictures! Screw her! and screw that stinking bastard in there!!! (*His nose begins bleeding.*) God, my nose. My nose. Lord Jesus! I've never known love. Never will. Oh, my nose. My nose. (*He exits U.C.*)

LEON. (*After a moment.*) People get deader and deader every day they're alive. That's deep.

BROCKER. Hell, anything's deep if you think about it long enough. A man's best friend's his dog is deep if you give it any thought.

LEON. (*Realizing that a man's best friend is his dog, is deep.*) Yeah.

BROCKER. People are always saying, "Life is this!"—"Death is that!" They think they'll clear everything up for themselves if they can just hone it all down to a small twist of phrase. Poor idiots! (*The lights fade downstairs and go on upstairs. The woman have settled in under blankets, pillows, etc. They are all drinking gin. It is darker now. All but one of the lights have been turned off.*)

KATTY. (*As she rubs lotion all over her face, and arms.*) I hate the me I have to be with him. If only I could have the baby it would give me someone to love and make someone who'd love me. There'd be a reason for having the fine house and the lovely yard.

MARSHAEL. God. I wanted children so badly. I was like some giant sea turtle looking for a place in the warm sand to lay my eggs. I felt all fertile inside. I wanted a home and babies and a family. But Jamey never wanted all that. Still I really thought I had to have it. I really thought I did.

COLLARD. Not me. No way. No how. After my abortion I went out and ate fried chicken. Got a ten-piece bucket filled with mashed potatoes and gravy, coleslaw, and a roll. First it tasted good and greasy and gooey. Then I felt like I was eating my baby's skin and flesh and veins and all. I got so sick— all there in the car. Now I — I never eat chicken. I take the pill and use a diaphram too. It'll never happen again. (*Dipping a stick into a bubble jar. Waving her hand, making bubbles.*) Wooh, look at those . . . beautiful. (*She can't resist popping one.*)

PIXROSE. I've never actually been pregnant. I guess 'cause I'm, well, I'm still a virgin. But I was pregnant one time in a dream. And when the child was born he was half human and half sheep and they said he was to be sold as a slave. But before they took him, I was allowed to hold him in my arms. His body was so warm and soft. I felt his heart beating against my heart. Then I looked down at his small sheeplike face, and he was crying. Then they took him away to become a slave.

KATTY. (*She rises.*) Well . . . hum. We'll just be exhausted tomorrow. That's all there is to it, just totally exhausted. (*Twisting an alarm clock, heading for the door.*) Come on, Pixrose, I'll help you get settled into the children's room. Good night, all.

MARSHAEL. Katty. Ah, what are you gonna do tomorrow —'bout Willie Wayne and all?

KATTY. Why, nothing. That's all I can do. I don't have children or a career like you do. Anyway I don't like changes. My hair's still the same as I wore it in college. Come on, Pixrose, it's late. (*Pixrose and Katty leave the bedroom and exit down the hall.*)

COLLARD. God, I feel so old and tired.

MARSHAEL. It's late. You try and get some sleep. It'll be morning soon. (*The lights dim upstairs as they rise downstairs. Leon and Brocker are in a deep discussion. Brocker is playing with the wooden spoons.*)

LEON. It's strange.

BROCKER. I know.

LEON. I mean she used to sing and whistle all the time when you were around painting those kitchen chairs red

BROCKER. It's strange.

LEON. She loved listening to you playing them spoons.

BROCKER. Yeah. Hey, look, I've got a thought. Why don't we get those snapshots taken for Willie Wayne? Do him a favor? After all, he's a bleeding man.

LEON. You mean it?

BROCKER. Sure. We got flash cubes; what the fuck.

LEON. Fine with me (*As they move into the parlor.*) So anyway, what happened with Marshael? I mean, you used to could make her laugh. I asked you over here 'cause you knew how t'make her happy.

BROCKER. Look, Leon, I can't make my ownself happy; so how the hell am I gonna make her happy?

LEON. (*As he removes the lift lid from the coffin.*) Well, I just don't understand what could have happened between you two. (*Noticing the corpse.*) Boy, I wonder what it's like really being dead.

BROCKER. Don't look like much. Smile! (*He takes the picture.*)

LEON. So what about Marshael? Why does she hate you now?

BROCKER. (*He takes pictures through the following.*) Who knows. She, ah, called me to come pick her up from the hospital Tuesday night. We were driving home. It was raining. She was upset, but, ah, but she still looked, you know, good. And for some reason, I started telling her how the first time I'd seen her was, when she was playing her violin at the pancake supper. I said she looked like some sort of wild, frightened angel, ripping up that violin with her black eyes blazing. Then,

ah, she started crying. She told me to pull the car over. I did. Well, I don't know. Nothing had ever happened, that way, between us before, and I felt funny with my tongue down her throat holding onto her hair. You know, with her husband there paralyzed in the hospital and with her all in distress. Seemed like maybe I was taking advantage of a situation or something; and so I left. I just took off. Walked home in the storm. Stepped in some goddamn horseshit, leaving her there in the car—alone—wanting somebody; needing something. God. What an asshole. Jesus, no wonder she hates me. (*Upstairs Marshael walks out onto the balcony.*) I leave the one woman I love alone in a great, unrelenting deluge. I give her nothing. Nothing. Not one thing. God, help us all. Listen, Leon; I gotta go. (*He heads for the front door.*)
LEON. Go where?
BROCKER. To find it. To get it.
LEON. What? To get what?
BROCKER. Exaltation! Love! Rapture! Glory! That's all there is! That's all that's left. (*He exits. As the lights go down, Leon returns to the parlor to put the lid back on the coffin. The moonlight drifts into the bedroom. Collard is sleeping in the bed. Marshael is standing on the balcony, talking to herself.*)
MARSHAEL. I won't sleep. My eyes are red I'm afraid to sleep. It's not like my nerves are raw, you know. It's like—like they've been stripped, leaving nothing but cold, cold bones. (*Pixrose enters the upstairs hall in her nightgown. She is terrified, distraught.*)
PIXROSE. I can't stay there. I can't. I can't.
LEON. Pixrose? What's wrong? Are you all right?
PIXROSE. I don't like sleeping in the children's room. All the toys and dolls look at me and scare me—
LEON. Here, now, here. Don't be scared. Don't be.
PIXROSE. See, it's not fair how my folks were trying to burn Franky and me up too. They were afraid of things. Thought life was evil and burned themselves up. But—but they shouldn't a tried burning me and Franky away with them.

First at home and then in that car. Still though, we survived. We survived—Oh, Leon. (*Then as she leaps down the stairs into his arms.*) Hold me quick!

LEON. Here, now, here. (*Leon picks her up in his arms. Then, after a moment, starts to carry her out.*) I'll get you a glass of milk. There's a cot on the back porch. You can drink the milk out on the cot. Out where Brocker's dog is sleeping. (*He carries her out through the dining room. The lights focus back on Marshael's room. She is talking to herself and putting Jamey's clothes in a sack.*)

MARSHAEL. All these ties. You never wore even half of 'em. Wasted ties. God, loose change. Always pockets full of loose change. And your Spearmint chewing gum sticks. Damn, and look—your lost car keys. Oh, well, the car's gone now. Damn you, leaving me alone with your mess. Leaving me again with all your goddamn, gruesome mess t'clean up. Damn, you, wait! You wait! You're not leaving me here like this. You're gonna face me! I won't survive! You cheat! I've got t'have something . . . redemption . . . something. (*She leaves the room, goes down to the parlor and walks in. The coffin is closed She begins to circle it.*) There you are. Coward. Hiding. Away from me. Hiding. (*Moving in on him.*) Look, I know I hurt you something bad, but why did you have to hold her fat, little hand like that? Huh? Treating me like nothing! I'm not . . . nothing. Hey, I'm talking. I'm talking to you. You'd better look at me. I mean it, you bastard! (*She pulls the lid off the coffin.*) Jamey. God, your face. Jamey, I'm scared. I'm so scared. I'm scared not to be loved. I'm scared for our life not to work out. It didn't, did it? Jamey? Damn you, where are you? Are you down in Mobile, baby? Have you taken a spin t'Mobile? I'm asking you — shit — Crystal Springs? How 'bout Scotland? You wanted to go there . . . your grandfather was from there. You shit! You're not . . . I know you're not . . . I love you! God. Stupid thing to say. I love you!! Okay; okay. You're gone. You're gone. You're not laughing. You're not . . . nothing. (*She moves away from the coffin, realizing it contains nothing of value.*) Still I gotta have something. Still something . . . (*As she runs out of the parlor then out the front door.*) The trees. Still have the trees. The purple, purple trees— (*The front door is left open. There is a moment of silence before Brocker appears in the side yard carrying wild flowers and a ladder. He is very drunk. He wears some of the flowers in his hair.*)

BROCKER. Hey! Love! My, love! I'm carrying you off to the moon! To the starts! To the shining planet of Mars! (*He now has the ladder up and is making his way to the top.*) *Exaltation!!!* Where angels aspire to glory! *Exaltation!!!*

COLLARD. (*Overlapping, as she comes out of her sleep.*) Who's there? Shut up. My aching head. God! Who is it?! Stay away! (*She runs out onto the balcony and starts throwing colored Easter eggs at Brocker.*) Who's there? Stay away! Go away! I mean it. Get out of here! God. Take that.

BROCKER. (*Overlapping.*) Hey, love! I'm carrying you in my arms to paradise! Remember?! Exaltation?!! Hey, watch it! OW! Look out, that's my chest!

COLLARD. (*Running on.*) It's Brocker! You lunatic! You raving imbecile!

BROCKER. (*Overlapping.*) Collard, you bitch!

COLLARD. (*She is at the ledge now and throws the real eggs out of the bird's nest.*) Take that! You stinking drunkard! You broken dog. Take that!!

BROCKER. (*Overlapping.*) AAH!!! YUK!! Help! Help!

COLLARD. Oh, God! Look at this! Look! Now you've made me murder these baby eggs! I've done murder! What else is left? What else?! OOOHH!! (*She collapses back down onto the bed.*)

BROCKER. Jesus! YUK!!! It's a madhouse. There's nothing more but to go sleep in a ditch with my dog. Here, Pooch! Hey, Pooch! (*Brocker whistles. A dog's bark is heard in the distance.*) Pooch, come here — Pooch, Pooch! (*He walks off looking for the dog, as the lights fade to blackout.*)

END OF SCENE

ACT III

Scent 3

It is the following morning. The coffin and the flower arrangements have been removed. The blue pin striped suit is also gone. The visible rooms in the house are empty. Pixrose is outside. She wears a pink dress with long white gloves and white stockings. She has on a hat with cherries. She is humming a song and spinning around and around in circles as the lights go up. Brocker enters R. He looks like he has been sleeping in a ditch.

PIXROSE. (*Still spinning.*) Hi Brocker! Good morning!!

BROCKER. Yeah, morning. Hey, what's going on?

PIXROSE. Just spinning around! Trying to make myself dizzy—(*Laughing as she staggers to the ground.*) It's fun. You wanna try it?

BROCKER. No, thanks. I don't need to spin t'get dizzy any more. I'm just blessed with it.

PIXROSE. Hey, Leon and me washed your dog for you this morning.

BROCKER. (*Picking up the ladder.*) Well . . . thanks.

PIXROSE What's his name anyway?

BROCKER. He's called Blacky. That's his name, Blacky. (*Brocker walks away carrying the ladder as Collard comes out of the upstairs bathroom. She is dressed in an ill fitted dress with ridiculous shoes and a funny looking hat. The outfit should be the exact opposite of the image Collard likes to present of herself. She wabbles out of the bathroom and stares at herself in the mirror.)*

COLLARD. You look perposterous. Absolutely and totally. I'm not going. That's all. I'm just not going. (*Leon and Katty enter from the dining room. Katty is dressed in her navy blue outfit. Leon has on his suit and tie. He carries a corsage and boxes containing the armbands and veils. He sets the boxes down on the card table.*)

KATTY. But did you see her at all this morning?

LEON. No, I ain't seen her at all.

KATTY. Are you sure she didn't go with Wayne to deliver the suit?

LEON. No, she didn't go with him. I spoke to him before he left—

KATTY. You did? What did he say? Was there anything interesting that was said? (*Wayne enters through the front door. He is dressed in a three piece suit.*)

WAYNE. Leon! Is she back? Has Marshael come back?

LEON. No, no one's seen her at all.

WAYNE. Well, we've got to find her!

LEON. Look, I gotta give Pixrose this precious rememberance. Marshael'll get back if she wants to. (*Leon exits to the kitchen. There is a tense moment of silence between Katty and Wayne.*)

WAYNE. I, ah, took Uncle Wilbur his suit.

KATTY. That's good.

WAYNE. Look, things have really been tense for me. Losing my only brother and all. It's been a shock.

KATTY. I know, Wayne, I know. Here, I'll ah, make some eggs up for you and heat the coffee. You gotta keep your strength up, Angel Pie. You know that? You really do. (*They exit through the dining room door, as Leon comes around the house, R., to find Pixrose sitting in the grass.*)

LEON. Hi.

PIXROSE. Hi.

LEON. You look pretty. That's a pretty dress . . . the hat too.

PIXROSE. Thanks. It's my Easter outfit.

LEON. Well . . . Here's a gift for you.

PIXROSE. For me?

LEON. Them's purple violets. It's my favorite kind of flowers. But—but that don't mean that they have to be your favorite kind too!

PIXROSE. They smell pretty. (*Holding the flowers up to Leon.*) Here, smell them. They're pretty.

LEON. Good. Hey, you wanna go 'round to the front and wait for the limousine? It's due to arrive directly.

PIXROSE. Sure! I've never seen a limousine before!

LEON. You think I have? (*They exit to the front of the house. Suddenly Marshael, Wayne, Katty and Brocker all enter the front hall from U.C. They are in an uproar. Marshael starts up the stairs; the rest follow her.*)

KATTY. Really, Marshael, I think, for your own sake, you should go —

BROCKER. (*Overlapping.*) Will you stop hounding the woman! For Christ's sake —

WAYNE. (*Overlapping.*) But you've got to go! You can't not go! Why won't you go?

MARSHAEL. Because I'm tired! I'm finally tired. I think I can sleep. And what's that horrible smell?!!

KATTY. I know! It's like — rotten eggs! What could it be?

WAYNE. But it's a disgrace, if you refuse to go to your own husband's funeral! A selfish, foolish disgrace! (*They are upstairs by now. Marshael enters her bedroom. The rest follow.*)

MARSHAEL. Look, I'm not going to go and put that rotting mess of formaldehyde in the ground, and that's all there is to it!

WAYNE. You're totally irreverant! Totally! There ought to be some sort of law —

BROCKER. (*Overlapping.*) The woman needs rest, you asshole!!

COLLARD. (*Overlapping.*) What's all this?! Don't bring *him* in here!!!

BROCKER. Oh, what do *you* know!

COLLARD. Lunatic!

WAYNE. (*To Marshael.*) Look, just comb your hair, and we'll go. It's getting late!

MARSHAEL. What's that rotting smell? It's making me sick.

KATTY. Collard, are you wearing that?

COLLARD. No! (*Suddenly Leon rushes in the front door.*)

LEON. (*Yelling up to them.*) Hey. Hey, everyone! It's here! The limousine! It's here! (*He runs back out and R.*)

WAYNE. The limousine?!

KATTY. Oh my, it's finally arrived. (*They start down the stairs.*)

WAYNE. Well, I'd better go check on it.

KATTY. Here, I'll go too. You might need some help.

WAYNE. Make sure things are all in order.

KATTY. Make sure they have the directions straight.

WAYNE. Make sure the headlights are all working. (*Katty and Wayne exit the front door.*)

MARSHAEL. It's you, Brocker. That smell; it's you.

BROCKER. I know it. I know.

MARSHAEL. Well, it's making me dizzy.

BROCKER. Sorry. Look, I'll go change. I'll just go change. (*He leaves the room and goes downstairs. In the front hall he starts to take his shirt off. He picks up his hat and coat and the two wooden spoons and then walks out the front door. It is all right if his actions overlap somewhat with the scene that is going on upstairs in the bedroom.*)

COLLARD. Look, Marsh, I can't go to the funreal. I just look too preposterous. I don't even have on clean underwear. I'm not gonna go.

MARSHAEL. But you gotta go. I—told the kids you'd go. I had breakfast with them over at Aunt Muffin's this morning. They wanna ride in the white convertible. They said they wanna ride with you.

COLLARD. But who are you gonna go with?

MARSHAEL. I don't need to go. Shit, Collard. I'm asking you to go!

COLLARD. (*A moment.*) All right then. I'll go. I'd be glad t'go

MARSHAEL. Good. I told them you'd bring their shoes when you came.

COLLARD. All right. Here, I can put 'em in here. God. You need rest bad, Marshy. Look here, your hands are shaking.

MARSHAEL. Right. Yes. I'm gonna try and get some sleep soon. Stop my eyes aching.

COLLARD. (*Picking up the children's shoes.*) Good then you rest. I gotta go. Don't worry. I'll see they get their little shoes. I'll take care of it all. You sleep. (*Wayne, Katty, Leon, and Pixrose all come in the front door. Pixrose is wearing the violet corsage.*)

WAYNE. I don't believe they've got Jersey Crow driving our limousine in that stupid hat.

COLLARD. That's them.

LEON. Look, if she doesn't want to go, I don't see why she should have to go. (*Handing Wayne a black arm band.*) Now here Willie Wayne, this is for you.

PIXROSE. Hey, Collard, look! Honeysuckle! (*She waves the honeysuckle to Collard who is coming down the stairs. Katty and Pixrose both start struggling with their veils. Katty is also putting on her gloves and getting her handbag.*)

WAYNE. Get Marshael, Collard, we've got to go immediately!

COLLARD. She's not going.

WAYNE. What is this? She's got to go! It's required!

COLLARD. Look, just because you'll always have the taste of leather in your mouth, doesn't mean the rest of us have to.

LEON. Collard, here's your veil.

PIXROSE. (*Overlapping.*) Am I wearing this right? (*Katty goes to her assistance.*)

COLLARD. (*Overlapping as she takes the veil with a new sense of command and warmth.*) Thanks. I'm gonna take the kids in the convertible. Look, you and Pixrose go in the limousine. (*She tries putting her veil on over her hat.*)

LEON. Great!

WAYNE. (*As he leaves.*) I wash my hands of it! I wash my hands of it entirely!

65

KATTY. Remember then, Collard. It's Grace Episcopal Church right on East Peace Street! Do you have that!

COLLARD. (*Putting her veil directly on her head then triumphantly putting the hat on over it.*) Yeah, I got it! I'll be there. I got it. (*They all exit out the front door. Upstairs Marshael rises. She has taken off her black dress and stands only in a white slip. She sits down on the bed and takes hold of a pillow. Brocker appears around the side of the house. He is wearing his hat and his dark suit coat without his shirt. He looks at the window, then starts playing a song on the spoons. Marshael wraps a blanket around herself and goes out onto the balcony.*)

MARSHAEL. Brocker—

BROCKER. Hi. Just dropped by. Thought you might need something. I don't know. Thought I'd see.

MARSHAEL. Thanks. I'm just gonna rest. Lord, you look awfully funny.

BROCKER. I do?

MARSHAEL. Sorta. What's that on your chest?

BROCKER. (*Opening his coat.*) A ship. (*Then making the ship move my moving his muscles.*) It's on a troubled sea.

MARSHAEL. (*Bursting out laughing.*) Oh, Lord! Look at that! A troubled sea!!

BROCKER. I like it when you laugh. I love to hear you laugh!

MARSHAEL. Really? I don't even know what my laugh sounds like.

BROCKER. It sounds . . . happy.

MARSHAEL. Hey, look, you could do one thing for me.

BROCKER. I could?

MARSHAEL. I need some more Easter candy for my kids. You know, things like bunnies and chickens and eggs and stuff.

BROCKER. Oh, sure, sure. I saw a whole bunch of that junk over at Ben Franklin's Dime Store. I'll, ah, get it for you right away. I'll buy a whole load of stuff! I'll run go and get it now! (*He starts to go R.*)

MARSHAEL. Brocker, wait! (*He stops.*)

BROCKER. What? What is it?

MARSHAEL. I don't know. Play something for me. Will you? Just till I go to sleep. Play something on the spoons. Would you?

BROCKER. All right. Sure. I'll play you a tune. Wanna hear, 'This Old Man?' I do it real well. Why—why you won't be able to keep your eyes open.

MARSHAEL. Play it. Yes, play that one. (*Brocker sits on the stump. He starts playing the spoons and singing "This Old Man."*)

BROCKER. (*Singing.*)
This old man
He played one
He played knick-knack
On my drum.
With a knick-knack paddy whack
Give a dog a bone
This old man comes rolling home.
This old man
He played two

MARSHAEL. That's nice.

BROCKER. (*Continuing.*)
He played knick-knack
On my shoe.

MARSHAEL. That's a nice song. (*She starts slowly into the bedroom.*)

BROCKER. (*Continuing.*)
With a knick-knack paddy whack
Give a dog a bone
This old man comes rolling home.

MARSHAEL. (*Getting into bed.*) I like it.

This old man
He played three
He played knick-knack
On my knee

67

MARSHAEL. (*Almost a-sleep.*) I do... (*She falls asleep as he continues to play the spoons.*)

With a knick-knack paddy whack
Give a dog a bone
This old man comes rolling home.

This old man
He played four
He played knick-knack
On my door
With a knick-knack paddy whack
Give a dog a bone
This old man comes rolling home.

(*The lights fade to blackout.*)

THE MISS FIRECRACKER CONTEST

WITH LOVE AND STARS
TO STEPHEN

THE MISS FIRECRACKER CONTEST was presented by the Manhattan Theatre Club, in New York City, on May 1, 1984. It was directed by Stephen Tobolowsky; the scenery was designed by John Lee Beatty; the costumes were designed by Jennifer Von Mayrhauser; the lighting was designed by Dennis Parichy; the sound was designed by Stan Metelits; and the production stage manager was Wendy Chapin. The cast was as follows:

CARNELLE SCOTT . . . . Holly Hunter
POPEYE JACKSON . . . . Belita Moreno
ELAIN RUTLEDGE . . . . Patricia Richardson
DELMOUNT WILLIAMS . . . . Mark Linn-Baker
MAC SAM . . . . Budge Threlkeld
TESSY MAHONEY . . . . Margo Martindale

SYNOPSIS OF SCENES

SCENE ONE: The living room of Ronelle William's house in Brookhaven, Mississippi — about five o'clock Monday afternoon on a hot day at the end of June.

There is something dreary and suffocating and frightening about the room with its dark oak furniture, its heavy, bright curtains and the endless clutter of nicknacks. An old spinning wheel sits in a far corner of the room.

There are three entrances and exits; a front door; a door leading to the kitchen; and a staircase leading to the upstairs rooms.

SCENE TWO: The same setting. About eight o'clock in the evening, on the following Saturday.

THE CAST

CARNELLE SCOTT, 24, the beauty contestant
POPEYE JACKSON, 23, Carnelle's seamstress
ELAIN RUTLEDGE, 32, Carnelle's first cousin; a beauty
DELMOUNT WILLIAMS, 28, Carnelle's first cousin;
  Elain's brother
MAC SAM, 36, the balloon man
TESSY MAHONEY, 23, the beauty contest coordinator

THE SETTING

The action of the play takes place in Brookhaven, Mississippi; a small southern town.

THE TIME

The ending of June and the beginning of July.

AUTHOR'S NOTE: It is strongly suggested that the actress playing Carnelle dye her hair bright red instead of opting for a wig.

ACT I

SCENE ONE

The lights go up onstage. Carnelle Scott, 24, stands with her back to the audience looking into a mirror. Carnelle is tallish with an oddly attractive face, a nice figure and very bright dyed red hair. She wears purple leotards, tights and tap shoes.
Carnelle turns away from the mirror with a glint in her eyes. She pushes the rolled up rug back even further, then rushes to place the needle back on the record spinning on the record player. A sung version of "The Star Spangled Banner" begins playing loudly.
Carnelle checks a notebook, then rushes madly back to the kitchen. She quickly returns with wooden spoons and stainless steel knives. She leaps into her talent routine that requires tap dancing, marching and baton twirling, none of which she is extremely adept at. When the record comes to, "And the rockets red glare . . . " she picks up a wooden spoon that she uses as an imaginary roman candle. She says, "Pow," each time she imagines it goes off. For the final, "Oh, say does that . . ." she puts down the spoons and picks up two knives that she uses as imaginary sparklers. She twirls them about. When the record is over Carnelle goes to remove the needle, as she repeats part of her routine to herself.

CARNELLE. Let's see, that was, "And the rockets red glare — (*Then as the imaginary Roman candle goes off.*) Boom! — The bombs bursting in air — Boom! — gave proof — Boom! — through the night — Boom! — that our flag was — Boom! — there — Boom! Boom! Boom!" (*She goes to mark down the ideas in her notebook.*)

73

Hmm. I don't know. I think that'll work. I think it will. (*There is a knock on the door.*) Coming. Coming—! Coming! (*Before going to the door Carnelle shakes her head of red hair back and forth, takes a towel from a chair and slings it carelessly around her neck. She begins panting deeply as she goes to open the door for Popeye Jackson. Popeye, 23, is a small, glowing person. She wears a homemade dress with many different size pockets and thick glasses with heavy black rims. She does not carry a purse.*) Oh, hello, Popeye. Come in. Come on in.

POPEYE. Thanks.

CARNELLE. (*Still breathing heavily.*) Wheew! Just make yourself at home. Oh, and please excuse the way I look, but I've been practicing my routine. It's something, I tell you, hard work. But it's coming along. It's coming right along.

POPEYE. Good.

CARNELLE. (*After an awkward moment.*) Well. I guess what I should do is show you the sketches so you'll have some idea of what I want.

POPEYE. Alright.

CARNELLE. (*Getting the sketches.*) They're right over here, I believe. Yes, here they are. (*Turning around.*) What's that thing?

POPEYE. (*Who has removed a magnifying glass from her pocket.*) It's my magnifying lens.

CARNELLE. A magnifying lens? You need that thing to see with?

POPEYE. Well, up close I do.

CARNELLE. Goodness gracious. Well, here're the sketches. Of course, now, I'm not an artist or anything; so the drawings aren't much. (*Pause.*) But I think you'll get the general idea.

POPEYE. (*Looking at the sketches through the lens.*) Oh, that's pretty.

CARNELLE. (*As if someone has given her a gift.*) You think so?

POPEYE. I like them stars.

CARNELLE. Well, I wanted to go with something really patriotic. Kinda traditional. You know, noble, in a sense.

POPEYE. And this costume's for a dance contest?

CARNELLE. Well, no; it's not a dance contest; it's for the Miss Firecracker Contest.

POPEYE. (*In the dark.*) Huh?

CARNELLE. The Miss Firecracker Contest? (*Popeye shakes her head.*) It's the beauty contest. They have it in Brookhaven every

Fourth of July. It's a tradition. It's a big event. It's famous. Why Representative Louis Pooley's gonna be here this very year to put the crown on the winner's head. It's a famous contest.

POPEYE. Well, I guess, I just don't know nothing about it.

CARNELLE. Well, it's odd to me. It's really odd to me.

POPEYE. Course I haven't been here in town but a short while. Only 'bout three weeks.

CARNELLE. (*Relieved.*) Oh! Oh, well, that explains it! that explains it all!!

POPEYE. Yeah.

CARNELLE. Anyway, this outfit is what I'm gonna be wearing in the talent section of the contest.

POPEYE. Oh.

CARNELLE. What I do's kind of a tap-dance-march-type-a-thing. It's gonna be done to, "The Star Spangled Banner." I'm gonna end up spinning these lit up sparklers around and around—one in each hand. (*She twirls the imaginary sparklers.*)

POPEYE. Gosh!

CARNELLE. And before that Roman candles going off—(*As she shoots off imaginary roman candles.*) Boom! Boom! Boom! Like that—right out over the top a the crowd!

POPEYE. Really?

CARNELLE. Oh, sure.

POPEYE. Boy.

CARNELLE. Well, so you think you'll be able to make up a pattern following these drawings?

POPEYE. I expect so.

CARNELLE. Well, then . . . the job is yours.

POPEYE. Thank you.

CARNELLE. You're welcome.

POPEYE. Maybe I should go on and get your measurements off you right now if ya don't mind.

CARNELLE. Oh, no, no. Fine. Go ahead. All right.

POPEYE. (*Getting her measuring tape from her pocket.*) I just need a few.

CARNELLE. Take all you want. I'll just stand right here. (*She strikes a dramatic pose.*) Just natural. Is this okay with you? This stance right here?

POPEYE. Sure. (*She begins measuring, looking at the measurement through her glass, writing it down, then starting a new measurement.*)

CARNELLE. My, I feel like a model or something. Very elegant. Of course, that's exactly what I should be doing. Modeling, that is. People have told me that. They say, "Carnelle, why do you keep slaving away at Slater's Jewelry Shop? You should be up in Memphis working as a model. You really should."

POPEYE. (*Trying to get Carnelle to relax her tightly tucked in stomach.*) You can just relax.

CARNELLE. What? Oh, I'm fine. Just fine.

POPEYE. Alright. (*She finishes with the waist measurement, looks at it through the glass, writes it down, then goes on.*)

CARNELLE. You know you do this very well. Expertly, in fact. Of course, you come highly recommended to me from Miss Celia Lily. She says you've done some really fine work in her shop. She says you seem really experienced to her.

POPEYE. Well, I'm that for sure. See, I been making clothes practically all my life. Started out when I was four years old.

CARNELLE. Oh, really?

POPEYE. Used to make little outfits for the bullfrogs that lived out around our yard.

CARNELLE. Bullfrogs! Yuk!

POPEYE. They was funny looking creatures.

CARNELLE. But why didn't you design clothes for your dolls?

POPEYE. We din't have no dolls.

CARNELLE. Oh; how sad.

POPEYE. Them frogs was okay.

CARNELLE. But what kind of clothes could you design for a frog? They'd look ugly in anything.

POPEYE. Well . . . one thing was a nurse's suit. Oh, and I remember a queen's robe and a cape of leaves. Different things.

CARNELLE. (*With a giggle.*) Well, I certainly hope you don't think of me as any bullfrog.

POPEYE. Huh?

CARNELLE. I mean, think I'm ugly like one of those dumb bullfrogs of yours.

POPEYE. Oh, I don't.

CARNELLE. Well, of course, you don't. I was just joking.

POPEYE. Oh.

CARNELLE. (*Suddenly very sad and uncomfortable.*) Are you about done?

POPEYE. Mostly. This here's all I need. (*Carnelle stares forlornly into space as Popeye measures her head.*) There. Done.

CARNELLE. Well, I've got to stretch a minute. (*She stretches from her waist, then kicks her leg up high.*) There! And, kick! And . . . kick!

POPEYE. You sure do kick high!

CARNELLE. Well, I work at it daily.

POPEYE. I could never kick like that.

CARNELLE. I don't know, maybe you could with practice. Want to try it? Come on and try it. Go ahead! And kick! And kick! And kick! And kick! (*Popeye kicks feebly in the air.*) Not bad. Keep on working at it. That's the only way to improve. Listen, I have a snack made up for us in the kitchen. Would you like it now?

POPEYE. Sure.

CARNELLE. I hope you don't mind, it's just ice tea and saltine crackers.

POPEYE. I love saltines.

CARNELLE. Alright then, I'll go get the snack. (*Carnelle exits to the kitchen. Popeye looks around. She goes over to the spinning wheel and spins it around. She watches it. She pretends to prick her finger on the needle. Carnelle comes back in carrying the snack tray. She now has an apron on over her leotards. Popeye turns around startled.*)

POPEYE. This sure is a scary house.

CARNELLE. You don't like it?

POPEYE. It's scary.

CARNELLE. Well, it's just like my Aunt Ronelle fixed it up. It's got her special touch: this old spinning wheel; these lace doilies; these old pictures in frames here. I'd prefer something more modern and luxurious, but—that's just me.

POPEYE. You live here with your aunt?

CARNELLE. Oh, no. She died. She had cancer.

POPEYE. I'm sorry.

CARNELLE. It happened just a few weeks before last Christmas. We were very close. It was a tragedy.

POPEYE. I'm sorry.

CARNELLE. (*As she pours Popeye's tea.*) You may of heard about her; Ronnelle Williams? It was a famous medical case— ran in all the newspapers.

POPEYE. No.

CARNELLE. Well, see what it was — Do you take lemon?

POPEYE. Please.

CARNELLE. Anyway, she had this cancer of the pituitary gland, I believe it was; so what they did was they replaced her gland with the gland of a monkey to see if they could save her life — Just help yourself to the sugar —

POPEYE. (*Moving to sit on the floor.*) Thanks.

CARNELLE. And they did, in fact, keep her alive for a month or so longer than she was expected to live.

POPEYE. Well, that's good.

CARNELLE. (*Pouring herself some tea.*) Of course, there were such dreadful side effects.

POPEYE. Mmm.

CARNELLE. She, well, she started growing long, black hairs all over her body just, well, just like an ape.

POPEYE. Gracious, Lord.

CARNELLE. It was very trying. But she was so brave. She even let them take photographs of her. Everyone said she was just a saint. A saint or an angel; one or the other.

POPEYE. It gives me the shivers.

CARNELLE. It was awfully hard on me losing my Aunt Ronelle — although I guess I should be used to it by now.

POPEYE. What's that?

CARNELLE. People dying. It seems like people'v been dying practically all my life, in one way or another. First my mother passed when I was barely a year old. Then my Daddy kinda drug me around with him till I was about nine and he couldn't stand me any longer; so he dropped me off to live with my Aunt Ronelle and Uncle George and their own two children: Elain and Delmount. They're incredible those two. They're just my ideal. Anyhow, we're happy up until the time when Uncle George falls to his death trying to pull this bird's nest out from the chimney.

POPEYE. He fall off from the roof?

CARNELLE. That's right. Tommy Turner was passing by throwing the evening paper and he caught sight of the whole event. Boom.

POPEYE. How awful.

CARNELLE. Anyhow, my original Daddy appears back here to live with us looking all kinda fat and swollen. And after staying on with us about two years, he suddenly drops dead in the summer's heat while running out to the Tropical Ice Cream truck. Heart failure, they said it was. Then this thing with Aunt Ronelle dying right before Christmas. It's been hard to bear.

POPEYE. (*After a moment.*) I had a brother who was bit by a water moccasin down by the Pearl River, and he died.

CARNELLE. Well; you know, they say everyone's gonna be dying someday. I believe it to.

POPEYE. Yeah. May as well. (*She finishes a cracker and wipes her lips with a napkin.*) That sure was tasty.

CARNELLE. Well . . . thank you much. Would you like to see the material I've chosen to make my costume with?

POPEYE. Why, yes.

CARNELLE. Good. Then I'll just run get it.

POPEYE. Oh, Carnelle?

CARNELLE. Yes?

POPEYE. Do you mind if I look at these pictures in frames here?

CARNELLE. Oh, no. That's what they're there for. (*Carnelle exits upstairs to the bedrooms. Popeye goes over and picks up her magnifying glass. She then goes and looks at the pictures. She looks at one, then another, then suddenly, at the third picture, she is struck. She picks it up and looks at it, studying it closely with her lens.*)

POPEYE. My. Oh, my. (*Carnelle comes back down carrying a sack.*)

CARNELLE. Who are you looking at?

POPEYE. A man. This man here.

CARNELLE. Oh, that's my cousin, Delmount.

POPEYE. What eyes. Look at his hair — It's wild wouldn't you say? It's wild.

CARNELLE. Well, I suppose, Delmount is rather a romantic figure.

POPEYE. Really?

CARNELLE. He was always writing sheets and sheets of poetry to the women he loved then he'd set them all afire and bury the ashes.

POPEYE. (*Swooning.*) How sad!

CARNELLE. Yes, Delmount's very odd. He can do this trick where he wiggles his ears.

POPEYE. (*Totally sold that this is the man for her.*) He can!?

CARNELLE. Sure.

POPEYE. (*Impulsively.*) Where's he live now?

CARNELLE. Well, it's strange . . . see, Delmount, he's had kind of a checkered past.

POPEYE. Checkered?

CARNELLE. Right. And about the first of the year a Louisiana judge sentenced him to a — well, to a mental institution.

POPEYE. Is he mad?

CARNELLE. No. Not really. He hit a man in the face with a bottle; so his lawyer got him put there instead of jail.

POPEYE. Oh.

CARNELLE. (*Upset.*) He was released in the spring, but he hasn't been home since. I don't know where he is now.

POPEYE. I hope he's alright.

CARNELLE. Here, let's look at the material.

POPEYE. Alright.

CARNELLE. (*Taking the red material from the sack.*) Here's the red.

POPEYE. Ooooh, that's pretty. (*Touching it.*) Silky too.

CARNELLE. And, of course, the blue.

POPEYE. (*Looking at the material through her glass.*) It's just like a midnight sky. I love blue.

CARNELLE. And then, the most expensive, the most elegant of all — silver for the stars.

POPEYE. Why, you went all out on this material — I can see that.

CARNELLE. Well, yes. I hope it's gonna be okay. Not having any white. I mean, I hope red, blue and silver will be patriotic enough.

POPEYE. Well, I just can't wait to —

ELAIN'S VOICE. Carnelle! Carnelle, Honey! (*Elain Rutledge, 32, enters through the front door. She is dressed in elegant pastels but appears somewhat wilted in the summer's heat. Elain could most definitely be described as beautiful, but her looks are now more strained and anxious than they once were. She carries expensive luggage, a cosmetic case, and a gift.*)

CARNELLE. (*Running to hug her.*) Elain!! It's Elain!!!

ELAIN. (*Hugging her.*) Why, hello, my little Carnation! How are you doing?!

CARNELLE. (*Overlapping.*) Oh, Elain! Elain! I'm just fine!

80

ELAIN. Why, you really did dye your hair, didn't you?

CARNELLE. Do you like it?

ELAIN. Well, it's just as red as it can be!

CARNELLE. That's what I wanted, crimson red.

ELAIN. Well, then, it couldn't be more perfect! Will you help me with these bags, here? My arms are just falling off!

CARNELLE. (*Taking the biggest bags.*) Of course! I'm sorry! Goodness, I thought you weren't coming in till the weekend.

ELAIN. Oh, I know, I know. I suddenly decided to cut my stay off short with my mother-in-law. I decided just to drive by Hollybluff and beep twice.

CARNELLE. (*With a giggle.*) Oh, you crazy thing!

ELAIN. No, really, I'm sorry, dar'lin, I should a called you up but — (*Suddenly noticing Popeye.*) Why, hello, Honey!

CARNELLE. Oh, this is my friend, Popeye Jackson. Popeye, this is my cousin, Elain Rutledge, the one I —

ELAIN. (*Overlapping.*) Why, hello, Popeye, so nice to meet you. What a smashing outfit!

POPEYE. Thank you.

CARNELLE. Elain knows everything about clothes. She just adores them.

ELAIN. Oh you crazy dear! Look here's a little something I picked up for you at a shop in the Quarter. (*Handing Carnelle a gift.*)

CARNELLE. What! Oh, you shouldn't have! Really, you shouldn't have. (*She opens the box and takes out a very strangely decorated Mardi gras mask.*) Why look! It's beautiful! Isn't that beautiful!

ELAIN. I just thought of you when I saw it. You'll have to wear it to a mask ball.

CARNELLE. (*Holding the mask in front of her face.*) How elegant! How simply elegant! Look, Popeye!

POPEYE. May I hold it too?

CARNELLE. Why, of course. (*She hands Popeye the mask. Elain and Carnelle hug then turn back to Popeye. There is a moment of silence as Popeye holds the mask over her eyes and slowly moves her head from side to side. Perhaps she makes a strange sound.*)

ELAIN. (*Taking off her dangling, shimmering earrings and handing them out to Popeye.*) Oh, here, Popeye, these are for you.

POPEYE. What?

ELAIN. Please, they're a gift to you. Here, put them on.

POPEYE. Oh, no.

CARNELLE. Oh, Elain! Elain!

ELAIN. (*Overlapping.*) Yes, yes! I insist! They're just right for you; they're just your color. Here, I'll put them on for you. (*She puts the earrings on Popeye.*) Oh, stunning! They look just simply stunning!

POPEYE. (*Slowly shaking her head back and forth.*) Why, thank you.

CARNELLE. Isn't she wonderful, Popeye! Isn't she just perfectly perfect!

ELAIN. Oh, how I wish I were!

CARNELLE. Don't be silly; you are!

POPEYE. (*Shaking her head.*) I never had me no earbobs.

ELAIN. Well, I'm glad you have them, Popeye. They look dazzling on you.

POPEYE. Well. I think I better be going. It's getting towards dark. Let me get all this rounded up. (*She starts getting the materials together.*)

CARNELLE. Popeye's going to be using this material to make my costume for the Miss Firecracker Contest.

ELAIN. You mean, you went on and signed up for that?

CARNELLE. Yes, I registered today.

ELAIN. I don't see why you're so interested in being Miss Firecracker; there's nothing to it.

CARNELLE. Well, not for you. See, Elain was Miss Firecracker way back when she was just eighteen.

ELAIN. Well, seventeen, actually.

CARNELLE. Anyway, it was way back that first year when I came to live with them. She was a vision of beauty riding on that float with a crown on her head waving to everyone. I thought I'd drop dead when she passed by me.

ELAIN. All that was ages ago. It's silly to think about.

CARNELLE. Anyway, I just thought I'd give it a whirl. I'm twenty-four. Twenty-five's the age limit. I just thought I'd give it a whirl while I still could.

ELAIN. (*Powdering her nose.*) They ought to change that name to—well, to something like, Miss Fourth of July. Miss Firecracker sounds so trashy.

CARNELLE. Course, I don't expect to win—that's crazy. I'm just in it for the experience—that's the main thing.

POPEYE. Well, I think you'd be perfect for a Miss Firecracker—with your red hair and all.

CARNELLE. Oh, well, that's actually why I dyed my hair red; I thought it'd be more appropriate for the contest.

POPEYE. It's a nice dye job too. I don't see no roots or nothing.

CARNELLE. I try to do a careful job on it.

POPEYE. Well, I got it all together here.

CARNELLE. Good, well here're the sketches.

POPEYE. And when will you be needing your costume by?

CARNELLE. Oh. Well, the audition'll be this very Saturday; so could you have it by Wednesday afternoon or Thursday at the latest?

POPEYE. Tuesday's fine.

CARNELLE. Alright, I'll see you on Tuesday. (*Carnelle and Popeye are at the front door now.*)

POPEYE. Alright. Bye.

CARNELLE. Bye, bye.

POPEYE. (*To Elain.*) And I love my earbobs!

ELAIN. (*From the sofa.*) Oh, good!

POPEYE. Well, alright, bye. (*She exits.*)

CARNELLE. Bye, bye. (*Turning and coming back to Elain.*) Oh, Elain! That was so sweet what you did—giving Popeye those earrings. It meant so much to her. You're so generous!

ELAIN. (*Meaning it.*) Don't talk about it, please. It was nothing. Oh, mind if I have a glass of this delicious looking ice tea? I'm about ready to drop dead from the heat.

CARNELLE. Oh, of course! Please! Here, I'll run get you a fresh glass out from the kitchen. (*Carnelle picks up the tray and exits. Elain takes off her hat and fans herself. She looks sadly around the room. Carnelle returns with a glass with a small umbrella in it.*) Here, now—

ELAIN. Bless you.

CARNELLE. There you are.

ELAIN. Why, Carnation, you're saving my life. This is heaven. Sheer heaven!

CARNELLE. (*Running to Elain's clothes bag.*) Oh, Elain, did you bring that dress along with you that I asked about on the phone?

You know, the beautiful red antebellum dress that you wore at the Natchez Pilgrimage the first year you got married. See, it's gonna be perfect for me to wear in the contest. I'm trying to make crimson red my thematic color. (*Opening the bag: she discovers the dress is not there.*)

ELAIN. I see — but I thought you said you weren't gonna be needing a formal dress for the audition this Saturday.

CARNELLE. I know, that's true. We'll just need them in the actual contest for the opening Parade of Firecrackers.

ELAIN. So, why don't we just wait till after the audition and see if you make it to the pageant.

CARNELLE. Why? Don't you think I'll make it?

ELAIN. Well, I hope so, Carnelle, but they only pick five girls.

CARNELLE. Well . . . I've thought about it, and I, frankly, can't think of five other girls in town that are prettier than me. I'm speaking honestly now. Course I know there's Caroline Jeffers, but she has those yellow teeth —

ELAIN. (*Not wanting to get into it.*) My this mint is delicious! Did you grow it yourself?

CARNELLE. Aunt Ronelle planted it before she died.

ELAIN. Well, it's quite refreshing.

CARNELLE. I know why you're worried. You think I've ruined my chances, cause — 'cause of my reputation.

ELAIN. I don't know what you mean — you're perfectly sweet.

CARNELLE. Well, everyone knew I used to go out with lots of men and all that. Different ones. It's been a constant thing with me since I was young and —

ELAIN. Let's not discuss it in all a this heat.

CARNELLE. I just mention it cause it's different now, since Aunt Ronelle died and since — I got that disease.

ELAIN. Please, Carnelle, nobody's profiting by this information!

CARNELLE. Anyway, I go to church now and I'm signed up to where I take an orphan home to dinner once a week or to a movie; and — and I work on the cancer drive here just like you do in Natchez.

ELAIN. That's all very admirable, I'm sure.

CARNELLE. My life has meaning. People aren't calling me, Miss Hot Tamale anymore like they used to. Everything's changed. And being in that contest — it would be such an honor to me . . . I can't explain the half of it.

ELAIN. Well, if you don't make it to the finals, just try to remember that Mama was at her most noblest when she was least attractive.

CARNELLE. I wish you had about a drop a faith in me. I'm not all that ugly.

ELAIN. And I wish you would stop fishing for compliments — 'cause I'm sick and worn out with giving people compliments about themselves!

CARNELLE. (*Overlapping.*) I'm sorry. I'm so, so sorry, I make such stupid blunders. I know you don't think I'm ugly.

ELAIN. (*Overlapping.*) I'm not myself — I'm just not myself. (*She begins brushing her hair. The phone rings. Elain freezes. Carnelle goes to answer it.*) If it's for me — say — say, I'm resting.

CARNELLE. Hello. . . . Oh, hello, Franklin. . . . Yes, she's here. . . . Well, I think she decided not to stop by there. . . . No, she's asleep now. She's gone on to sleep. . . . Well, wait just a minute, I'll go see. (*She puts her hand over the phone.*) He wants me to go wake you up.

ELAIN. (*In a whisper.*) He what! Oh, how inconsiderate can he be! Why, I've been driving all day long in this blazing heat and he doesn't even care if I get my rest. You tell him I'm out dead with exhaustion and you absolutely can not wake me.

CARNELLE. (*She waits a few beats and then says breathlessly into the phone.*) Franklin . . . I absolutely can not wake her. She's out dead with exhaustion. . . . Alright, I'll tell her. Bye, bye. (*She hangs up the phone.*) He says for you to please call him when you wake up.

ELAIN. Oh, he does, does he? Well, he can just sit and wait, cause I'm not calling him — not ever.

CARNELLE. Why not?

ELAIN. Listen Carnation, I think you should know something — I'm not just here on a visit.

CARNELLE. You're not?

ELAIN. No. (*Then after a moment.*) I've left Franklin.

CARNELLE. What?!

ELAIN. Now, remember, it's a sworn secret and not a living soul is to find it out.

CARNELLE. I won't say a word to anyone. I swear.

ELAIN. You see, I haven't told Franklin yet and he actually still believes everything is—bearable between us.

CARNELLE. I just can't believe all this. You were so in love. It seemed like Franklin loved you so much. I thought I wanted a man to love me that much.

ELAIN. Yes; he did love me. But it just caused him to follow me around asking, "Do you love me? How much do you love me? Tell me how you love me," till I could shake him till he rattled.

CARNELLE. Then you don't love him anymore?

ELAIN. (*Taking off her jewelry.*) No. He makes me ill.

CARNELLE. How awful.

ELAIN. Yes.

CARNELLE. But what about your two little boys. They need a mother.

ELAIN. Oh, children manage in this world. Don't ask me about them.

CARNELLE. Gosh, Aunt Ronelle said you had it all up there in Natchez; everything—just'like a queen in a castle.

ELAIN. I know. I did. I only hope I can stand to give it all up. (*Deeply moved.*) We had such beautiful clocks. I must have a bath. (*She rises.*)

CARNELLE. Elain. (*Elain stops.*) What was it like—when you had it all?

ELAIN. Ah, Carnation! The abundance of treasures merely serves to underline the desperate futility of life. (*She exits upstairs to the bedrooms.*)

CARNELLE. Oh—Tell me more—Please! Tell me more! (*She picks up all of the bags and follows Elain out of the room. The stage is empty for a few moments. Suddenly, the front door opens, Delmount Williams enters. Delmount, 28, is tall and thin with piercing blue eyes and a sallow complexion. He wears a white shirt and a pair of worn out pants. He carries a brown paper bag containing all of his belongings. Leaving the front door ajar, Delmount enters the room. He finds something about the atmosphere loathsome. He sits down and lights up a pipe. He sits smoking for a few moments, taking in the room. Popeye peeps in the front door.*)

POPEYE. (*As she enters.*) Carnelle? Carnelle—(*Spotting Delmount.*) Oh!

DELMOUNT. Hello.

POPEYE. Hi. Are you—You're—

DELMOUNT. Delmount Williams. I'm Carnelle's cousin.

POPEYE. Yeah.

DELMOUNT. Well, I don't know where Carnelle is right now.

POPEYE. Oh.

DELMOUNT. You're a friend of hers, I suppose?

POPEYE. Yes. I just met her recently. I'm Popeye Jackson.

DELMOUNT. Popeye? That's an unusual name.

POPEYE. Oh, well. . . . It's not my original name. I wasn't born with it. (*Embarrassed she begins to run on.*) See, what happened was my brother Lucky, he threw a handful a gravel in my eyes and they started stinging and then he give me this brown bottle a drops t'put inside my eyes and telling me it's eye drops but, in fact, it's drops for the ears and then this burning sensation come into my eyes, causing me t'scream out and cry like the devil and after that I got me a pair a glasses and my eyes was bulged out a bit; so folks was calling me, Popeye and the name just stuck with me—Popeye. That's how I got the name.

DELMOUNT. (*After a moment.*) Well, that's a mighty tragic tale.

POPEYE. Ah, no. Actually, the fortunate part is I can now hear voices through my eyes.

DELMOUNT. Through your eyes.

POPEYE. Well, now and then I hear em—laughing and—carrying on.

DELMOUNT. Yeah. Well, I think I'll see if I can rustle up Carnelle for you. Carnelle! Honey! Are you home?! Carnelle! Carnelle!

POPEYE. Oh, no! No! I just forgot these measurements and I see em right here on the side table! (*Carnelle enters from the bedrooms.*)

CARNELLE. Delmount! No! No, it isn't you! Why, I can't believe my eyes! Oh, Popeye, this is my cousin, Delmount! He's come back at last! How are you? Are you doing alright? You look tired.

DELMOUNT. I'm fine. Is that a wig?

CARNELLE. What? Oh, no; it's real.

DELMOUNT. My, God, Child, are you trying to look like a bareback rider in the Shooley Traveling Carnival Show?

CARNELLE. You don't like it?

DELMOUNT. Hardly, Honey. Hardly.

CARNELLE. Maybe you'll grow accustomed to it. I have more and more myself. First I didn't like it at all—thought it was loud, in fact. Ah, did you meet my friend, Popeye?

DELMOUNT. (*Sitting down to smoke his pipe.*) We've spoken. (*Carnelle looks over to Popeye. Popeye manages to smile but stands frozen.*)

CARNELLE. (*Turning back to Delmount.*) Why, look at you! When did you start smoking a pipe?

DELMOUNT. Don't be silly. I've *always* smoked a pipe. Good Lord and butter. (*After a moment to the women.*) Why don't you sit down?

POPEYE. (*Making her exit in a flurry.*) No. I—really have to be going. I just forgot these measurements here. Now I got em.

CARNELLE. Well, alright. I'll be seeing you. Bye! (*Popeye is gone. Carnelle turns back to Delmount.*) So, what have you been doing?

DELMOUNT. Not much. Had a job scraping up dead dogs from the road.

CARNELLE. We were—concerned about you.

DELMOUNT. I was alright. Course the dogs were a rotting mess.

CARNELLE. (*After a moment.*) So, what brings you back home to Brookhaven?

DELMOUNT. Business.

CARNELLE. Oh.

DELMOUNT. I don't know if you realized this but my mamma the monkey left the whole of this house to me.

CARNELLE. I realized it.

DELMOUNT. Well, I'm going to sell it. I'm going to sell this house and every stick of furniture in it. And I don't want to hear anything from you about it. It's mine; it's been given to me. And I'm not going to feel sorry for you just cause you went and dyed your hair fire engine red!

CARNELLE. Well, alright, Delmount! You don't have to get mean about it! If you want to sell the house, it's your house to sell; so go on and sell it!

DELMOUNT. I will! I'm through working at disgusting job

after disgusting job. I hate working! I loathe it! (*Elain appears on the staircase in a flowing robe.*)

ELAIN. Carnation, Honey, where'd you put the —

DELMOUNT. Oh — No!!

ELAIN. Delmount!

DELMOUNT. You bitch! You!

ELAIN. What!?

DELMOUNT. How could you betray me like that!?! Your own flesh! Your own blood!

ELAIN. What's wrong with you? Are you still insane?

DELMOUNT. Ooh! Ooh! I'm not speaking to you! I'm not speaking to you!!

CARNELLE. (*Overlapping.*) What's going on? What is it?

ELAIN. Don't ask me! Don't ask me!

DELMOUNT. No! No! Don't ask her! She could never tell. She could never tell that the beautiful, the sweet, the perfect, Elain Rutledge refused to help her own brother get out of a dirty lunatic asylum!

ELAIN. Why, it was clean, it was cheerful, it was the most expensive money could buy! Oh, but you've always lied — even as a child we could never believe a word you said!

CARNELLE. (*Overlapping.*) Oh, what's wrong? What happened? Tell me! Please!!

DELMOUNT. It's all quite simple, Child a Mine. They would have released me after two months time into Mrs. Rutledge's loving custody, cause, you see, she is my next a kin, but she wouldn't have me. She wouldn't sign the papers.

ELAIN. (*Overlapping.*) Please, Delmount. I'm sorry, but we thought you needed the professional help. You were so upset about Mama dying —

DELMOUNT. Oh, Lord! She knows I wasn't upset cause of that! She know's that!

ELAIN. And Franklin just thought, cause of the children —

DELMOUNT. (*Under his breath.*) Franklin — that sheep pussy.

ELAIN. (*Angry.*) I mean, after all, Delmount, you did commit a violent act — hitting that poor man in the face with a bottle —

DELMOUNT. (*To Carnelle.*) Do you actually think I'm of such base character? I challenged that man to a duel! A duel! I can't help it if the weapons he chose were broken bottles! It was an honorable act in defense of a woman with beautiful, warm, bronze skin. I do not regret it.

ELAIN. (*Trying to break in between Carnelle and Delmount.*) Well, besides all of that, you know good and well, you've always had a checkered past!

DELMOUNT. What checkered past?

ELAIN. For one thing, you tried to choke Carnelle's poor father to death right in there at the dining room table!

DELMOUNT. Why, I never!

ELAIN. You did! It was right on New Year's Day!

CARNELLE. That's right, cause I found the dime in the black-eyed peas —

DELMOUNT. Alright, I did! I did it! But he was boring me to death! I just wanted to shut him up!

ELAIN. Now, see! See! That is not reasonable behavior! It's just not reasonable. And how you almost got run out of town on a rail cause of what happened with T.S. Mahoney's two young virgin daughters! It's no wonder you have bad dreams! It's no wonder!!

DELMOUNT. Rub my face in it, why don't you! You're so damn perfect and I'm such a no account failure! Rub my face in it!

ELAIN. I'm sorry Delmount. I'm sorry. Oh, you bring out the worst in me. You always have. You always have! (*Elain exits in a flurry. Carnelle and Delmount look after her for a moment then Carnelle goes to pick up the crackers and Delmount goes back to his pipe.*)

DELMOUNT. The irony of it. The intense irony.

CARNELLE. What irony?

DELMOUNT. Mahoney's two ugly daughters. I went up there thinking all they wanted was for me to see their box of newborn kittens. Well, when we got up in the attic, I saw most all of the kittens had swollen heads and crippled bodies. It was nothing but a cardboard box full of deformed damn cats. That's all there was to it. Well, I felt sorry for those two ugly daughters with their deformed box of cats. And they were dying for it. Hell, I was doing them a favor. There's the irony. You just can't go around obliging other people in this world. That's one thing I've learned.

CARNELLE. (*Sticking a dirty cracker into her mouth.*) I feel sorry for ugly girls. I really do.

DELMOUNT. Yeah. Ah, listen, little Child a Mine. About selling the house and all, I was planning on giving you half of what I make. That way you can get out of this town for good and always. How about it?

CARNELLE. Well, Delmount. I don't know! I've never thought about leaving Brookhaven.

DELMOUNT. Well, think about it. There's never been anything here for you but sorrow.

CARNELLE. Yes, that's true. Still . . . I don't know. (*After a moment.*) Maybe if I could, if I could leave in a blaze of glory. Yes! That's what I'd like to do—leave this town in a blaze of glory!

DELMOUNT. How do you mean?

CARNELLE. Well, if I won the Miss Firecracker Contest— See, I'm a contestant in it and if I could just win first prize then I would be able to leave this town in a crimson blaze of glory!

DELMOUNT. The Miss Firecracker Contest—Hell and damnation! (*He gets up.*)

CARNELLE. (*Following after him.*) Where are you going?

DELMOUNT. For a walk! (*He exits out the front door.*)

CARNELLE. (*Yelling after him.*) Delmount! Well, what in the world is eating you?! (*After a moment.*) Hmm, yes . . . a crimson blaze of glory! (*She performs with solemn beauty as the lights begin to fade.*) "And the rockets red glare—Boom!—the bombs bursting in air—Boom!—gave proof through the night—that our flag was—Boom!—there!" Boom! Boom! Boom!

BLACKOUT

END OF SCENE

ACT I

SCENE TWO

The lights go up on the living room. It is about eight o'clock in the evening on the following Saturday. Several cold, formal arrangements of long stemmed roses have been placed around the room. Most pieces of furniture now have price tags tied onto

91

them. Delmount stands smoking a pipe, and spinning the spinning wheel around as he listens to it creak.

DELMOUNT. Hmmm. . . . (*He gives the spinning wheel a kick. It wobbles. He goes to the desk to fill out a price tag. Elain enters carrying a silver tray with a decanter of wine and three glasses on it. One of the glasses has already been poured. Elain is somewhat tipsy.*)

ELAIN. Hello, Delly, I've brought you out a cool glass of Japanese plum wine.

DELMOUNT. No, thank you.

ELAIN. (*Setting the tray down.*) It's really exquisite wine. I just love things that are Japanese. (*He doesn't respond.*) Sure you don't want a glass?

DELMOUNT. Yes. (*He goes to put a price tag on the spinning wheel.*)

ELAIN. How much are you asking for the spinning wheel?

DELMOUNT. Five dollars.

ELAIN. Five dollars! Why, that is just wildly ridiculous! I mean, that's an actual antique you've got before you!

DELMOUNT. If you don't mind, Miss Priss, this is all my affair!

ELAIN. Ooh. And I thought you weren't mad at me anymore.

DELMOUNT. What made you think that?

ELAIN. Yesterday afternoon when we were sitting out back snapping green beans for supper you started laughing and telling your stories—I thought we were friends again. Please, you know you're just being hard-hearted about the whole thing.

DELMOUNT. I don't know what I'm being. I had bad dreams last night. I always have them. They never stop. Every night I have them.

ELAIN. (*Fanning herself.*) Must a been the heat. (*The phone rings. They look at each other.*) Get it!! (*Delmount dashes for the phone. Carnelle appears at the door with a dish rag in her hand. It is obvious that she has raced to get there.*)

DELMOUNT. (*Answering the phone.*) Hello? . . . This is he speaking . . . Yes . . . What? . . . No, I would not consider giving it away . . . I'm sorry but I happen to need the profit . . . (*Carnelle goes and picks up Delmount's dinner tray that is sitting on the desk.*) Well, it'll be up for auction at the July Fourth Carnival, if you want it so badly you can bid for it there . . . Yes

92

. . . Fine. Good-bye. (*He hangs up the phone.*) That was Mrs. J.R. Biggs. Imagine! She wanted me to donate that old spinning wheel to the D.A.R. How ludicrous! As though that entire organization couldn't afford to bid five dollars for it! What presumption! It's most maddening!

CARNELLE. Well, I guess, I better go and finish up the dishes. That — ah, that tuna nood'll really stick t'your plates. (*She exits to the kitchen, holding back tears.*)

DELMOUNT. Dammit! When were they supposed to have called by?

ELAIN. Six o'clock. It's after eight now.

DELMOUNT. I hate this. So she didn't even make it to the stupid finals.

ELAIN. I guess not.

DELMOUNT. God.

ELAIN. Not only that — Ruby Kay told me this year they had the worst turn out in history. Ever since they had to integrate the contest she says the turn out's been decreasing and the quality of the entire event has gone down, down, down.

DELMOUNT. Oh, stop it, please! I don't want to hear about it. Jesus God.

ELAIN. I know, I know.

DELMOUNT. (*Frantically.*) I don't know what to do. I mean, she actually thinks she's tap dancing. (*He imitates her.*) She's moving around like this, or something and she thinks she's tap dancing. Remember how Uncle Willie just dropped her off here and left her with nothing but a pillow case full of dirty rags? I'd never seen anything so pathetic. Had ringworms in her head.

ELAIN. Uh. Mama had to shave off all of her hair and put ointment on those sores in her head — I don't know, seemed like several times a day.

DELMOUNT. God, she was an ugly sight.

ELAIN. Wasn't she though. She always went around wearing that yellow wool knit cap pulled down over her head even in the summer's heat. Mama told her people would just think she had short yellow hair.

DELMOUNT. Mama was such a brilliant woman.

ELAIN. Well, from a distance it kinda looked like that.

DELMOUNT. I do doubt it. Anyway, she never did attain any self-esteem. Had to sleep with every worthless soul in Brookhaven trying to prove she was attractive.

93

ELAIN. (*Finishing another glass of wine.*) Please! It was just some sort of degrading stage she was going through. I'm certain she's over it now.

DELMOUNT. Well, I wish she was back in it.

ELAIN. Delmount!

DELMOUNT. I do! Least then she wasn't putting herself into stupid, miserable contests and publicly getting kicked in the face. Least for the disease she just privately took some shots.

ELAIN. Don't talk about it! I can't bear that side of life! It's repulsive to me. So shut up your mouth for once!!

DELMOUNT. Well, don't have a hissy fit! (*The phone rings.*)

ELAIN. My, God.

DELMOUNT. You think it's them?

ELAIN. No. I don't know. (*Carnelle appears at the door with a brownie in her hand.*)

CARNELLE. Here, I'll get it. I'll go on and—get it. (*She picks up the phone.*) Hello? . . . Oh. Yes, just a minute. It's for you Elain. It's Franklin.

ELAIN. Thanks. (*Carnelle exits to the kitchen, stuffing the brownie into her mouth.*) Hello. . . . Yes, Dear, I got them. . . . Oh, they're beautiful; they're—very fragrant; they're—I-I don't want to come home. . . . I mean not ever, or for awhile, or for not ever. . . . I feel like I'm missing my life. . . . I don't know about the children. They'll manage. . . . Oh, for God's sake, Franklin, no one's going to bake them into a pie! . . . Oh, please! I don't want to discuss it anymore. I'm tired of it all, I'm through with it all. Good-bye! (*She hangs up the phone. She is stunned and shaken by what she has done.*)

DELMOUNT. (*Who has been listening to all of this while pretending to work with the price tags.*) Did you mean it? You're gonna leave him?

ELAIN. Yes.

DELMOUNT. By God, Swayne. By God. I love ya, Honey! How I do love ya! Now are you sure you meant it?

ELAIN. Uh huh.

DELMOUNT. Don't just tell me you meant it, then later take it all back. You've done that before, you know.

ELAIN. I haven't.

DELMOUNT. What do you mean you haven't?!? It's a personality trait with you. It's your trademark! You tell me you're gonna do something one way and then you go back on it cause of what Mama said or what Franklin said or what some other fly-by-night-fool-idiot said!

ELAIN. Don't pick on me!

DELMOUNT. Ooh! I knew it! You didn't mean it! I knew it!

ELAIN. I meant it! I said it!

DELMOUNT. All you want is for everyone to think you're perfect. Well, perfect is dull!

ELAIN. Don't you dare call me dull. Just because I'm not insane and obsessed and possessed by dreams.

DELMOUNT. (*Overlapping.*) Shut up, Elain. Shut up your red blood lips!

ELAIN. You are a selfish human being! Mama always loved you ten times better than me.

DELMOUNT. Oh God.

ELAIN. I had to win contests and be in pageants before she'd give me any notice at all. When I graduated Jr. college she said, "You've had your spoonful of gravy now go out and get a rich husband;" so I did.

DELMOUNT. You're a fool to let Mama ramshackle your life. Mama was nothing but mean.

ELAIN. Not to you. She was sweet to you.

DELMOUNT. She pretended to be sweet.

ELAIN. Well, everyone always thought she was. Till the day she died, people were saying she was a blessed angel on earth.

DELMOUNT. Yeah, an angel in apes clothing.

ELAIN. You are so cruel.

DELMOUNT. Well, hell, she just turned herself into a monkey to get at us—just to be mean. I always knew Mama was mean.

ELAIN. No. She wasn't always. Things change. She wasn't always.

DELMOUNT. Why, I remember when I was a child a three how she tortured our favorite dog, White Face, right before my very eyes.

ELAIN. Wha'd she do to White Face?

DELMOUNT. Well, remember how White Face would always stand out by the back porch door hoping somebody would throw him some measly scraps?

ELAIN. I guess so.

DELMOUNT. Well, one day she was making a lemon pie and she says to me, "Ha! Let's see how he likes *this!*" and she slings a lemon rind right out to White Face and he jumps up and bites into it then runs off howling. And she's just standing there—laughing.

ELAIN. (*Stunned.*) Oh my God. So, Mama's always been mean. G'me a drag off a your pipe. (*He hands her the pipe. She takes a long drag.*)

DELMOUNT. Are you really gonna leave him?

ELAIN. (*Handing back the pipe.*) I said I would. (*The phone rings. They look at each other.*)

DELMOUNT. I can't stand it. (*He grabs the phone angrily.*) Yeah!? . . . Oh. Yes, just a minute. Carnelle? Carnelle, telephone!! Carnelle!

ELAIN. (*Overlapping.*) Carnelle! Honey! Phone! (*Carnelle appears. Her face is beet red.*)

CARNELLE. For me?

DELMOUNT. Uh huh. (*He hands her the phone.*)

CARNELLE. (*Into the phone.*) Hello. . . . Oh, Ronnie. . . . No, I don't think so. . . . Cause, I don't go out riding around like that anymore. I got other interests now. . . . You just don't understand anything about me. . . . Now don't you call me that. . . . I said don't call me that. So long. (*She hangs up the phone and stands totally still.*)

ELAIN. Who was it?

CARNELLE. Nobody. Just that creep Ronnie Wayne I used to date. He's calling me Miss Hot Tamale. Listen, I guess, I won't be needing that red dress of yours. It looks like I didn't make the Miss Firecracker Contest after all.

DELMOUNT. Ah well . . . count yourself lucky—that type a false pageantry; it's way beneath you.

ELAIN. Yes, it is. Why-why since it's been integrated the quality of the contest has really gone down, down, down.

DELMOUNT. Why, it's nothing but a garish display of painted up prancing pigs! That's all there is to it.

CARNELLE. Well, the main thing is—it was gonna be—I don't know—visible proof. And I would a liked to ride on a float and wave out to people.

ELAIN. Why, all this is gonna help build up your character! Remember, the more Mama suffered the more divine she became. (*There is a knock at the door.*)

CARNELLE. That must be Popeye. I told her I'd pay her tonight for sewing my costume. Tell her I'll be right back with the money. (*She exits up the stairs, holding back tears.*)

DELMOUNT. Popeye—that's all we need. Did she lose her brains or what?

ELAIN. I like Popeye. She's a nice girl.

DELMOUNT. Then you talk to her. I'm gonna go get my dessert. (*He exits to the kitchen, mumbling to himself.*) So, it's over. It's finished. She lost. Good. I'm glad!

ELAIN. (*As she opens the door for Popeye.*) Hello, Honey. Come on in. (*Popeye enters. She is wearing the earrings.*)

POPEYE. Hi.

ELAIN. Well, it looks like our little Carnation didn't make the beauty pageant after all.

POPEYE. (*Shocked.*) She didn't?

ELAIN. No.

POPEYE. I can't believe it.

ELAIN. Well, here, Honey, let me get you a glass of cool, plum wine.

POPEYE. I just knew she was gonna make it—with her red hair and her dancing and those roman candles shooting off right up into the sky.

ELAIN. (*Handing her some wine.*) I know. She put a lot of work into it. It's a disappointment. But life is hard and it's never easy to lose anything.

POPEYE. No, I suppose not. (*After a moment.*) I once knew these two midgets by the names of Sweet Pea and Willas. I went to their wedding and they was the only midgets there. Rest a their family was regular size people. But they was so happy together and they moved into a little midget house where everything was mite size like this little old desk they had and this little ole stool. Then Sweet Pea got pregnant and later on she had what they called this Caesarean birth where they slice open your stomach and pull the baby out from the slice. Well, come to find out, the babies a regular size child and soon that baby is just too large for Sweet Pea to carry around and too large for all a that mite sized furniture. So Sweet Pea has to give up her own baby for her Mama to raise. I thought she'd die to lose that child. It about crushed her heart.

ELAIN. (*Finishing off her glass of wine.*) I don't feel that way about my two boys. I don't want to spend time teaching them manners. I don't like them.

POPEYE. Y'don't?

ELAIN. No. My husband either.

POPEYE. What's wrong with him?

ELAIN. (*Gayly, as she pours herself some more wine.*) He smells of sweet cologne and wears three rings on every finger.

POPEYE. (*Pretending she has three rings on every finger.*) Gosh. They must feel heavy.

ELAIN. It's such a burden trying to live up to a beautiful face. I'm afraid I'm missing everything in the world. (*Delmount enters from the kitchen.*)

DELMOUNT. What happened to all of those brownies?

ELAIN. They're right in there on that blue china tray.

DELMOUNT. All of them?

ELAIN. Yes, Delly, the whole batch. (*Delmount exits to the kitchen.*)

POPEYE. (*Whispering hoarsely.*) What's the matter? He can't find the brownies?

ELAIN. I'm sure they're right under his nose. (*Delmount enters, carrying an empty tray.*)

DELMOUNT. They're all gone! The whole batch!

ELAIN. My, goodness! Well, I guess Carnelle ate them up. She's a compulsive eater when she's unhappy.

DELMOUNT. Dammit! I wanted a brownie! (*Then he stops, embarrassed.*) Ah, hello, Popeye. How're you?

POPEYE. Fine.

DELMOUNT. (*Smoothing down his wild hair.*) Well. . . . good. Ah, lovely earrings you're wearing.

POPEYE. Thank you. They was a present t'me from Elain. She give em to me.

DELMOUNT. Oh, right. Carnelle mentioned it . . . Well, maybe we—have some ice cream in the freezer. (*He exits to the kitchen.*)

POPEYE. (*Weakly.*) Oh. Oh. Oh. (*She begins fanning her heart and blowing air onto it.*)

ELAIN. What's the matter? Are you alright?

POPEYE. My heart—it's—hot. It's hot. It's burning. (*Blowing air onto her heart.*) Puff, puff, puff. (*She puts the wine glass against her heart.*) There. Ah. It's better now. It's better.

ELAIN. My word, you look faint.

POPEYE. Tell me, when your heart gets hot, does that mean you're in love?

ELAIN. Dar'lin, are you in love?

POPEYE. I reckon.

ELAIN. Not—not with Delmount?!

POPEYE. Yes. (*Puff, puff.*) Yes.

ELAIN. How astonishing! Why, his complexion's so sallow — and he's got a rude, irritable disposition.

POPEYE. It does seem like it.

ELAIN. How utterly odd. Tell me, Popeye, have you ever been in love before?

POPEYE. Well, my heart's never been hot or nothing, but I did have me a boyfriend once.

ELAIN. And what was he like?

POPEYE. Not much. He like t'pet me like I was a cat or something. He's asking me to purr and meow. Like, "meow, meow, purr, purr, purr." I don't know, he's crazy. I's expecting him t'give me a box a cat nips for Christmas.

ELAIN. What did he give you?

POPEYE. . . . . Nothing.

ELAIN. (*Pouring them both more wine.*) Well, if you want my opinion, that is just about what Delmount will give you. He's an unstable character and he's had a very checkered past.

POPEYE. I know bout that.

ELAIN. Well, did you know about his strange, obsessive eye for beauty? (*Popeye shakes her head.*) How he's been known to follow a normal looking woman through the streets all day and all night because he finds the mere shape of her nose exotic or beautiful; or perhaps he finds the texture of her lips to be unusually soft and smooth. You don't want anything to do with him. I worry about him. He's not right. He's obsessed. (*She finishes her drink. She is uncomfortable and upset.*) What in the world is keeping Carnelle? She must be up in her room crying. I'd better go get her. (*Elain exits up the stairs. Popeye sits alone sipping wine. She begins shaking her head back and forth. After a moment she makes a solemn toast to the voices inside her eyes.*)

POPEYE. Cheers. (*Delmount enters from the kitchen. He is eating a dish of vanilla ice cream.*)

DELMOUNT. Oh. Hello. Where's Elain?

POPEYE. She's getting Carnelle.

DELMOUNT. (*Smoothing down his hair.*) Oh. (*He sits at the desk and begins writing.*)

POPEYE. Are you writing poems?

DELMOUNT. What?

POPEYE. Carnelle said you write poems.

DELMOUNT. Oh. Well, on occasion I have.

POPEYE. I'd like to read em.

DELMOUNT. (*Embarrassed.*) They're personal.

POPEYE. Oh. (*She starts to run on.*) Course, I never read many poems before. There weren't all that many poem books you could get off a the traveling book mobil. Most books I got was about animals. Farm animals, jungle animals, arctic animals and such. Course they was informative, I learned some things; they's called: a gaggle a geese; a pride a lions; a warren a rabbits; a host a whales. That's my personal favorite one: a host a whales! (*They look at each other.*) Carnelle says you can wiggle your ears.

DELMOUNT. Does she?

POPEYE. Yes.

DELMOUNT. (*Straightening his hair.*) It's an old trick.

POPEYE. I would liked t'have seen it.

DELMOUNT. I don't do it anymore. (*He straightens his hair again.*)

POPEYE. What d'ya dream about at nights?

DELMOUNT. (*Taken aback.*) Why do you ask?

POPEYE. I don't know, you're face looks tired. I thought maybe you was having bad dreams.

DELMOUNT. What are you saying? You make me uncomfortable. A gaggle of geese! What's that?! What are you talking about? This whole night has been unbearable! Ooooh! Now the ice cream has given me a headache. Lord Jesus! A gaggle of geese! Oh, my head! My, head! (*He exits to the bedroom, holding his head. Popeye watches him leave then she puts both of her hands over her heart and starts to sob.*)

POPEYE. Oh. Oh. Oh. I must be stupid. I must be. (*CAR-*

NELLE enters from the bedrooms. Her nose is red. She carries a wad of kleenexes and a change purse. She spots Popeye crying.)

CARNELLE. Popeye! What is it? What's the matter?

POPEYE. *(Sobbing.)* Oh, I'm stupid. I'm stupid.

CARNELLE. Why? What happened? What?

POPEYE. It seems — It seems I love him. *(Pointing to the door.)* I love Delmount.

CARNELLE. Oh, no! I knew it. I knew it.

POPEYE. But I don't know what to say. I don't know how to come to say it. I just say, "Carnelle says you can wiggle your ears." He doesn't love me. I've lost him!

CARNELLE. *(Starting to cry.)* Oh, oh. Dear, little Popeye. I've lost too. I've lost too.

POPEYE. What?

CARNELLE. The contest! I lost the Miss Firecracker Contest!

POPEYE. Oh, right.

CARNELLE. I didn't even make the finals! They don't want me. I'm a failure!

POPEYE. Oh! There, there.

CARNELLE. I'm ugly, Popeye! My thighs are fat! No one loves me!

POPEYE. *(Overlapping.)* Oh, he'll never love me! Never! Never!! Oh, I hope I don't scream out — aaahh!!!

CARNELLE. *(Overlapping as she pulls at her hair.)* I hate my hair! I hate it! *(Elain enters from the bedroom. She spots them crying.)*

ELAIN. My, God! What is it? What's wrong?! Did someone die?!

CARNELLE. *(Falling across the couch.)* Oh, don't ask! Don't ask!

ELAIN. What happened?! Please! What?!

POPEYE. *(Wiping away tears.)* Well . . . well, she's crying cause she lost the beauty contest — and, and I'm crying cause he — he — he doesn't care about me! *(Popeye breaks down crying.)*

ELAIN. Oh, I see. You poor dears. You poor dears. There, there now. Here, here, now. There, there. *(Popeye and Carnelle whimper softly.)* You don't have to worry anymore. Things'll get better. Your lives aren't over, not like mine is. No neither of you have to face the sort of tragedy I'm facing. Neither of you is starting life all over again, feeling nothing but terror and fear and loneliness! *(Popeye and Carnelle sob loudly.)* Oh, God. Oh,

God. I can't believe I've left him. I've left him! Oh, my, dear God! There'll be no more roses! No more! (*She caresses an armful of roses.*)

CARNELLE. What? You've really left Franklin?

ELAIN. Yes! (*Weeping as she throws a handful of roses.*) Good-bye!

CARNELLE. You've told him?

ELAIN. (*Throwing another handful of roses.*) Yes! Farewell!

CARNELLE. Oh, Elain! Elain!

ELAIN. (*Throwing roses.*) No, more! No, more!!

POPEYE. Roses! Look! Roses!

ELAIN. (*Throwing roses.*) I don't know what to do! I don't know what I can do!

CARNELLE. Me neither; me neither. Oh, life!

POPEYE. (*Holding roses.*) Roses! Roses! Roses! (*Pause. The phone rings. All throw roses at the phone as they continue weeping.*)

POPEYE. (*Pointing to the phone with a rose.*) It rings!

ELAIN. Oh, let it ring! Just let it ring!

POPEYE. Yes, ring! (*The phone rings four more times.*)

CARNELLE. (*Suddenly alive.*) Wait. I'll get it. Quick! Here, I'll get it! (*She grabs the receiver.*) Hello. . . . Yes, this is she. . . . What? . . . Oh, I'm so sorry. . . . Oh, no. How sad. How tragic. . . . What? . . . Yes, alright. . . . Thank you. Bye bye. (*She puts down the phone.*) That — That was Miss Blue and, well, do you remember her little dog, Turnip?

ELAIN. The brown and white one —

CARNELLE. (*Breathlessly.*) Yes, well, Turnip was hit by a van and he died; so Miss Blue was late in notifying the five finalists but — oh my God.

POPEYE. Huh?

CARNELLE. Oh my God.

ELAIN. What?

CARNELLE. I made. I made it! By God I made the pageant!!! I did! I did! I made it! AAAHHH!!!!!

ELAIN. (*Overlapping.*) Praise God! Praise God! Some victory!

POPEYE. (*Overlapping.*) Oh you made it! You made it! Hurray!

ELAIN. (*Running on.*) Oh, Carnation! Carnation, what a triumph for you! Of course, I always knew you'd make the pageant! I never doubted it for one minute!

CARNELLE. They're — they're gonna be taking my picture for

the newspaper at ten o'clock in the morning at the Court House square. I'll be famous!

ELAIN. It's just stupendous! Here; here let's have a toast!

CARNELLE. A toast for *me?* Make a toast for *me?*

ELAIN. Yes! Yes! (*She starts to pour the glasses.*)

POPEYE. Yes, a toast! A toast!

ELAIN. Quick, call Delmount! I'll pour out these glasses.

CARNELLE. Delmount! Delmount, come quick! We're having a toast! We're having a toast to me!

ELAIN. (*Overlapping.*) Here, you go, Popeye. And for our Carnation. (*Delmount enters from the bathroom. He is in his bathrobe and wears a towel wrapped around his head.*)

DELMOUNT. What is it? What? I'm right in the middle of my hot oil treatment!

ELAIN. (*Handing him a glass.*) Here, Delmount, we're having a toast!

DELMOUNT. Huh?

ELAIN. Well, no more glasses. I'll just have to drink from the bottle. A toast everyone! To Carnation! May she win first prize in the Miss Firecracker Contest!

DELMOUNT. What?!

ELAIN. (*She raises the bottle.*) Cheers!

POPEYE. (*Raising her glass.*) Cheers!

CARNELLE. (*Raising her glass.*) Cheers!

DELMOUNT. (*As he clicks each of their glasses.*) Oh — my — miserable — God! (*They go about clicking each other's glasses as Delmount downs his drink and the lights blackout.*)

END OF ACT I

103

SYNOPSIS OF SCENES

SCENE ONE: The carnival grounds—about three o'clock in the afternoon on the Fourth of July.

We see the outside area behind a large carnival tent and the inside of a backstage dressing room. There is simply a bench and a garbage can in the outside area. To get to this area the characters enter from right. It should be established that when entering from down right the characters are coming from a different part of the carnival then when entering from up right.

The characters can get to the dressing room from this outside area by taking a step up and entering through a doorway. Inside the dressing room there is a dressing table, a chair, a stool, and a clothes rack. There is a curtain in the dressing room at left. This entrance and exit leads to the backstage area of the beauty contest.

SCENE TWO: The same setting. Several minutes later.

SCENE THREE: The same setting. That evening.

ACT II

SCENE ONE

The lights go up on an empty stage. Mac Sam, the balloon man enters up right carrying a bunch of colored balloons, and coughing painfully. Mac Sam is in his mid-thirties. He is amazingly· thin; stooped shouldered; and in drastically poor health. Yet there is something extraordinarily sensual about him. His eyes manage to be magnetic and bloodshot at the same time. He walks slowly over to the doorway of the dressing room.

MAC SAM. Hey, Carnelle. Hey, beautiful. (*He sees that no one is inside.*) Hmm. (*He finishes his cigarette and tosses it to the ground and spits up a lot of blood. He wanders off up* R.*, coughing and whistling a tune. Carnelle enters* L. *into the dressing room with Tessy Mahoney. Tessy is the uglier of T.S. Mahoney's two ugly daughters. She has a large nose, a weak chin, tiny eyes and bad posture. She covers up her bitterness by being as sweet as she can be. Carnelle is wearing a simple button down shift but she has applied lavish makeup and elaborately styled her hair in preparation for the contest. Both women are carrying armloads of beauty contest paraphernalia: the red antebellum dress; a hoop for the skirt; pantaloons; the red, silver and blue costume; a robe; a make-up case; shoes; stockings; roman candles; etc.*)
TESSY. (*As she enters the dressing room carrying only the tap shoes.*) It's over here. It's this way. It's this way, here!
CARNELLE'S VOICE. Oh. Oh, I see. I see!
TESSY. Can you make it?
CARNELLE. (*Making her way into the dressing room.*) Yeah. I got it. Here, I got it. (*Dropping her belongings where she can.*) Wheew! Brother. Thanks very much for the help.
TESSY. Sure. It's what I'm here for.
CARNELLE. Oh, look! Is this my dressing room? Is this mine?
TESSY. (*Picking up her clipboard and taking a pencil from behind her ear.*) Uh huh. It's the only one left. The good ones have all been taken. (*Looking at her watch.*) You're running late, you know.
CARNELLE. (*Struggling with her belongings.*) Yes, I know. I was sewing on my dress. Things aren't going smoothly at all today.

Oh, look! Now my hair piece is falling out. I worked all morning on that. So, is your sister nervous?

TESSY. Not really. I guess she knows she doesn't have a chance.

CARNELLE. (*As she straightens up her things.*) What makes you say that?

TESSY. Well, she's not at all attractive. I'm amazed she ever got in the contest. I'm sure it's just cause the judges think she's some sort of concert pianist. But she just knows that one opus by Johann Sebastian Bach. I swear that's all she knows.

CARNELLE. Hmm, I suppose that talent part of the contest will count quite a bit.

TESSY. Well, she looks like a tank in her swim suit.

CARNELLE. She does?

TESSY. She's hump shouldered from practicing that one Johann Sebastian Bach opus on our piano all day long.

CARNELLE. What a shame.

TESSY. This is strictly confidential, but the word is out that the only real contenders for the Miss Firecracker crown are you and Caroline Jeffers.

CARNELLE. (*Overcome.*) Oh, gosh, I don't know —

TESSY. It's the truth. Everyone's saying it. We're all agreed.

CARNELLE. Of course Caroline's really a lovely girl . . .

TESSY. Yeah, except for those yellow teeth.

CARNELLE. Well, I hear she took medicine for seizures that she had as a child and it scraped off most of her tooth enamel.

TESSY. I heard that too, but it doesn't matter.

CARNELLE. It doesn't?

TESSY. I really don't think the judges are interested in sentimentality — just the teeth themselves. (*Referring to the red dress.*) That's such a beautiful red dress. It's really very fine.

CARNELLE. Yes, it's beautiful. I'm just a little worried though. It just arrived from Natchez yesterday and, well, it didn't seem to fit me exactly right.

TESSY. What's wrong with the fit?

CARNELLE. Well, the waist was a little snug. But I worked on it this morning and added in this extra bit of material. (*She shows that a large strip of pink material has been awkwardly added to the bodice of the red dress.*)

TESSY. (*Disdainfully.*) Oh. Well.

CARNELLE. Course, I know it's not the exact matching color. Actually, my cousin, Elain's gone to get my seamstress, Popeye Jackson, and see what she can do. We couldn't find her last night. She'll fix it right up. This is just temporary.

TESSY. Well, I hope so. It looks a little funny.

CARNELLE. (*Looking outside.*) Oh, I know Elain'll bring Popeye; she promised she would. She's never let me down in her life. Gosh, I think I'm starting t'sweat. My makeup is melting right down my face. (*She starts fixing her face.*)

TESSY. (*Looking at her watch.*) Hmm. Actually, you don't have much time. It's only twenty-eight minutes till the opening Parade of Firecrackers. (*Tessy blows her whistle.*)

CARNELLE. Oh, my word! Well, I'm ready except for my dress. I mean, my head is ready.

TESSY. (*Removing schedule from her clipboard.*) Well, anyway, here's your schedule.

CARNELLE. Thanks.

TESSY. Oh and have you seen the Grand Float they've made for Miss Firecracker to ride at the head of the Independence Day Parade?

CARNELLE. Oh, yes, I saw it — it's . . . beautiful.

TESSY. Why, yes, it's very fine. Well, I'd better go let Miss Blue know you're checked in. (*After glancing at herself in the mirror.*) Oh. Mind if I borrow some of your hairspray?

CARNELLE. No, go ahead.

TESSY. Thanks. (*As she sprays her already rock hard hair.*) I, ah, hear your cousin Delmount's back in town.

CARNELLE. Yes, he's back.

TESSY. (*Still spraying.*) Well, you can tell him for me that I've forgiven him. I understand now that some men just don't have any self control. Just none at all. Think that'll hold?

CARNELLE. Uh huh.

TESSY. Anyway, tell him my Uncle Ferd's given us a new litter of siamese kittens if he wants to drop by and see them. I know he always enjoyed animals.

CARNELLE. I'll tell him.

TESSY. Well, good luck. I'll be standing by backstage running the contest. Let me know if any emergencies arrive.

CARNELLE. Alright.

TESSY. Give em H.

CARNELLE. I'll try. (*Tessy exits* L. *Carnelle turns back and looks in the mirror. She stares at herself as she wipes sweat off the back of her neck.*)

CARNELLE. Oh, Lord. (*She tries a big friendly smile. It falters.*) Oh, Lord. (*She begins fooling with her hair and makeup. Mac Sam enters from the carnival grounds* U.R. *He stops; looks at the dressing room; ties his balloons to the bench; and goes toward the dressing room.*)

MAC SAM. (*Looking inside the dressing room.*) Hi, ya!

CARNELLE. AAH!

MAC SAM. Admiring y'physiognomy?

CARNELLE. (*Catching her breath.*) Mac Sam. What are you doing here?

MAC SAM. Just came t'wish you well. Heard you were in the beauty contest and came by t'wish you well.

CARNELLE. (*Breathlessly.*) Thanks. I'm nervous.

MAC SAM. Sure y'are. Well, good luck. I wish y'well. (*He leaves the dressing room. She follows.*)

CARNELLE. I—didn't think I'd be seeing you again.

MAC SAM. Yeah, well, wonders never do quite cease. (*He looks at her with his magnetic eyes then starts to leave again.*)

CARNELLE. I tried to notify you. After I found out. Couldn't . . . locate you though.

MAC SAM. Oh, "that". Yeah, well, I'm enjoying, "that." Find it most fascinating.

CARNELLE. But didn't you get the shots?

MAC SAM. Nah.

CARNELLE. But all you do is—they give you these shots and you're cured. It cures you.

MAC SAM. I don't care t'be cured.

CARNELLE. What do you mean? You've got to be.

MAC SAM. (*Taking out a cigarette.*) Listen, Honey, this life a mine is strictly on the house. Strictly a free roll a the eternal dice. I was almost choked to death by my mama's umbilical cord at birth. Spent three days purple and gasping for breath. I'm tired out of gasping. (*He lights his cigarette and blows out the match.*) Mmm. You're hair looks really nice. I like that color. It looks good on you.

CARNELLE. It doesn't seem too loud?

MAC SAM. (*Smelling her hair.*) Not a bit. No, Sugar, not a bit.

DELMOUNT'S VOICE. Carnelle!? Carnelle, are you about?!

CARNELLE. (*Calling.*) Delmount! Is that you? (*To Mac Sam.*) It's my cousin, Delmount.

DELMOUNT'S VOICE. Carnelle!!

CARNELLE. I'm over here!

MAC SAM. Well, I'll be ambling along. It was good seeing you.

CARNELLE. (*Impulsively.*) Will ya come back by?

MAC SAM. (*His eyes becoming magnetic.*) Oh, yeah. (*He exits* R.)

DELMOUNT'S VOICE. Carnelle!

CARNELLE. I'm over here!!! (*Delmount enters excitedly from the carnival grounds* D.R. *His hair is wild; he carries a stuffed dog.*)

DELMOUNT. Oh! Well, there you are! Sounded like your voice was coming from over there by the snow cone stand.

CARNELLE. No, I'm here.

DELMOUNT. Well . . . well, look, here's an artificial dog I won pitching dimes onto plates. Take it; it's for you if you want it.

CARNELLE. Why, thank you, Delmount. (*She kisses him.*) Oh my lips. (*Carnelle hurries into the dressing room to fix her lips. Delmount follows.*)

DELMOUNT. Things are going very good over at the auction. I mean, the furniture, it all seems to be selling like hot cakes. Why, it looks to me, Child a Mine, that our lives may actually be on the verge of being fine.

CARNELLE. Gosh, everything feels so all of a sudden. Selling the house and all of the belongings and . . . leaving. . . . It makes it much more important that I win the contest. I mean, the main thing is I gotta leave in the blaze of glory. (*She leaves the dressing room and starts pacing back and forth.*) Let's see, I know I'll beat Saphire Mendoze just cause she's the token Negro and Mexican. I'm not trying to be mean about it, but it's the truth. Then there's Joe Anne Jacobs.

DELMOUNT. Frank Jacob's sister's in the pageant?

CARNELLE. Uh huh.

DELMOUNT. She's a shrimp.

CARNELLE. Well, sorta. Then there's Missy Mahoney—

DELMOUNT. Oh, my God! Is she in the pageant?

CARNELLE. Yeah.

DELMOUNT. Why next to her sister, Tessy, Missy's the ugliest girl in the whole town!

CARNELLE. Sssh! Sssh! (*Pointing to the dressing room.*) Tessy's in charge of the pageant coordination. She may hear you.

DELMOUNT. Oh, Jesus. Keep me away from those two. They are trouble.

CARNELLE. Well, Tessy was asking about you just now.

DELMOUNT. She was? Holy cow; holy cow. Where's my pipe? I've got to lay low; that's all. Lay low till I can get out of this town for good and always.

CARNELLE. Let's see, then there's Caroline Jeffers. She is awfully pretty except . . . Oh, I don't know! I don't know! (*She begins chewing her nails.*) Have you seen Elain?

DELMOUNT. Not since this morning.

CARNELLE. She was gonna go find Popeye to help sew up that red dress. It looks funny the way it is.

DELMOUNT. Well, I haven't seen Popeye since that night you got into this blessed contest.

CARNELLE. (*Biting her nails.*) Oh, shoot! I said I wasn't gonna chew on my nails! (*She takes a nail file from her dress pocket and begins filing.*)

DELMOUNT. She's strange anyway . . . that Popeye. She's very strange. A strange bird.

CARNELLE. (*Working on her nails.*) I guess so. I guess she is. Still . . . well, I guess, I shouldn't tell you. No, never. mind.

DELMOUNT. Oh, that's fine. That's just fine. You start to say something and then you don't. Very nice, Carnelle, very nice.

CARNELLE. Well, it's just . . . it's just, well, she said she liked your hair and—

DELMOUNT. What? My hair? She said she likes my hair?!

CARNELLE. Yes, and how you can wiggle your ears and write poetry.

DELMOUNT. Wiggle my ears!? Good Lord and butter.

CARNELLE. Oh, I may as well tell you . . . she's in love with you.

DELMOUNT. What!?! No, she's not. I don't believe that. Who told you that?

CARNELLE. Well, she said it. And she was crying over you. It's the truth, Delmount. She was in the living room crying over you.

DELMOUNT. No, I don't believe it. Crying?

CARNELLE. I know. But I didn't have the heart to tell her

about your obsessive eye for beauty. You know; that one you have.

DELMOUNT. Oh. Yes, I have acquired a weakness for the classical, exotic beauty in a woman. I've been a fool for it. It's my romantic nature.

CARNELLE. And I guess you don't think that Popeye's exactly classical? (*Delmount looks forlornly at her.*) Well, I've got to at least go put on my pantaloons and hoop. I've got to at least do that.

DELMOUNT. This tobacco is too sweet. It's making my head spin. Anyway, my hair's an unruly mess!

ELAIN'S VOICE. Carnelle! Carnation, Honey!?!

CARNELLE. (*Stopping.*) Elain — (*Elain enters* R. *in a flowing summer dress. She looks radiant and fresh. She carries the Mardi gras mask in a paper sack.*)

ELAIN. Oh, Da'lin, there you are!

CARNELLE. Oh, Elain, I knew you'd come!

ELAIN. Why, hello, Delly!

DELMOUNT. Hello Swaney.

ELAIN. Will you just look up at that sky! It's as blue as the mighty sea! Oh, I feel like a child today! I swear, I do! You'll never believe it, but Miss Blue has asked me to come up and give a speech before the contest starts. She wants me to talk on, "My Life as a Beauty." Isn't it too exciting!

CARNELLE. Oh, yes, yes. But — but where's Popeye? The dress — I couldn't make it look right.

ELAIN. Oh, Carnation, I went over to Miss Lily's Dress Shop and heard the most disheartening news: poor, little Popeye was fired yesterday afternoon. They said she was giving away the merchandise.

CARNELLE. Oh, no!

DELMOUNT. Well, where'd she go?

ELAIN. No one knows. They haven't seen her. But anyway, I came up with the most creative idea to save the day. You can wear this lovely Mardi gras mask in the opening parade. That way you can just hold it up to your face like this, covering the side of your dress where the extra material is with your arm and elbows, plus adding some mystery and elegance to — well, to your total look. Just walk around like this. (*She moves around making dips and swirls, alternately moving the mask from in front of her face to the side of it with flip of her wrist, as she makes her dips.*) And

111

scoop! And scoop! And scoop! You think you can manage it?
CARNELLE. (*Taking the mask.*) I'll try. I'll really try. (*She begins practicing.*) And scoop! And scoop. And scoop, etc.
ELAIN. That's it. Now just flip out your wrist. Make it crisp! That's good. Just keep at it. That's the only way to improve. (*Turning to Delmount.*) It's amazing but everyone recognizes me. They say I'm still exactly the same as I was. "Just in full bloom like a rose!" That's what one dear man said. I wish Mama were here. She'd love all of this!
CARNELLE. (*Still practicing.*) I know. She'd be so surprised if she could see me. I'm totally changed from when she knew me. Totally new. I think I got it. (*Tessy sticks her head into the* L. *side of the dressing room.*)
TESSY. Carnelle?
CARNELLE. Out here, Tessy! I'm here!
CARNELLE AND ELAIN. Tessy!
DELMOUNT. Tessy! (*He leaps under the tent.*)
TESSY. (*Entering the dressing room* L. *carrying a shoe box with a rubber band around it and holes punched in it.*) Carnelle?!
CARNELLE. I'm over here!
TESSY. Oh! (*As she steps out of the dressing room to the outside area.*) Why, Elain! Hello! How're you doing?
ELAIN. Why, if it isn't Tessy Mahoney! I'm doing fine. Just fine.
TESSY. Will you look at you. If you aren't the most beautiful thing in the whole wide world!
ELAIN. Oh, you silly, dear!
TESSY. (*Handing Carnelle the shoe box.*) Here, Carnelle. Some man brought this as a gift to you.
CARNELLE. Why, thank you. Who could have sent it?
TESSY. I just can't get over how beautiful you are. I just can't.
ELAIN. Why, how sweet can you be?
CARNELLE. (*Reading the scrawled message.*) "Thought you'd enjoy this. Good luck always. Mac Sam."
ELAIN. So, what's in the box?
CARNELLE. I don't know. But I—I think it's alive.
ELAIN. What? Let me see—(*She opens the box.*) AAH!!! (*She slams the top back on the box and drops it to the ground.*)
CARNELLE. What is it?
ELAIN. It's a horrible little frog in a pink outfit!

CARNELLE. Oh, my lord. (*She picks up the box and looks inside.*) Oh, lord. (*To Tessy.*) Where'd he go? Where'd the man go?

TESSY. I don't know. He gave me the box up front.

CARNELLE. Show me. Quick! Show me!

TESSY. (*As she hurries back through the dressing room and runs off L.*) Well, it's this way. But you better hurry up; it's only seventeen minutes till the opening Parade of Firecrackers—

CARNELLE. (*Overlapping as she follows Tessy out.*) Come on, Elain! Come on! He'll know where Popeye is! He'll know!

ELAIN. (*Following Carnelle off L., overlapping.*) But why? What do you mean? What's all this about? What an awful gift! Some friend you must have! (*They all exit L. Delmount comes out from under the tent. He is dusting off his pants when Popeye suddenly enters from down right dancing, humming, and eating blue cotton candy. She is wearing her earbobs and a pretty summer dress.*)

DELMOUNT. Popeye.

POPEYE. (*Stopping her dancing.*) Hello. (*She fans herself with the blue cotton candy as they stare at each other for a moment.*) I was looking for Carnelle.

DELMOUNT. Oh. Well. I don't know. I think she went looking for you. Found some sort of frog in a suit.

POPEYE. Was it a pink suit?

DELMOUNT. I think it was.

POPEYE. Oh, well, I sold me about ten different outfits out at a booth this morning. But I only had me that one frog in the pink suit, kinda there on display; case you didn't have no dolls.

DELMOUNT. I see.

POPEYE. Well. So why was Carnelle a'hunting for me?

DELMOUNT. Oh. Well, she, ah, she needed you to help sew on this red dress she has for the contest. She's been looking for you since last night.

POPEYE. Oh. Well, I rode the bus up to Jackson last night. Went to visit the observatory. They had the telescope aimed up on the moon. Thought I'd take a look.

DELMOUNT. How'd it look?

POPEYE. Big. Orange. Kinda shiney and sparkley.

DELMOUNT. Sounds nice.

POPEYE. It was.

DELMOUNT. (*There is an awkward pause. He begins smoothing down his hair.*) Hmm. Gosh. (*He stops smoothing. Looks at her.*)

Oh. (*Suddenly messing his hair all up.*) I prefer it unruly. Don't you?

POPEYE. I don't much know. (*A pause.*) Ah, where's the dress? Maybe I should go take a look at it.

DELMOUNT. Oh, well, it's in here. It's right in here. (*They go inside the dressing room. He shows her the dress.*) It's ah, too small right here in the waist.

POPEYE. Hmm. Let me take a look.

DELMOUNT. Well, here, I'll hold your cotton candy.

POPEYE. Thanks. You can finish it, if you want. (*At that moment Carnelle, Mac Sam, and Elain are heard coming from the carnival from down* R. *They are in an uproar.*)

MAC SAM'S VOICE. But I told you, I took the thing from some small kid who was tired of it! How do I know where he got it!?!

ELAIN. (*Overlapping.*) Well, in my opinion, it's a tasteless sort of gift! (*By now they are all on stage.*)

MAC SAM. I thought it was festive!! A unique gift for a unique girl! Who are you anyway?!

ELAIN. Who are *you?!?*

DELMOUNT. Wait! It's them! (*Stepping outside the dressing room.*) She's here! She's inside! Popeye! She's looking at the dress!

CARNELLE. She is?!

ELAIN. She's here!?

MAC SAM. Who is this Popeyed anyway? (*They all rush into the dressing room. The following dialogue goes at a rapid pace.*)

CARNELLE. Popeye! You're here!

POPEYE. Hello. I need scissors.

ALL. Scissors. Scissors.

CARNELLE. Scissors. Scissors. Let me look. Let me look! (*She begins searching through her makeup case.*)

DELMOUNT. Listen, Bub, those balloons don't fit in here.

MAC SAM. Is that Popeyed?

ELAIN. Popeye! It's Popeye!

CARNELLE. Oh, I don't think I have any scissors! They're none here!

TESSY'S VOICE. (*Coming from off* L.) Elain! Oh, Miss Elain!

DELMOUNT, ELAIN, CARNELLE. Tessy!

114

DELMOUNT. Quick! Hide me behind those balloons. (*Delmount jumps behind Mac Sam's balloons.*)

MAC SAM. Watch it, Sonny!

TESSY. (*As she enters from the* L. *side of the dressing room.*) Miss Blue says it's only five minutes till she introduces you for your speech on beauty.

ELAIN. Oh, thank you, Darlin. Thank you. (*Looking in the mirror.*) For heaven's sake, my face isn't even on!

MAC SAM. Her face?

TESSY. Why, Carnelle, you'd better hurry and get dressed! All the other beauty contestants are already in their gowns and ready to go! (*She exits* L., *blowing her whistle. All scream. Delmount reappears.*)

CARNELLE. What can I do? There're no scissors. What can I do?!

ELAIN. (*Sitting at the dressing table, putting on her makeup.*) Just wear the mask; you'll be fine, really.

CARNELLE. Oh, will somebody, please, take this frog!?

MAC SAM. Here, Honey, Mac Sam'll take care of it. (*He takes the box from her.*)

CARNELLE. Quick, now my pantaloons! Oh, God, I'm hot. I'm sweating. I stink. (*Someone throws her the pantaloons.*)

DELMOUNT. I believe I mentioned your balloons don't fit!

MAC SAM. I'm holding the frog!

CARNELLE. (*Struggling with her pantaloons.*) Oh! Oh, which is the right end?! Look, I can't even find the right end of my pantaloons! It's hopeless!! It's hopeless!! It's utterly hopeless!! (*She throws the pantaloons into the air, collapses on the floor then starts crawling around on the floor searching for her pantaloons.*)

ELAIN. Now just try to be calm, Carnation, Honey. Try to enjoy yourself; it's all going to go as smooth as silk! I promise you — I give you my word of honor!

DELMOUNT. You'll do alright, Child a Mine — It's a stupid, idiotic contest, you'll do fine!

MAC SAM. You're beautiful, Baby — just beautiful!

POPEYE. (*About the pantaloons.*) Here. Here, now. You step in 'em like this.

MAC SAM. Yeah, put your foot in there.

CARNELLE. (*Trembling.*) In there? Right in there?

POPEYE. Uh huh.

DELMOUNT. Come on, child, you can do it.

CARNELLE. (*Gritting her teeth.*) Well, alright. (*She grabs the pantaloons and furiously starts to put them on.*)

MAC SAM. That's it!

ELAIN. Good. Good.

DELMOUNT. You've got it now!

CARNELLE. Hey! Hey, look, they're on me! My pantaloons are on!! (*General applause, sighs of relief, etc. Mac Sam raises Carnelle's hand in victory. Fast blackout.*)

END OF SCENE

ACT II

Scene Two

> The setting is the same. Several minutes have passed. The red dress, the hoop, the pantaloons, and the Mardi gras mask are gone. Mac Sam sits on the bench smoking a cigarette and drinking whiskey from a flask. His balloons are tied to the bench. Delmount is pacing back and forth in front of the bench.

DELMOUNT. Wonder how it's going?

MAC SAM. Why don't ya take a look?

DELMOUNT. Not interested.

MAC SAM. Oh.

DELMOUNT. She look alright to you in that big, red thing?

MAC SAM. Oh, yeah.

DELMOUNT. God. How she can put herself through this I'll never understand. Never.

MAC SAM. Well, women are funny about their looks. My granpapa used to say to me, "Sammy, all ya have to do is tell a woman she's beautiful and she goes like that!" (*He makes a horizontal victory sign with his fingers.*)

DELMOUNT. How pithy.

MAC SAM. Well, of course I try not to abuse the knowledge but it has come in handy in some borderline cases.

DELMOUNT. Well, fortunately, I have yet to make advances

116

to any woman who did not possess at least one classically, beautiful characteristic. It's sort of a romantic notion I've had. I don't know. Perhaps, it's caused me to be fragmented in love. Perhaps, it's been obsessive. What do you think?

MAC SAM. Well, what I like is a woman who can take it right slap on the chin. That's what I like. (*He begins to cough, spreading germs all over his flask. He takes a slug, relieving his cough, then he says.*) Care for a slug?

DELMOUNT. (*Aghast.*) No, thank you. (*Popeye and Elain enter in a flurry from up R. Popeye carries a half eaten hot dog.*)

POPEYE. Ooh! Ooh, me! Ooh!

ELAIN. (*Overlapping.*) It's a travesty! A travesty! An utter Godforsake travesty!

DELMOUNT. What's going on? Is it going alright? How's it going?

ELAIN. Air! Air! I must have some air! (*She falls back onto the bench as Delmount and Mac Sam fan her furiously.*)

POPEYE. (*Acting it out.*) See, see, she tripped on that big ole red skirt and fell down flat on her face! Whoops! (*She falls to the ground.*) And people was laughing. 'Ha, ha, ha, ha, ha!'

DELMOUNT. (*Overlapping.*) Laughing! Oh, my God! Laughing!

POPEYE. They was laughing out loud!

ELAIN. (*Coming out of her faint.*) There—there's a group of hoodlums out there yelling, "Miss Hot Tamale! Miss Hot Tamale!!" It's a disgrace. It's a humiliation! And that horrible Ronnie Wayne is actually throwing peanuts and trash and ice right up there on the stage in front of everyone!

DELMOUNT. At her? Is he throwing them at her?

ELAIN. Well, a peanut caught her right between the eyes!

DELMOUNT. What? What! He dies!! DIES!!!! Ronnie Wayne! Ronnie Wayne!! (*Delmount exits U.R. as Carnelle enters L. into her dressing room. The red dress, which was quite lovely and seductive when Elain wore it eleven years ago, now looks like a whore's gown on Carnelle. It is faded and ill fitted and totally askew. She slings down the torn and broken Mardi gras mask furiously. There are peanuts and trash on her dress and in her hair.*)

CARNELLE. AAAAH! OOH! It's awful! It's so awful! They never forget! They never do! (*Elain and Popeye start for the dressing room. Mac Sam stays on the bench. He lights up another cigarette.*)

ELAIN. (*Overlapping.*) It's her! She's there!! (*Stepping inside the dressing room.*) Carnation—

POPEYE. (*Stepping inside.*) Hi.

CARNELLE. Did you hear them? Oh, did you hear them? They were laughing and calling me, "Miss Hot Tamale." Did you hear it?

ELAIN. Why, look at you, you're dripping wet . . . let me help you out of this gown before you perish. (*She starts to unbutton the gown.*)

CARNELLE. Oh, if only the dress had come sooner. I could have fixed it right. I wouldn't of needed that fancy mask. I felt so foolish wearing it.

ELAIN. (*Defensively, as she tries to get the dress over Carnelle's head.*) I'm sorry, but I thought it would do—I just didn't realize that, well, that you were so big boned! Anyway, the color's all wrong—it was just too loud.

CARNELLE. But I love the color red. I love how it blazes!! Oh, I've got a pushing sensation right between my eyes as though it like to crack open my brains! Ooh!!

ELAIN. Now, listen, Carnation, if you don't calm down, you're headed for a clear cut nervous breakdown! Just try to remember how Mama was enlightened by her affliction. Why, remember what she was always telling you, "Pretty is as pretty does." (*Carnelle collapses in despair.*)

POPEYE. You want this hot dog? I ain't enjoying it.

CARNELLE. Thanks. (*Carnelle takes the hot dog and stuffs it into her mouth, as Tessy enters* L. *She is in an uproar.*)

TESSY. Will you stop him! Will you please try and stop him!! He's messing up Missy's whole opus. He's out there in the audience causing a horrible, horrible scene!!

CARNELLE. (*Overlapping.*) Who? What? Stop who?!

TESSY. Delmount, that's who! He's smashing Ronnie Wayne's head into the dirt! And everyone's hollering!

CARNELLE. Oh, Lord, I've got to stop him—(*She starts to leave* L.)

TESSY. No! Don't go through the stage!

CARNELLE. Oh—(*She turns and runs out the* R. *side of the dressing room.*)

ELAIN. Wait! Carnelle! You're in your hoop!

118

CARNELLE. (*Who is now in the outside area.*) Oh, no! I'm in my hoop!

MAC SAM. Well, you don't have to tell me!

CARNELLE. (*Covering herself.*) Oh, please, run around there and stop Delmount! He's out there in a fight—he's stirring up trouble!

MAC SAM. Alright, Baby. I'm going. (*About his balloons.*) Hey, see that no one steals my capital! (*He exits up* R.)

CARNELLE. Thanks, Mac Sam! Thanks a lot! (*She goes back into the dressing room.*) It's alright. It'll be fine. Mac Sam's gone to stop him.

TESSY. That Delmount is just wild. He is just recklessly wild!

ELAIN. (*Sitting down on a stool, fanning herself.*) Well, as we all know, he's had a very checkered past. (*Tessy looks to Elain who turns away with a grimace.*)

TESSY. I suppose, Missy's whole opus is just ruined. Well, be that as it may, the show must go on. (*Looking at her clipboard.*) Let's see . . . let me get this straight. Joe Anne Jacobs follows Missy with her comedy pantomine to, "Take Me Out to the Ball Game," then ther'll be Caroline Jeffers' dramatic interpretation from, *Gone With the Wind.* Then, of course, there's Saphire's holla hoop act and finally, last but not least, is your tap dance routine to, "The Star Spangled Banner." Alright, do you have that order?

CARNELLE. (*Who has removed her hoop and put on a robe.*) Uh huh.

TESSY. Since you go on last, it looks like you'll have to really rush to get into that bathing suit for the final crowning.

CARNELLE. It doesn't matter. It's all over. It's all ruined.

ELAIN. Don't worry, we'll help her out. It won't be a problem.

TESSY. Why, thank you, Elain. You're probably the most admirable person I've ever met. Truly you are! Oh my! (*She exits* L.)

ELAIN. It's sweltering in here. Let's get some air. (*She steps from the dressing room to the outside area.*)

CARNELLE. (*Following her.*) Alright.

POPEYE. Good. Maybe we can catch a breeze. (*She steps outside the dressing room.*)

CARNELLE. I hope so, Popeye. Oh lord. I do.

DELMOUNT'S VOICE. I showed them! I showed them all!!
Those cold blooded swine!! (*Mac Sam and Delmount appear from*
U.R. *Mac Sam is supporting Delmount who is dragging his leg and has
blood on his face.*)

POPEYE. Oh!!

CARNELLE. Delmount!

ELAIN. Delly, are you alright?!

CARNELLE. What's happened?

MAC SAM. They started throwing rocks at him. They hit him
there on the leg.

CARNELLE. Oh, Lord, are you hurt? You're not hurt are
you?!

DELMOUNT. They don't make um hard enough.

ELAIN. Well, you look dreadful. I'll run get that disinfectant
from the car! (*She exits* D.R.)

POPEYE. Well, I'll—I'll get ya some ice. You can put it on
your swolled up leg! (*She exits down* R.)

CARNELLE. (*Sinking to the ground.*) This is awful. Throwing
rocks. They were throwing rocks. I'm about to cry.

DELMOUNT. It's alright, Child a mine. Nobody's hurt. We
enjoyed it.

MAC SAM. Yeah. (*Cough, cough.*) Yeah. (*Cough, cough, cough,
cough, cough. He spits up blood.*)

CARNELLE. Mac Sam, what's wrong? Are you choking?

MAC SAM. Nah. I'm just spitting up clots of blood.

CARNELLE. What?

MAC SAM. It's nothing. Happens all the time. Look at that
clot there; it's a nice pinkish-reddish sorta color.

CARNELLE. You're making me sick, here. Sick. (*Tessy enters
L. into the dressing room. She is holding a record.*)

TESSY. Carnelle?! Oh Carnelle!

CARNELLE. It's Tessy.

DELMOUNT. Christ, I'm too weak to move.

TESSY. (*Stepping outside, spotting Delmount.*) Why, will you look
at you! I just hope you're proud of yourself. Causing all of that
racket! Here, Carnelle, Tommy Turner wants you to show him
which song on this record you want played for your routine.

CARNELLE. Alright. (*She takes the record, goes through the dressing
room and exits* L.)

TESSY. So how's life been treating you?

DELMOUNT. Oh, fair.

TESSY. Well, I just thought you should know that I'm still bearing emotional scars because of the time you took unfair advantage of me up in the attic. They're deep scars, Delmount. They hurt.

DELMOUNT. (*Quietly as he squirms.*) Have a little mercy. I'm bleeding here. Look: blood. (*He mops off his head with a handkerchief.*)

TESSY. Well, you don't have to worry. I've already forgiven you. It's my religion: First Presbyterian. And to show you I mean it, tonight I'll let you take me to watch the fireworks.

DELMOUNT. What—

TESSY. (*She starts to leave.*) I'll even trust you to sit by me all alone in the dark! See you back here at 7:45 p.m. on the nose!

DELMOUNT. No, wait—(*He tries to get up but flinches in pain.*)

TESSY. (*As she exits through the dressing room and out* L.) I've got to run now! There's a show on!

DELMOUNT. (*Overlapping, he crawls after her.*) Please—Don't forgive me! Don't forgive me! Don't! It was rotten behavior! I stink, I tell ya! I stink! (*Dropping to the ground.*) Christ.

MAC SAM. (*After a moment.*) Classically—beautiful—characteristics?

DELMOUNT. She was an exception.

MAC SAM. I'll say.

DELMOUNT. It was a long time ago.

MAC SAM. You don't have to make excuses to me. I've done nearly as bad myself. Course, now, Alligator Woman did have a way with her tongue. (*He helps Delmount to the bench as Popeye enters from* D.R. *She carries a purple snow cone.*)

DELMOUNT. All right! All right! So I'm confused about women. I'm an idiot! A fool!

MAC SAM. Relax, chump. I'm just enjoying the day.

POPEYE. Here! Here, I got ya some ice. It oughta help take down that swelling.

DELMOUNT. But that's purple ice!

POPEYE. Well, they was out a cherry.

MAC SAM. Hmm. That's pretty good, Popeye! Pretty good! Here, pull up the pants. (*He jerks up Delmount's pants leg.*)

121

DELMOUNT. AAH!

MAC SAM. (*Taking the snow cone and dumps it down on Delmount's leg.*) Now slap down that ice!

DELMOUNT. Jesus Christ, Man!!

MAC SAM. Feel better? (*Elain enters from* D.R. *She carries a can of medicated spray.*)

ELAIN. I'm back, Delly! I'm back! You can just relax now! You're gonna be fine! Let me just put on this medicated spray —

DELMOUNT. Look, it's all right. I'm fine. I don't need anything *else.*

ELAIN. Oh, my God! Your leg's turned purple! I think I'm gonna faint!

DELMOUNT. No, it's ice! Purple ice! (*Holding up the paper cone.*) Ice!

ELAIN. Oh! Well, you had me going. For awhile there, you did have me going. Now let me just apply this spray —

DELMOUNT. Look, I'm fine! I don't need anything else; so just leave me alone. *Okay?*

ELAIN. Well, alright. Alright. You can't do anything with him when he gets like this. (*Her eyes meet Mac Sam's.*) Hello.

MAC SAM. (*Saying everything with his magnetic eyes.*) Hello.

ELAIN. (*Nervously.*) So, Popeye, we hear you, ah, lost your job.

POPEYE. Well, I was fired from it.

ELAIN. It's such a shame.

DELMOUNT. Yeah. It is.

ELAIN. (*Primarily for Mac Sam's benefit.*) So, what transpired? I mean, what all happened? Do tell!

POPEYE. Oh, well, I reckon what it was was when I was sewing up there in the front a the big store. This little child walked in and she started looking in at all that shiny jewelry behind the glass counter. I saw her looking and I said, 'My, what lovely eyes you have. Them's pretty eyes. What color are them eyes?' And she looks up at me and say, 'I don't know. I don't have no idea.'

ELAIN. Imagine, not knowing the color of your own eyes. Amazing. Continue, please.

POPEYE. Well, I gets out this compact case from behind the glass counter. It's covered with the most beautiful colored sea shells in all the world. And I give it to her and says, "Look in there and tell me what color your eyes is." She takes a long look and says, "Them's blue eyes." And that was the truth, she was right about it. So I give her the sea shelled compact case to take on with her, just by chance she forgets what color her eyes is and needs to take a look. Well, Miss Celia Lilly comes looking for that compact case later on in the day. I told her what happened and that's when she give me the news, "Popeye, you're fired."

MAC SAM. Hey. I like this Popeye character. She's hep.

DELMOUNT. Hep? She isn't hep.

ELAIN. Well, it's a shame, Popeye. They should have given you a second chance.

POPEYE. Oh, I don't mind it. I like traveling. (*About Mac Sam who is casually blowing out smoke rings.*) Hey, look! He's blowing smoke rings out from his mouth! Watch him! Wooh! What a trick!

MAC SAM. (*Taking the cigarette out of his mouth.*) Oh, that—that's nothing. Here, take a look at this! (*As he sticks the lit part of his cigarette into his mouth.*) Enter the infernal jaws of hell! (*With the backwards cigarette in his mouth, he blows out smoke.*)

POPEYE. Oh, look! Smoke! He's blowing out smoke! He's gonna burn up his throat!!!

MAC SAM. (*Taking out the cigarette. To Popeye.*) Ta! Da! How'd ya like that, Beautiful? (*Delmount's eyes go crazy.*)

POPEYE. It was wonderful! It was!! Do you know anymore?

DELMOUNT. Here! I know one! I can do one. Just watch! Now I'm going to wiggle my ears!

ELAIN. Oh, that's right! Delmount can do the most stupendous trick where he wiggles his ears!

POPEYE. Oh, let's see it! (*They all watch as Delmount makes a facial grimace, while trying to wiggle his ears.*)

MAC SAM. (*After a moment.*) I don't see em wiggling.

ELAIN. No, they're not wiggling.

POPEYE. Nah, they ain't.

DELMOUNT. Well, I—guess I'm out of practice. (*Mac Sam laughs cheerfully.*)

POPEYE. (*Disappointed.*) Ooh.

DELMOUNT. But here, I can do this trick where my thumb comes off. Like this! (*He does the trick where his thumb comes off.*)

POPEYE. Oh, I know that one too! (*She takes off her thumb.*)

ELAIN. That's an old one. (*She takes off her thumb.*)

MAC SAM. Yeah. (*He takes off his.*)

DELMOUNT. Well, perhaps I should just go! . . . I don't know. I don't know. (*He wanders away from the group. Carnelle enters L. into the dressing room.*)

CARNELLE. (*Mumbling to herself, as she sinks down at the dressing table.*) "I'll never be hungry again. I'll never be hungry again. As God is my witness . . . As God is my witness . . ."

POPEYE. (*Spotting Carnelle through the doorway.*) Carnelle! Is it time for your act to go on? (*Running inside the dressing room.*) Do you need some help?

CARNELLE. Oh, Popeye, I was just watching Caroline Jeffers do that heartbreaking speech from, *Gone With the Wind,* — I tell you, that's what I should have done: a dramatic interpretation piece. See, because I could break down and cry real tears right now if I wanted too. It's acting like I was laughing or happy or something — that's what'd be hard.

POPEYE. I like you act. It's beautiful. Them roman candles shooting off. Here, put on your suit. (*She hands Carnelle the red, blue and silver costume.*)

ELAIN. (*To Mac Sam.*) So, Mr. Mac Sam, what sort of day have you been having?

MAC SAM. Oh, not bad. Just been sitting here rotting away in the July sun.

DELMOUNT. (*Walking up to them.*) Excuse me. I believe I need to apply some medical spray to my wounds. (*He takes the spray and moves away.*)

POPEYE. (*About Carnelle's costume.*) Oh, that looks so good. Them silver stars really shine.

CARNELLE. I don't know, Popeye. I'm afraid it's a lost cause.

POPEYE. But I love it when you twirl them sparklers all around. I practically lose my breath. Here're your tap shoes.

ELAIN. Nice assortment of balloons you've got — and in a variety of colors.

MAC SAM. And which may I ask, is your favorite color?

ELAIN. Pink. I adore, pink.

MAC SAM. Ah, pink. I once knew a woman whose skin was awfully pink and pretty looking.

DELMOUNT. (*Sticking his head into the dressing room.*) Hey, what does that guy do? He looks like a corpse. How does he look like that?

CARNELLE. He's sick.

DELMOUNT. I'll buy that. (*He leaves.*)

POPEYE. Gosh. I've been trying so hard t'forget him.

CARNELLE. You mean, Delmount?

POPEYE. Uh huh.

CARNELLE. How's it going?

POPEYE. Well, today I found out he'd forgotten how t'wiggle his ears. But it don't matter.

TESSY'S VOICE. Carnelle! (*Tessy enters the dressing room* L.) They're voting on Saphire's hoolahoop act right now! You better get out there. You're on next! (*She blows her whistle and exits* L.)

CARNELLE. Oh, my God, I'm on next. I'm next.

POPEYE. (*Running outside.*) Hey, everyone! Carnelle's on next! She's gonna be doing her dancing routine to, "The Star Spangled Banner!"

MAC SAM. (*Getting up and making his exit* U.R.) I'm on my way!

CARNELLE. I don't know if I can go back out there.

POPEYE. Here's your sparklers and your roman candle.

CARNELLE. Do I look okay?

POPEYE. Just right.

CARNELLE. Let's go. (*They exit* L.)

ELAIN. Well, aren't you going?

DELMOUNT. I don't think I can watch it. I mean, she thinks she's tap dancing and she's just clomping her feet around. It makes me very anxious.

ELAIN. Poor, Carnation. She wants to be beautiful without understanding the limitations it brings.

DELMOUNT. Well, it'll all be over soon. Carnelle will go up to Memphis; I'll start my life in New Orleans and you'll go — wherever the winds take you. (*He looks over at Elain who seems somber.*) Hey, don't worry, Swayne. You're free. You're finally gonna find out just why you're alive. (*Tessy enters* L. *She carries a box of long-stemmed roses and brings them out to Elain.*)

TESSY. Elain! Oh, Elain! Look, here's a box of flowers that were sent to you. Isn't it exciting! Oh, here's the card; it dropped off. (*She hands the card to Delmount because Elain is holding the box.*)

Well, I've got to rush back! Got a show on! Don't forget the fire-works! (*She exits through the dressing room and off* L.)

DELMOUNT. I thought he stopped sending the roses.

ELAIN. He did.

DELMOUNT. Mind if I take a look at this card?

ELAIN. Go ahead.

DELMOUNT. "My Dear Elain, I've been very, very happy since your phone call this morning. How I do need to hear how much you love me. I'll be by for you tomorrow morning at eleven a.m. You're adoring husband, Franklin." (*After a moment.*) What kind of idiot am I? What kind of dupe? You would think that after you left me in that lunatic asylum I would know not to trust you.

ELAIN. Be fair! You always had everything! Mama left the whole of the house to you and all of the furniture and all of the silver and even the handmade quilts! She left nothing to me! Nothing at all!

DELMOUNT. You can have it. You can have all of the money that's made! Just leave him.

ELAIN. (*Overlapping.*) I don't want it. Stop planning my life! I'm used to better things now . . . my face cream . . . my clocks. And he adores me. I need someone who adores me. (*Mac Sam enters U.R. in excitement.*)

MAC SAM. (*Throwing a handful of confetti.*) Stupendous! Rav-ishing! A little bit of sheer heaven!

ELAIN. What—(*Carnelle and Popeye enter the dressing room* L. *They are elated. Carnelle twirls a burning sparkler.*)

CARNELLE. I don't believe it! I don't believe it! They were all clapping! It was a hit!

POPEYE. (*Overlapping, as she shoots off imaginary Roman candles.*) Pow! Pow! Pow!

MAC SAM. She was out there just dancing and marching and the music was swelling—

POPEYE. (*Overlapping.*) She was so beautiful!

CARNELLE. (*Overlapping as she tap dances and twirls her baton.*) Yes sir! Yes sir!

MAC SAM. (*Running on.*) And everyone started cheering when the Roman candles went off—

POPEYE. Pow! Pow! Zoweey!

CARNELLE. They were cheering for me!

MAC SAM. Brilliant performance! And can she dance! (*Delmount looks dumbfounded.*)
ELAIN. (*Running to join Carnelle and Popeye in the dressing room.*) Did it really go well? Did it really?
POPEYE. Oh brother! I about died!
CARNELLE. Quick! Let's go girls! I gotta change into my bathing suit! I don't have much time.
MAC SAM. (*Sitting down.*) Boy, (*cough, cough*) so beautiful, (*cough, cough, cough*) so fine!
DELMOUNT. (*Accusingly.*) Tell me, just exactly what do you mean when you're telling Carnelle how beautiful she is?
MAC SAM. I mean she's . . . beautiful.
DELMOUNT. You're a liar.
MAC SAM. Yeah, well, I do work the carnivals. (*He spits up a clot of blood.*)
CARNELLE. (*Pulling up her bathing suit.*) Lord, is this tight! Come on. There! There, I got it. I hope this French bra'll help. How do my thighs look?
TESSY. (*Sticking her head into the room* L.) Quick! Get out there! They're starting the lineup! (*She exits* L. *blowing her whistle.*)
CARNELLE. Oh, my God. It's time for the final crowning. It's time! Hey, let me wave goodbye to the boys. (*Carnelle waves goodbye.*) Goodbye, boys! I'm going. I'm going out to the final crowning!
MAC SAM. Hey—good luck! We'll be right there cheering!
DELMOUNT. You look good, Child!
ELAIN. Do your best.
CARNELLE. (*Hugging them.*) Oh, Elain! Oh, Popeye!
TESSY. (*Sticking her head in.*) Come on! Their moving out on the stage!
CARNELLE. Farewell, Everyone! Farewell! (*Carnelle exits* L.)
POPEYE. Quick! We've got t'run around and see her! (*She starts out.*)
MAC SAM. I'm moving out! (*Elain pauses a moment to exchange a look with Delmount. She then turns and exits. Delmount looks after them. He paces around for several moments. He glances into the empty dressing room.*)
DELMOUNT. I'll never understand it. Never. It lacks sense. It makes me ill. I mean, for Christ's sake who would want to ride in a parade? It's so pitiful. Man parading his ridiculous

pomposity down his pathetic little streets, cheering at his own inane self-grandeur. (*He looks at himself in the dressing room mirror.*) Oh, God I hope she comes in first! I hope she does. I do. I do. I swear I hope she beats them all!! (*Mac Sam enters* U.R.)

MAC SAM. Wooh. Amazing. Unbelievable. (*Delmount looks at him.*) She lost. I don't know what for.

DELMOUNT. Holy cow. Holy cow. (*Elain and Popeye enter* U.R.)

ELAIN. Oh! I just don't understand it. She tries so hard. I guess, they really just took those, "Miss Hot Tamales," to heart. (*To Delmount.*) Did you hear the results?

DELMOUNT. I heard.

ELAIN. Course everyone knew Caroline Jeffers would come in first. And I suppose, in a way, it's understandable that Joe Anne came in second.

DELMOUNT. The shrimp?

ELAIN. But, I mean, when Missy Mahoney came in third!

DELMOUNT. Third!

ELAIN. Well, I nearly died! But to me the crowning blow was having Saphire Mendoza come in ahead of our Carnation! That was the crowning blow!

DELMOUNT. Holy cow. What are we gonna say to her? What are we gonna say? (*Carnelle enters the dressing room* L. *They all stare at her. She wears a fifth place banner. She looks at herself in the mirror, then she bravely turns to face her family and friends, hoping for acceptance.*) Well, it was a stupid meaningless contest.

MAC SAM. Completely laughable.

ELAIN. Mama always said that what's really important in life is —

CARNELLE. I — don't — want — to — hear — it!! I wanted to win that contest. I cared about it. It was important to me. (*To Delmount.*) And I don't care how stupid and meaningless you think it was!! (*To Elain.*) And what are you looking at?! You never wanted me to win! You think I'm ugly that's why you told me to wear that stupid mask over my face! I can't believe I ever wanted to be like you or that mean old monkey either! (*Mac Sam starts to cough. Carnelle turns to him.*) And why don't you get well!?! You make me *sick* you're so *sick!!* You look like shit!!! I tell you, I'm so mad I could spit! (*Spit.*) There! (*Spit, spit.*) There, I spit! (*Spit.*) Die you monkey! Die!

TESSY. Carnelle!! (*She enters the dressing room* L. *carying a large American flag on a pole.*) Carnelle, come on! You and Saphire are gonna follow along behind the Grand Float carrying these American flags. You better get out there; everyone's waiting. (*She holds out the large American flag.*)

CARNELLE. (*Grabbing the flag.*) Thanks!

DELMOUNT. Wait. You don't have to do that. You don't have to follow that float.

CARNELLE. Look, if you come in last, you follow that float. I took a chance and I came in last; so, by God, I'm gonna follow that float!! (*She exits* R. *carrying the American flag.*)

MAC SAM. Hey! You're beautiful when you're mad. Beautiful, Baby!

DELMOUNT. She's gonna fall flat on her face carrying that big ole flag.

ELAIN. (*Straight front.*) I'm not like Mama. I'm not.

TESSY. (*Checking her stopwatch.*) Only four hours and forty-nine minutes till tonight's colorful display of fireworks. (*She hurries back into the dressing room and exits* L. *Delmount looks after her, then looks forlornly to Mac Sam. Mac Sam offers his flask — Delmount takes a long slug. Meanwhile, Popeye slowly turns her head upward to look towards the coming fireworks.*)

QUICK FADE TO BLACKOUT

END OF SCENE TWO

ACT II

Scene Three

The setting is the same. It is now early evening and darkness is beginning to fall. The stage is empty for a moment then Elain enters the dressing room left. She carries her purse and a half empty bottle of red wine. She is weary and a bit drunk.

ELAIN. Carnelle? Good; not here. (*She looks around the empty dressing room then goes and sits down at the dressing table. She gazes at her face in the mirror. She straightens her hair.*) You're not yourself today. Not yourself.

DELMOUNT'S VOICE. Carnelle! Carnelle, you here? Honey? (*He enters* L. *and spots Elain.*) Oh. Has Carnelle come back yet?

ELAIN. I don't know. I haven't seen her since she ran off and hid after the parade.

DELMOUNT. Think she'll be all right?

ELAIN. I doubt it.

DELMOUNT. Lord, you waiting here for her?

ELAIN. No. I just came by to get my dress. (*She rises and starts gathering up the red dress.*) I don't think she's that interested in seeing me. Looks like she doesn't admire me so much anymore.

DELMOUNT. I don't understand you. I know you're probably a kind person. You gave Popeye your earrings; you have a need to be excited by life. So why do you go back to being what Mama wanted? You know she was mean!

ELAIN. (*Turning to him angrily.*) Yes, I know she was mean and you know it too. So why do you straighten your wild hair? Why do you have horrible, sickening dreams about pieces of women's bodies? Some all beautiful; some all mutilated and bloody! I hate those dreams. I wish you didn't tell me about them. They scare me.

DELMOUNT. I'm sorry. I'm sorry.

ELAIN. It's okay.

DELMOUNT. I—I don't have those dreams anymore. I've stopped having them.

ELAIN. You have?

DELMOUNT. Yes.

ELAIN. Well, good. That's good. Do you want some wine?

DELMOUNT. Sure. Give me some wine. (*She hands him the bottle—he takes a drink. He hands the bottle back to her—she takes a long drink.*)

ELAIN. You know about those earrings I gave Popeye . . .

DELMOUNT. Yeah?

ELAIN. I hated the damn things. They pinched my ears. I was glad to get rid of them.

DELMOUNT. (*After a moment.*) Swayne.

ELAIN. What?

DELMOUNT. You're incredible.

ELAIN. Well, you've always forgiven me.

DELMOUNT. Yeah. I always have.

ELAIN. So I better be going.

DELMOUNT. Where're you going?

ELAIN. (*Referring to the red dress.*) To take this out to the car. Then on out to have some real fun before I drop dead off this planet. I've got myself a date for the fireworks. I'm meeting him in the grove down under the wisteria trees.

DELMOUNT. Well, Honey, I hope you have yourself a real good ole time.

ELAIN. Don't you worry. I'm gonna be a reckless girl at least once in my dreary, dreary life. Bye, bye now. (*She leaves the dressing room. He follows her to the doorway.*)

DELMOUNT. Bye.

ELAIN. (*As she exits down* R., *carrying the red dress.*) Be seeing you!

DELMOUNT. Bye. (*He stands looking after her. Popeye enters* L. *from the dressing room. She wears binoculars around her neck and is eating peanuts from a sack. Turning to see her.*) Popeye —

POPEYE. Hi.

DELMOUNT. Hello.

POPEYE. Is Carnelle come back?

DELMOUNT. No. I'm waiting here for her.

POPEYE. Oh.

DELMOUNT. I'd like to see her.

POPEYE. Yeah.

DELMOUNT. Course, I'm not even sure if she's coming back here or what.

POPEYE. Oh. (*Uneasy, she starts to leave.*)

DELMOUNT. Would you like to wait here too?

POPEYE. (*Stopping.*) Sure. Alright. Peanut?

DELMOUNT. Thanks. (*A pause.*) So you'll be leaving Brookhaven?

POPEYE. I reckon.

DELMOUNT. It's funny cause I'm leaving here too.

POPEYE. You is? Where was you planning to go?

DELMOUNT. I thought I'd be going to New Orleans — get back to the University and learn to be a philosopher. That way, after I have time to study and think it all through, I'll be able to let everyone know why we're living. It'll be a great relief . . . I believe. And where are you going to go?

POPEYE. Well, I don't know the particulars. But I heard a this place name of Elysian fields.

DELMOUNT. Elysian fields?

POPEYE. Right. See, they got this ambrosia t'eat and wine and honey t'drink and all sorts of people carrying on. Do you know what state it's located in?

DELMOUNT. It—isn't in a state.

POPEYE. It ain't?

DELMOUNT. No. It isn't even in the world. It's—it's fictional. It's a made up place. Why it's only in books and stories.

POPEYE. Oh. Well, shoot. Guess I won't be going there. (*Tessy enters* L. *into the dressing room. She is wearing a big straw hat.*)

TESSY. Oh, Delmount!! Are you here? Delmount?! (*She steps from the dressing room to the outside area.*) Oh, there you are! (*Looking at her watch.*) Right on the nose! You punctual thing! Do you like this hat?

DELMOUNT. It becomes you.

TESSY. Isn't he sweet. Well, do come on. Well. Tell your friend good-bye and let's head to the fireworks.

DELMOUNT. Ah, Tessy . . .

TESSY. Yes?

DELMOUNT. Well, I—I can't go with you to the fireworks.

TESSY. Oh, you can't?

DELMOUNT. No, I—I promised Popeye I'd go with her. I'm sorry. I tried to tell you this afternoon.

TESSY. I see. I see. I try to turn the other cheek and you slap it too. You're ungrateful and unworthy and low and dirty and mean! Why, I'm never gonna forgive you again! Never! I hope you rot in H!! (*She exits down* R.)

DELMOUNT. Brother.

POPEYE. Why did you lie t'her?

DELMOUNT. Huh?

POPEYE. You told her you was promised t'go t'the fireworks with me.

DELMOUNT. Oh. Well, I just didn't want to go out to the fireworks with her and . . . And you can't go around obliging other people in this world.

132

POPEYE. Oh.

DELMOUNT. Of course I do want to go watch the fireworks. They always have a nice, colorful display. You weren't planning to—I don't know, go to the fireworks yourself?

POPEYE. Sure. It's why I brung my binoculars. Had me a place picked out and everything.

DELMOUNT. Oh. Hmm. Well, I guess you . . .

POPEYE. Huh?

DELMOUNT. No, nothing. I'll be seeing you. Bye. (*He exits down* R. *Popeye sits on the bench and stares ahead. She reaches into her peanut bag. There are none left.*)

POPEYE. (*Miserably.*) Guess that's the last of em. (*Delmount reappears abruptly from* D.R.)

DELMOUNT. Popeye would you mind going to watch the fireworks with me tonight?

POPEYE. No. I wouldn't. Sure. Alright.

DELMOUNT. (*Overlapping.*) Good. Good then. Good. Let's go! (*They exit* D.R. *The stage is empty for a moment before Carnelle sneaks on from under the tent. She is wearing a short trench coat over her red bathing suit. She looks around, sees no one and heads into the dressing room. Mac Sam suddenly appears out of the darkness.*)

MAC SAM. Hey! Red! Where ya going?

CARNELLE. Mac Sam! Dammit! I didn't want anyone to see me.

MAC SAM. Well, I saw ya. How ya been?

CARNELLE. Oh, alright.

MAC SAM. Hey, you sure blew up this afternoon.

CARNELLE. I know it.

MAC SAM. Well, you really did explode.

CARNELLE. I know. I'd never been so mad as I was. And I spit out at everyone. I just spit at them Oh! That's so awful it's almost funny!

MAC SAM. Hell, it was the best part of it!

CARNELLE. Oh, I don't know. I better get my stuff out of here.

MAC SAM. You know, I went looking for you after the parade. Where'd you get off to?

CARNELLE. Oh, nowhere. Just out walking by the railroad tracks.

MAC SAM. What were you doing down there?

CARNELLE. (*As she gathers up her belongings.*) Kicking rocks. Thinking. I thought maybe I was a victim of broken dreams but then I thought maybe I wasn't. I was trying so hard t'belong all my life and . . . I don't know. Oh, looks like Elain came for her red dress. Anyway, I just don't know what you can, well, reasonably hope for in life.

MAC SAM. Not much, Baby, not too damn much.

CARNELLE. But something —

MAC SAM. Sure. There's always eternal grace.

CARNELLE. It'd be nice. (*Holding up the shoe box.*) Look, here, my frog's gone.

MAC SAM. Yeah. That Popeye set it loose.

CARNELLE. Oh, well, I still have the suit. (*She holds up the pink suit. They look at each other and smile.*)

MAC SAM. God, you're beautiful. I wouldn't trade those times we had together not for anything.

CARNELLE. (*Throwing her arms around him.*) Really?

MAC SAM. Not for a golden monkey.

CARNELLE. But how about — I mean I gave you —

MAC SAM. Oh, the syph. Hell, I've got t.b., alcoholics disease, rotting gut. I tell ya, I'm having fun taking bets on which part of me'll decay first: the liver, the lungs, the stomach, or the brain.

CARNELLE. (*Suddenly uneasy.*) It's getting late. I gotta go. (*Carnelle leaves the dressing room carrying all of her belongings. He follows.*)

MAC SAM. Hey, listen, you want to go to the fireworks with ole, Mac Sam? We could spend a fine night together.

CARNELLE. No. I — I just need some rest. You'd be tiring me out awful fast.

MAC SAM. Yeah.

CARNELLE. I gotta get this out to the car. Goodbye, Mac Sam. Goodnight. (*He doffs his cap to her. She exits* D.R.)

MAC SAM. Goodbye, Baby. I'll always remember you as the one who could take it on the chin. (*He looks after her a moment, spits up a clot of blood, wipes off his mouth and starts to exit* U.R.) Ah, well, on to the wisteria trees. (*He is gone. Suddenly Popeye and Delmount appear climbing out onto the roof of the tent from off* R. *Popeye is leading; she carries a box of popcorn. Delmount follows nervously.*)

POPEYE. This way. That's right. Hold on, now.

134

DELMOUNT. Holy Christ.

POPEYE. There. Aren't these seats great?

DELMOUNT. Oh, yeah, wonderful.

POPEYE. And we can keep an eye out for Carnelle—case she comes back by.

DELMOUNT. Yeah. Great.

POPEYE. Here. Take a look through the binoculars. See how the sky looks. (*Delmount looks through the binoculars.*) Well, how's it look?

DELMOUNT. (*Becoming interested.*) Hmm. Not bad.

POPEYE. (*As she throws handfuls of popcorn in front of the binoculars.*) Watch out! It's snowing! Look! It's snowing! See it! See it snowing!

DELMOUNT. (*Overlapping.*) Oh, great! Snow flakes! Yeah! I see it! (*Impulsively, as he takes the binoculars from in front of his eyes.*) Oh, Popeye, I just have to tell you about these beautiful dreams—I just have to—No, it's absurd! (*He turns away in anguish and spots Carnelle who has entered* D.R.) Why, Carnelle!

POPEYE. Oh, Carnelle! Hi!

CARNELLE. (*Taken aback.*) Why look at you two! What in the world are you doing way up there?!

POPEYE. We're gonna watch the fireworks! Come on up!

DELMOUNT. Yeah, come on! Please, we've been missing you. It's great up here!

CARNELLE. No, I really don't care about the fireworks. I think I'm gonna just go on home.

POPEYE. Oh, please, they's so beautiful to see!

DELMOUNT. Come on, Child! Just for awhile. You can come up for awhile.

CARNELLE. No, really, I just left something in the dressing room; I'm gonna get it and go on home. (*She enters the dressing room.*)

DELMOUNT. Lord, I hope she's alright. She didn't even mention the contest. God, I wish she'd come watch the fireworks with us.

POPEYE. Me too. (*Carnelle pulls the artificial dog out from under the dressing table. She pats it.*)

DELMOUNT. Here, you want to look through the binoculars for awhile?

POPEYE. Okay. (*Popeye takes the binoculars and looks through them.*

135

Carnelle sits at the dressing table and looks at herself in the mirror.) Ooh, I love the heavens. I'd love to live up there. Do you think it's cold or warm up there?

DELMOUNT. Hmmm. I don't know. Cold maybe? Warm? I don't know.

CARNELLE. (*Looking at herself in the mirror.*) It used to be brown. I had brown hair. Brown.

POPEYE. The man at the observatory he's talking about things such as black holes in space, globular clusters, blue giant stars and other galaxies, he says, "If you can think of it; you've got it." My mind's about to burst just trying.

CARNELLE. (*Looking around the room.*) Grace. Eternal grace. Grace. Hey, hey. I wanna watch the fireworks. (*She picks up the dog and runs out the dressing room ablaze with excitement.*) Hey! Hey, how do I get up there? I wanna come up!

DELMOUNT. (*Overlapping.*) Oh child, you're coming up?!

CARNELLE. Yes! Yes! I wanna come up! I've changed my mind! I'm coming up. How do I get up?!

POPEYE. (*Overlapping.*) Hurray! Hurray! It's easy! You just run around there and jump off of them piled up boxes and climb up the pole!

CARNELLE. Great! I'm on my way! I'm coming up! (*She exits* U.R.)

POPEYE. WOW! She's coming up! I'm so happy! I'm happy!

DELMOUNT. Oh, Popeye! (*He grabs her and kisses her full on the mouth.*) I've been dreaming about you at night. I see you riding across the sea with a host of green whales. Popeye, I love you.

POPEYE. (*Past ecstasy.*) I feel like m'teeth is gonna fall out a my head. (*Carnelle appears on the roof; she is carrying the dog.*)

CARNELLE. Hey! I'm up here! I made it! I'm up.

DELMOUNT. That's right! Now just slide on out here. That's it. Good. You made it.

CARNELLE. Oh, will you look at all those stars in the sky.

POPEYE. Yeah.

DELMOUNT. Oh, yeah.

CARNELLE. Listen, I—I don't know what I was thinking about this afternoon—when I was screaming and all.

DELMOUNT. Please, it's alright. You don't have to say anything. Everythings all right.

CARNELLE. It's just I was upset about not being able to leave

in the blaze of glory. Of course, I know it doesn't matter. I mean, the main thing is—well, the main thing is . . . Gosh; I don't know what the main thing is. I don't have the vaguest idea. (*Carnelle is laughing when the first firecracker explodes in the sky.*)
DELMOUNT. Wait! It's started!
POPEYE. (*As gold light floods their faces.*) A gold one! Look, it's a gold one!
CARNELLE. (*Now red light.*) Why, it's bursting into red! Red! Crimson red!
POPEYE. Pow!! Pow! pow. (*And then silently mouthing it.*) Pow. . . . (*The explosion is over. They sit in silence for a moment.*)
CARNELLE. Gosh, it's a nice night.
DELMOUNT. As nice as they come. (*Hold a moment. Blackout.*)

END OF PLAY

THE LUCKY SPOT

With love to Susan Kingsley and her two kids Roxie and Gar.

THE LUCKY SPOT was presented by Manhattan Theatre Club (Lynne Meadow, Artistic Director; Barry Grove, Managing Director) at City Center Theatre in New York City on April 9, 1987. It was directed by Stephen Tobolowsky; the sets were by John Lee Beatty; the costumes were by Jennifer Von Mayrhauser; the lighting was by Dennis Parichy; the sound was by Scott Lehrer; the production stage manager was Peggy Peterson; and the fight staging was by B. H. Barry. The cast, in order of appearance, was as follows:

CASSIDY SMITH. . . . . Mary Stuart Masterson
TURNIP MOSS. . . . . Alan Ruck
REED HOOKER. . . . . Ray Baker
WHITT CARMICHAEL. . . . . .Lanny Flaherty
LACEY ROLLINS. . . . . Belita Moreno
SUE JACK TILLER HOOKER. . . . . .Amy Madigan
SAM. . . . . .John Wylie

The world premiere of THE LUCKY SPOT was presented by the Williamstown Theatre Festival, Nikos Psacharopolous, Artistic Director.

CHARACTERS

CASSIDY SMITH, 15, works at the Lucky Spot dance hall.
TURNIP MOSS, 20's, works at the Lucky Spot.
REED HOOKER, 40's, owner of the Lucky Spot.
WHITT CARMICHAEL, 30's, a wealthy visitor from New Orleans.
LACEY ROLLINS, 30's, a taxi dancer.
SUE JACK TILLER HOOKER, 30's, Reed Hooker's estranged wife, a former taxi dancer.
SAM, late 60's, a patron of the Lucky Spot.

SETTING

The entire action of the play takes place at the Lucky Spot Dance Hall in Pigeon, Louisiana, a small southern town about sixty miles west of New Orleans. The dance hall is located along the main road at the edge of town.

The dance hall is actually an old Victorian farmhouse. The main room of which has recently been converted into a ballroom with a dancing area, a bar, a jukebox, and a carousel horse that spins. A few tables and a lot of chairs are stacked up together against the wall.

There are four entrances and exits to the ballroom: a swinging door Left that leads to the kitchen; a staircase leading to the upstairs; a front door; and a side door Right, leading to an outdoor area.

The outdoor area consists of an old wood stump and a leafless tree.

TIME

Christmas Eve, 1934.

MUSIC SUGGESTIONS*

ACT I

MUSIC A: "We're In The Money" with Ginger Rogers vocal, 1931.

MUSIC B: Ike "Yowse suh" Hatch and His orchestra's recording of "Some of These Days," London, 1935.

ACT II

MUSIC A: "I Need A Little Sugar In My Bowl," Bessie Smith, vocal, 1931.

MUSIC B: Valaida Snow's trumpet solo on "I Must Have That Man," London, 1937. Repeat the whole song (pg.)

MUSIC C: Fletcher Henderson's "Twelfth Street Rag," Crown Records, 1931. Repeat (pg.)

MUSIC D: Jimmie Noone and Earl Hines' recording of "King Joe," Chicago, 1928.

MUSIC E: Jimmie Noone and Earl Hines' recording of "Sweet Lorraine" — Take 2, Chicago, 1928.

MUSIC F: Coleman Hawkins' recording of "Honeysuckle Rose," London, 1934.

MUSIC G: James Price Johnson, piano solo, "Crying' For The Carolines," New York, 1930.

MUSIC H: Jimmie Noone and Earl Hines' recording of "Sweet Lorraine" — Take 1, Chicago, 1928.

MUSIC I: Louis Armstrong and His Orchestra's recording of "On the Sunny Side of the Street," with Louis Armstrong 100 vocal, Paris, 1934.

---

*See Special Note on copyright page.

ACT I

Cassidy Smith, 15, sits behind the counter writing slowly on a piece of oatmeal carton. She wears a derby hat and loose fitted dull colored garments. Music A plays on the jukebox.*
Turnip Moss enters the outdoor area, dragging a freshly cut pine tree. Turnip, 20's, is a wiry young man with deep watchful eyes.
Turnip hauls the tree in through the side door to the ballroom.

TURNIP. Morning.
CASSIDY. Oh look! Look at this! You're bringing in a tree. We're gonna have a Christmas tree!
TURNIP. Think it's big enough?
CASSIDY. Why it's bigger than me. (*Cassidy comes out from behind the bar. We see that she is about eight months pregnant.*)
TURNIP. Yeah; I guess. Wonder where it oughta go?
CASSIDY. Don't know. Never put a tree inside a room before.
TURNIP. Well, how 'bout . . . how 'bout . . . 'how 'bout . . . How 'bout we put it over here by the staircase? That way people can see it as they're sashaying down the stairs.
CASSIDY. Oh, yeah, that'd be good!
TURNIP. You think it looks good there?
CASSIDY. Uh-uh.
TURNIP. I think it looks good there too. Damn good.
CASSIDY. Yep. You heard anything from Hooker? (*Turnip goes to pour himself the last of the coffee.*)

---

*See Special Note on copyright page.

145

TURNIP. No. He's been out all night long. Sure hope he struck it lucky.

CASSIDY. Yeah. Hey, Turnip. (*Indicating writing on the oatmeal carton.*) How's that look to you?

TURNIP. (*Reading.*) "Cassidy Smith Hooker." What's this for?

CASSIDY. It's my name. I'm practicing writing it for when I sign the papers.

TURNIP. Sign what papers?

CASSIDY. My marriage papers.

TURNIP. Who're you marrying?

CASSIDY. (*Pointing to the paper.*) Hooker. See there?

TURNIP. What makes you think you're marrying Hooker?

CASSIDY. He tol' me. He give me this yellow piece a rope for a engagement ring.

TURNIP. Let me see that. Hmm. (*Turnip looks at the rope ring then looks back to Cassidy.*) Well, I don't mean this t'hurt your feelings or nothing, Cassidy; but I think he was just kinda — kidding around with ya.

CASSIDY. No, I don't think he was.

TURNIP. Well, thing is Hooker, he — he's already got a wife.

CASSIDY. Yeah, I know. Sue Jack's her name. But I don't think he cares much for her.

TURNIP. Why not?

CASSIDY. Soon as she's released out from Angola State Penitentiary — he's divorcing her and marrying me.

TURNIP. Who told you that?

CASSIDY. He did. He promised me.

TURNIP. I don't believe it.

CASSIDY. Then don't. (*Cassidy gets a broom and starts sweeping up pine needles.*)

TURNIP. Cassidy . . . you think he's in love with you?

CASSIDY. (*Sweeping.*) I didn't say that. I don't care nothing 'bout that. I don't even believe in all that.

TURNIP. Well, when you get married to a person, you're supposed to be in love with the person you're getting married to. I know that much. And people have called me dumb.

CASSIDY. Just look at all these pine needles. It's a damn mess you've made hauling in that ole tree.

TURNIP. You better believe how he was in love with Sue Jack. She's beautiful, and smart, all full of laughing times. Why she was a real lady. Always wore fine lace gloves on her hands so that she could keep her fingertips soft for playing cards.

CASSIDY. Yeah, well I went out this morning and talked to them dancing women out back. Some of 'em used to work with her at the dime a dance halls over in New Orleans. They tol' me she was a broken down wreck. And they put her away for throwing some rich lady over a balcony railing.

TURNIP. That's right—that lady's named Caroline Carmichael. Sue Jack come in a found her lyin' in bed with Hooker and she don't like nobody messing with her man. See, she's very touchy. 'Specially when she drinks. Meanest damn drunk I ever heard of or saw. (*Reed Hooker, mid-40's, enters from the front door. His white shirt is torn and a bloody handkerchief is tied around one of his arms. There is a worn mournful look in his eyes that belies his dashing exuberance.*)

HOOKER. Well, now top of the morning and a Merry Christmas Eve t'the both of ya.

CASSIDY	TURNIP
(*Overlapping*)	(*Overlapping*)
Hooker, you're back!	Did ya win any money?

HOOKER. (*Running on.*) What's this? A Christmas tree? Well, I do love the color green. It's the color of cash!

CASSIDY. What's all this blood?

TURNIP. Do ya like it by the stairway?

HOOKER. Knife wound. No, no, by the window so they can see it from the road.

CASSIDY. Who cut ya? Who done it?

HOOKER. Ah, self-inflicted misfortune.

TURNIP. (*As if this were obvious.*) Oh sure, from the road. They gotta see it from the road.

CASSIDY. Well, I'll get ya some cobwebs from out in the barn t'help staunch the bleeding. (*Hooker picks up Cassidy and twirls her around in his arms.*)

HOOKER. Now aren't you the sweetest girl in the whole wide world and her with her six little toes.

CASSIDY. Don't talk about my toes.

HOOKER. She's got the prettiest little toes.

TURNIP. Six all on one foot. I've seen 'em.

CASSIDY. I said stop talking about my toes less you want me to slice your eyes out — I don't like to hear nothing about that. You're just making your fun outta me.

HOOKER. No, no, I ain't making my fun outta you. Why, I been out all night long bucking the tiger just to bring you back a Christmas gift.

CASSIDY. A Christmas gift for me?! (*Hooker gets a jug of whiskey, from behind the counter, and throughout the following downs a couple of belts.*)

TURNIP. I bet she's never had a Christmas gift.

CASSIDY. I have, too.

TURNIP. Mr. Pete never gave her anything but a cat-o'-nine tails from what I hear.

CASSIDY. My mama used t'give us an orange and a pepper-mint candy every Christmas morning.

TURNIP. Your mama's been dead almost ten years.

CASSIDY. I remember it though. (*To Hooker.*) So what'd ya bring t'me?

HOOKER. Well, Saucer Eyes, I was gonna bring ya a solid gold hat with red ostrich plumes, and Turnip, I was gonna bring you a pocket full of Mexican jumping beans. Unfortunately, I got hooked up in a godless card game. Lost my luck late. Came outta there with nothing but the mist of the morning dew.

CASSIDY. Well, what in the world was I gonna do with another hat? I already got this one.

HOOKER. Ah, six months from now, we'll be eating outta hats. Soon as we get the Lucky Spot Dance Hall rolling.

TURNIP. Yeah, well, I sure hope the place goes over big tonight 'cause we're flat broke around here.

HOOKER. Hey, look, it's Christmas Eve. People are so lonely out there you can smell it rotting on 'em. Here at the Lucky Spot we'll be selling hot music, fine dancing and sweet solace of kindhearted women.

CASSIDY. I can't wait to see it with all the lights and music and the women in their long shiny gowns dancing with all the lonely souls.

HOOKER. We're gonna make a fortune.

TURNIP. I just hope they don't tear down the doors fighting t'get in.

CASSIDY. It'll be more like a dream than something real.

HOOKER. Well, now enough gold bricking. Let's get up our Christmas tree. We got any coffee left?

CASSIDY. I'll make a new pot. And I'll fix ya some breakfast.

HOOKER. Fine, fine, but do me a favor and don't put that greasy gravy all over everything on the plate.

CASSIDY. I won't. I'll make it real good this time. Real good. I promise.

HOOKER. Yeah. (*Cassidy exits to the kitchen. Throughout the following Hooker and Turnip make a wooden Christmas tree stand and put the tree into it.*) She's not a bad kid but I swear to God she is the worst damn cook I ever knew.

TURNIP. Well, what can you expect? You won her in a poker game.

HOOKER. Yeah, well maybe I should have taken the chestnut mare.

TURNIP. Why didn't ya?

HOOKER. Oh, you know . . . her face.

TURNIP. What about it?

HOOKER. That woebegone countenance. I don't know. Anyway, it's done. Come on and help me with this tree.

TURNIP. Hooker?

HOOKER. Huh?

TURNIP. It's about Cassidy. I think she's suffering from some sort of grand delusion.

HOOKER. Hold this here. Hold it tight now.

TURNIP. See, cause she is claiming you told her you'd marry her.

HOOKER. Oh yeah?

TURNIP. Yeah, she seems to be counting on it.

HOOKER. Look, I'm already married. Remember? To the ditch digger's daughter.

TURNIP. Yeah, well, Cassidy said you were gonna divorce Sue Jack and marry her. She claims you promised her.

HOOKER. Christ, I never promised her. (*A beat.*) Maybe I intimated something about the faint possibility.

TURNIP. Why would ya do a thing like that?

HOOKER. I don't know, Turnip. Maybe I just got fed up with the way she kept rolling herself down the staircase and eating boxes of match heads and banging at her belly with a two-by-four.

TURNIP. Oh, ya mean she didn't want t'have no kid.

HOOKER. I don't think she did, no. (*Hooker gets a banner from behind the counter.*) Here, let's get up the sign.

TURNIP. (*A beat.*) Gosh, so what're ya gonna do about Sue Jack when she gets out of prison? Would you divorce her for real?

HOOKER. God, no. I'd just shoot the bitch on sight.

TURNIP. Yeah, well, yep. But you ain't still mad at her about it all?

HOOKER. The hell I'm not.

TURNIP. But she loved him same as you. After it happened she got all torn up inside.

HOOKER. Bullshit! She was glad to be rid of both of us. The night after they laid my kid in the ground she went out to a cockfight in a red tassled dress and squandered away her wedding ring. She went on boozing and brawling and lavishing away everything decent we ever had together. Don't ever mention her to me! Don't ever mention her to me!

TURNIP. Okay, okay. I won't; I won't! So, ah, what's gonna happen with Cassidy, I mean concerning the predicament ya got her in.

HOOKER. Look, she'll have the kid. The Lucky Spot'll be in full swing. I'll send her off to some respectable school, let 'em teach her how t'cook. She'll find a nice guy — that'll be that.

TURNIP. (*A beat.*) What about your baby?

HOOKER. I'll just hang on to him.

TURNIP. How do you know she won't want it?

HOOKER. The sign's not even. Your side's too low.

TURNIP. So how're ya gonna tell Cassidy ya ain't marrying her? How're ya gonna spring it on her?

HOOKER. Stop dogging me. I'll spring it on her. I'll spring it on her.

TURNIP. I mean, look at the condition ya got her in. I wouldn't know what the hell t'tell her by now.

HOOKER. Goddamnit, Turnip! Now your side's too high. Bring it down.

TURNIP. I wonder if I'll ever have a girlfriend. My brothers told me I'd never have a girlfriend as long as I had the name Turnip. But I didn't know how to change my name 'cause folks was always calling me by it.

HOOKER. (*Looking up at the sign.*) I reckon that'll do.

TURNIP. I just wish I wasn't plaqued by self-doubt. But I'm afraid of . . . I don't know what, but I bet it's something. (*Cassidy re-enters from the kitchen. She carries a tray with a breakfast plate, silverware, cup and saucer and coffee pot.*)

CASSIDY. Oh, look, ya got up the tree! And look at that. (*She points to the banner and tries to read it as she makes cowboy coffee.*) Let's see. "Well . . . welcome. Welcome to . . . "

TURNIP. (*Reading easily.*) "Welcome to the Grand Opening, Lucky Spot Dance Hall."

HOOKER. (*To imaginary guest.*) Welcome, welcome, welcome.

TURNIP. Yes, sirree, welcome one and all.

CASSIDY. Hooker.

HOOKER. Huh?

CASSIDY. I need to talk to you on a matter. It's kinda . . . pressing. (*Hooker and Turnip exchange a meaningful glance.*)

HOOKER. Yeah, we're gonna have some fun tonight!

CASSIDY. Here's your breakfast for ya.

HOOKER. Thanks. (*Hooker takes the plate, looks at it and smirks derogatorily, then shakes his head to Turnip.*)

CASSIDY. It look bad to you?

HOOKER. It looks like it always looks when you cook breakfast.

CASSIDY. I'll take it back.

HOOKER. No, no. I'll eat it. (*Cassidy reaches for the plate to take it and Hooker notices her hand.*) Don't you ever wash your hands?

CASSIDY. . . . Sure.

HOOKER. Well, you could plant a vegetable garden underneath those fingernails. Don't you ever clean them?

CASSIDY. Yeah, I just . . . when I'm working, well the

dirt gets stuck there and I can't never get it out.

HOOKER. Try scraping it with a hairpin.

CASSIDY. I ain't got no hairpins.

HOOKER. Then use a nail or a fork or something, for Christ sake!

CASSIDY. (*Picking up Hooker's fork.*) Okay.

HOOKER. Not my fork, God damn it! Look, I don't mean to harp on you about this or anything. We're pals, right? Come on. I'll try and eat some of this slop. I'm sure it isn't too horrible. Jesus Christ, you're not gonna start t'cry just 'cause I tell you you should wash your filthy hands once a goddamn century?!

CASSIDY. No, I'll . . . I'll go wash 'em. I'm just needing to talk to you, that's all. I'll wash up and come on back. (*Cassidy exits up the stairs. Hooker turns to Turnip.*)

HOOKER. Jesus. Women. They're all alike. Them girls out back. You stay ten miles clear of any whiff of 'em — that's my best advice. (*Whitt Carmichael, 30's, enters through the front door. He is a tall man with an imposing elegance. He wears an expensive but understated suit and carries an alligator attache case.*)

TURNIP. Howdy.

CARMICHAEL. Reed Hooker?

HOOKER. What can I do for you?

CARMICHAEL. Well now, I'd like to discuss with you briefly my involvement in the ownership of this property. (*Hooker stares at Carmichael, poker-faced.*) The story is that you won it off my cousin, Davenport Fletcher, in a five-day card game down on the Gulf Coast.

HOOKER. Yes, well, that's how that story goes.

CARMICHAEL. This was my aunt's estate and she did leave it to Davenport. Now, the only problem I perceive is my cousin's three hundred and fifty-five dollar debt to me that he used this house as collateral against. Right here's a copy of the papers alerting you of the situation. (*Carmichael hands Hooker a document. Hooker takes it.*) Of course, I can see you've made some . . . improvements.

HOOKER. Yeah, well, they're a lot of initial expenses you accrue when starting out a new business. And there's always a bit of difficulty with handing out the ready cash; so as I'm sure you can imagine, your request for payment in full is difficult for me at this time. However, if you're a hunch bettor, I believe I could finagle you some points in the Lucky Spot that could triple your money for you in about a year's time.

CARMICHAEL. Then you honestly think this place is going to make money?

HOOKER. I'm afraid it's bound for glory. The Lucky Spot will be the first genuine taxi dance hall set in an isolated rural area. The glamour, magic and music of the city sporting life will now be available to the simple country folk who secretly ache for such dazzling companionship on so many of these lonely moonless nights.

TURNIP. Yeah, we got the flyers up all over town. Everyone's talking the place up big.

HOOKER. Yes, all of our dance teachers have been hired directly out of New Orleans. They split their take fifty-fifty with the hall. We also get all of the door and, of course, the extras.

TURNIP. (*Holding up a hanger of old neckties.*) Yeah, like these neckties you can rent for ten cents at the door in case, say, you forgot your own necktie . . . or in case, say, you never had no neckties at all.

HOOKER. Of course, the real saving grace, economically speaking, is the jukebox. Isn't she a beauty? See, we won't have to pay a nickel to any local musicians for playing their lousy marshmallow music. Why, we've got twenty-six of the newest tunes, played by the hottest bands, right at our fingertips. So what d'ya say, pal? Are you a hunch bettor?

CARMICHAEL. As a matter of fact, Mr. Hooker, I am somewhat of a gambler and I believe I'm going to have a bet against this depressing little monkey hop and the foolhearted ex-rumrunner who doesn't have a Chinaman's chance of making a business out a racket.

HOOKER. Well, now, would anybody care to add to that; or maybe subtract?

CARMICHAEL. I'll make it simple: give me the cash or I close down the hall.

HOOKER. How long do I have?

CARMICHAEL. I believe that order the sheriff signed allows you 'till January one. Time's almost up.

HOOKER. You're a real sport. But I'm too many miles down the road t'turn back now. (*Hooker produces a deck of cards.*) Here let's cut for it. Double or nothing.

CARMICHAEL. Afraid not.

HOOKER. (*With a forced grin.*) Look . . . it's Christmas.

CARMICHAEL. Well, I'm not Santa Claus. (*Cassidy comes running down the stairs excitedly. She carries a comb.*)

CASSIDY. (*About her fingernails.*) Look! Look here, I scraped out every scrap of dirt from underneath there using the teeth on this here comb.

HOOKER. Ah, great work.

CASSIDY. Thanks. (*Extending her spotless hand to Carmichael.*) Hi, Mister!

TURNIP. This man's trying t'close down the Lucky Spot. Says Hooker owes him a lot a money.

CASSIDY. Well then, Hooker'll just have t'have himself another lucky streak. Just like he did that time down in Gulfport when he won me and this place and the Chevy motor car.

CARMICHAEL. All that. Well now, Mr. Hooker, you do seem to be quite a lucky man. But then I guess you did pick up a few gambling tips from your very talented wife.

CASSIDY. How d'you know his wife?

HOOKER. What d'ya know about her?

CARMICHAEL. Hmm. Well. I've played cards with her on occasion. And then there was a time when I was bringing my sister, Caroline Carmichael, back and forth from the hospital every day to testify against Mrs. Hooker at her trial.

HOOKER. Good Christ, he's Caroline Carmichael's brother!

TURNIP. No wonder he hates your damn guts.

HOOKER. Yeah, well, he can hate my guts as much as he wants to, but it wasn't me who shoved Caroline over that goddamn balcony railing! Sue Jack did it all on her own. (*To Carmichael.*) So you stop harassing us 'cause of that no good wife of mine?! God, I'd love t'break her rotten neck and shut

154

her up for good!

CARMICHAEL. Lucky you didn't shut her up before you mastered all of her card playing pointers.

HOOKER. What pointers do you mean?

CARMICHAEL. Your wife was an expert card sharp; had great hands, knew all about shaved cards, hold outs . . . ringing in a cold deck.

HOOKER. What are you inferring?

CARMICHAEL. I'm not inferring.

HOOKER. Look, like you say, Sue Jack had the hands. You gotta have the hands. I never did. Nah, there's only one thing I learned from Sue Jack that ever did me any good.

CARMICHAEL. Now what would that be?

HOOKER. A simple rule of thumb: whoever throws the first punch in a fist fight has a twenty-to-one shot at aceing the match. (*The two men stare at each other.*)

CARMICHAEL. Is that a fact? (*Hooker shrugs his shoulders and turns.*)

HOOKER. Seems t'be. Hey! (*Hooker turns back and clobbers Carmichael in the jaw. Carmichael falls to the floor.*) Sorry I pasted him, but he was becoming insufferable.

CARMICHAEL. You're gonna regret this. Believe me, you're gonna regret this a lot. I'm calling in the Sheriff.

HOOKER. Hey, Turnip, help the man outa here. (*Turnip pulls Carmichael to his feet and ushers him towards the door.*)

CARMICHAEL. You're outta here. You're through. Pack your goddamn bags! You're finished! (*Hooker yells after them as Turnip and Carmichael exit out the front door.*)

HOOKER. (*Overlapping.*)Relax, Carmichael. I'll have that money for ya by January one! No damn problem with the Lucky Spot opening. No damn problem!

TURNIP. (*Offstage*) No damn problem!

HOOKER. Jesus!

CASSIDY. Looks like you got that man pretty riled up.

HOOKER. Looks like it.

CASSIDY. You reckon he's gonna get us kicked outta here for good?

HOOKER. Look, the Lucky Spot Dance Hall opens at 8 p.m. tonight; by 9:15 we'll be strolling on Easy Street; by January one, you'll be dancing in satin red shoes. Every day's gonna be like a goddamn holiday in Paris, France! Now do ya have that straight?

CASSIDY. Uh huh.

HOOKER. Well, good. 'Cause I'm sure as hell not standing here telling ya all this crap just t'get your rotten hopes up for nothing.

CASSIDY. No, I — I sure I don't wanna get my rotten hopes up for nothing. 'Cause my hopes . . . well, sometimes, when they get way, way up there, I don't even know how t'get 'em back down without dying or not living or breathing or exploding. I don't know why. Sometimes.

HOOKER. Yeah. Sure. Well, I would never want t'get your hopes up for nothing.

CASSIDY. Thanks. I appreciate it. (*They look at the floor for a moment.*) Hooker?

HOOKER. Yeah?

CASSIDY. I got this thing for you. (*Cassidy takes a dirty worn piece of paper out of her pocket.*)

HOOKER. What is it?

CASSIDY. Just a card. A birthday message.

HOOKER. Well, my birthday was way back in the damn summer.

CASSIDY. I know. I been carrying the card around since then.

HOOKER. Uh-huh.

CASSIDY. But I just never could find the right time t' . . . give it to ya.

HOOKER. Oh. (*Cassidy hands out the card then withdraws it.*)

CASSIDY. Nah, maybe I should wait and go on and give it to you some other time.

HOOKER. Well, I may as well look at the thing.

CASSIDY. There's nothing particular about it.

HOOKER. Okay, if you don't want me t'have it . . .

CASSIDY. No, no. Go on. Here. It's for you. (*She hands him the card.*)

HOOKER. (*Hooker unfolds the paper and reads the message aloud.*) "To Reed Hooker. Happy Birthday. From Cassidy Smith." The "K"'s backwards. (*He hands the paper back to her.*)

CASSIDY. Well . . . okay.

HOOKER. I gotta go wash up. (*Hooker starts up the stairs.*)

CASSIDY. I'll, ah, I'll run iron ya your clean shirt. (*Hooker exits up the stairs. Cassidy exits out the kitchen door carrying the breakfast tray. Lacy Rollins, a shortish woman in her 30's, with peroxided hair and heavy rouge, appears outside dressed in a frilly, tattered robe and high heels. She stumbles across the yard and moves into the dance hall through the side door. She looks around, sees the room is deserted, spots the coffee pot and starts looking for a cup. Turnip walks in through the front door. He eyes her nervously.*)

TURNIP. Hi.

LACEY. (*Startled.*) I was just coming in from out back t'hunt me some coffee. I need t'have coffee every morning. Otherwise, my heart just won't start pumping and it's likely I'll drop into a dead heap right here on this floor.

TURNIP. Well there's the coffee pot right there.

LACEY. I see it, but I'm gonna need me a cup. Do you know where there's a cup? Or even a bowl? I don't mind drinking outta bowls. I don't have t'be prissy. (*Turnip finds a cup.*)

TURNIP. Here, use this.

LACEY. Thanks. I don't guess there's any sugar?

TURNIP. No.

LACEY. Oh, well. It's just I love sugar. You can't ruin sugar. I wish I could put it on every morsel I ever ate. Wouldn't it be wonderful poured all over your scrambled eggs, and your sausages and your grits?

TURNIP. I never thought t'give it a try. (*Lacey moves around the room.*)

LACEY. Well, I've thought t'give it a try. I've thought and thought and thought and— (*Lacey trips on her robe and falls to the floor. On the verge of tears.*) Oh dear. Look here, I've tripped again. I'm always falling down. I've got very weak ankles. My ankle bones are practically the smallest bones in my body. It's a condition that I've had since early birth. (*Starting to cry.*) Oh Lord. I'm sorry if I seem t'be falling apart. My goodness, it's only Christmas Eve and already I'm emotional.

TURNIP. Is something wrong?

LACEY. Well, where am I supposed to go? What am I supposed to do? Tomorrow's Christmas Day, and I'm sure no one's even thought to get me a present. I'm stuck out here in this backwoods without a nickel in my stocking —

TURNIP. What're you talking about? You'll be dancing here at the Lucky Spot tonight. You'll clear some jack. (*Hooker comes down the stairs without wearing a shirt.*)

HOOKER. Hey, Cassidy, where's the clean shirt? (*Noticing Lacey and Turnip*) Oh, good morning, Lacey, right? Hope you girls had a good night's sleep. Ya'll all gotta look real beautiful for tonight.

LACEY. Don't you know?

HOOKER. Know what?

LACEY. The other girls have all gone. They're all catching the train back t'New Orleans. And not a stinking one of 'em would lend me the fare. They don't like me. I'm unpopular everywhere I go. (*Cassidy enters from the kitchen with a clean shirt.*)

HOOKER. What're you saying? The girls aren't out back in the bungalows? (*Turnip runs out to check the bungalows.*)

LACEY. Bungalows? He calls those bungalows! Why, every-one of us recognized them to be authentic slave quarters. I don't care what fancy colors you paint them.

HOOKER. Look, what's happening here? (*Turnip enters.*)

TURNIP. They're gone alright.

HOOKER. Why'd everyone go?

LACEY. They all heard she was coming back.

HOOKER. Who?

LACEY. Your wife, Sue Jack. They're all scared t'death of her — think she's dangerous.

HOOKER. For Christ sake, she's in prison. She's no more coming here than Santa Claus.

LACEY. Well, the kid in the derby hat seems to be differently informed.

HOOKER. (*To Cassidy.*) What do you know about Sue Jack coming here? (*Hooker takes the shirt from Cassidy and starts to put it on.*)

CASSIDY. Well, it's just I been keeping in check with the lady over at Angola Penitentiary . . .

HOOKER. You what?

CASSIDY. Yeah. And she tells me there's a special order

releasing some prisoners out early for Christmas time and Sue Jack's one of 'em.

HOOKER. Well, she sure as shit's not coming here for Christmas!

CASSIDY. Yeah, she is. 'Cause I told 'em where we was.

TURNIP. Oh Lord!

CASSIDY. And we wanted her to come on out here.

HOOKER. I oughta bust you, Cassidy. I oughta bust you good! Is this any of your goddamn business?! (*To Lacey.*) How long ago did the girls leave here for the train depot?

LACEY. I don't know. A while, I guess.

HOOKER. I gotta drive over there and stop them. (*To Turnip who echoes his words.*) Look, if she . . . if she comes here . . . (*Hooker shoves Cassidy, who is trying to stop him, into the door.*) God damn it! . . . you tell her to get out and stay out. She's not welcome ever.

CASSIDY. But you don't understand! She's gotta be here t'get her divorce so you can oblige your marriage t'me. Please. Then she can go away forever! (*Hooker pulls Cassidy up by her hair.*)

HOOKER. Look, I don't want you getting involved with that woman. Stay clear of her! You understand me? Huh?!

CASSIDY. Uh-huh. (*He lets her go.*)

HOOKER. Good. (*Hooker storms out the front door.*)

CASSIDY. He pulled my hair. He never done that before. He never shouted at me like that. I thought he was different, but he's just the same! Oooh! I hate him! I hate him! He's mean and awful! And I hate him forever!

TURNIP. Well, you should never have taken it on your own t'stick your nose in like you did, calling up the prison, telling them t'send Sue Jack here.

CASSIDY. (*Turning on him.*) Yeah, well, how else is she gonna get her divorce so I can get my marriage? Huh? Did you ever think of that?! See, 'cause he's just got to marry me soon. Otherwise, this thing will be born out a bastard. And everyone in the world will look down on it and it won't have no excuses at all. (*Breaking into tears of raging fury.*) Oh, he promised me he'd marry me. He promised! He wouldn't break his promise, would he? Oh, promise me, he wouldn't!! Promise me!!!

TURNIP. Sure, I promise. I promise. Just don't cry so much.

LACEY. That's right, sugar, all that crying's gonna use up your face. And you've only got this one little face t'get by on for your whole life long. Ya gotta use it up sparingly. (*Turnip gets a bucket of red berries and brings it over to Cassidy.*)

TURNIP. Hey, you wanna start stringing up these berries? We gotta decorate the tree.

CASSIDY. We gonna string these berries then put 'em up on the tree?

TURNIP. Yeah.

CASSIDY. That'll look good.

TURNIP. And there's popcorn. I'll go make the popcorn. We'll string that up, too.

CASSIDY. Okay. (*Turnip exits to the kitchen. Cassidy takes a needle and thread out of her pocket and starts stringing the berries. Lacey watches Cassidy, who is contentedly stringing berries.*)

LACEY. May I help?

CASSIDY. Okay. I got one more needle. (*Cassidy goes to get a needle and thread.*) Tell me.

LACEY. What?

CASSIDY. You reckon Hooker's gonna be able t'bring them dancing ladies back here for tonight?

LACEY. Well, I hope so. Otherwise, my life is simply at a complete loss for direction.

CASSIDY. I should never of spoken nothing about her coming back. I sure didn't guess it'd run 'em all off like that.

LACEY. Oh, those girls are all being horrible, silly, scaredy cats. Why, back when she was dancing in New Orleans, everyone of 'em would of died to be just like her.

CASSIDY. They would of?

LACEY. Sure. Sue Jack Tiller was top girl at the Glitter Dance Palace. She was the most beautiful, the finest dancer, the funniest wit. She made a hobby of collecting diamond engagement rings. She was always fishing guys for silk gowns and mink furs. Why, she possessed this one floor-length white mink coat that all the girls stood dripping with envy over. 'Course it didn't bother me a lick as I've never had the slightest affection for rodents. Pass the berries. (*Cassidy*

160

passes the bucket of berries to Lacey.)
CASSIDY. Here.
LACEY. None of us could ever fathom why she hauled off and married an insane rumrunner like Reed Hooker. Oh not that he wasn't well-to-do. Prohibition was a very flush time for the rumrunners. Still she could have had anyone. After all she possessed a great many assets.
CASSIDY. Like what?
LACEY. Well now, her greatest asset, in my opinion, was her ability to hold a prolonged conversation with a man. My auntie always told me, if a man would hold a conversation with a woman, well, she was special. She had more than his grudging physical desire — she had his admiration and respectability.
CASSIDY. Well, me, I — I've talked to men. I say things t' 'em and mostly they talk right back.
LACEY. That's different, sugar. What I'm talking about is real conversation. Not things such as "Hi, cutie," or "Hot night," or "Where's my clean shirt?" See, a real conversation would be dealing in topics with much more depth and importance.
CASSIDY. Like what? What would be a real conversation?
LACEY. Hmm. It's hard t'say exactly. But more along the lines of a discussion as to how the sun is really a star and it's made up out of balls of burning fire and once there was an ice age and everything got frozen and died in the cold but then things began to thaw out and the sun came back out and people could start to living again but the dinosaurs were gone forever because they had become . . . extinct.
CASSIDY. Gosh. Well. I'd be confused speaking in a conversation like that.
LACEY. Sure. Most girls would be. Or say, for instance, one might have a conversation discussing deep, frightening things about living and dying that most people would never even mention because they're too stupid t' think 'em up in the first place.
CASSIDY. Like what deep frightening things 'bout living and dying?
LACEY. Oh . . . I don't know exactly. Just a very compli-

cated sort of conversation. I don't get t'practice conversation that much. Most fellows won't pay any attention to me unless I'm being perky. But her . . . they'd have endless conversation with her.

CASSIDY. Still all an' all, I bet she's not one whit better'n me.

LACEY. Well . . . you're a good deal younger than she is. You've got the bloom of youth.

CASSIDY. Yeah; I hope.

LACEY. Does Hooker . . . does he ever tell you he loves you?

CASSIDY. (*Factually.*) Oh no. No person ever told me that. But one night, not long ago, I—I dreamed some furry animal said it loved me, but I don't remember what kind it was.

LACEY. Well, even though I've never really known it, I do believe in love. I don't think I could go on living if I didn't. Unfortunately, I've got a way of making any fellow I'm with so mad he'll haul off and hit me. The last one, he tried t'drowned me in the bathtub. Since then, it's been hard t'let myself trust a man. But I still keep trying. I still believe in love. (*Sue Jack Tiller Hooker, 30's, enters through the front door. She has the jarring presence of a ravaged beauty. She is tall and thin and wears a hand-me-down dress, a thin wool coat and flat ugly shoes. She carries a large handbag.*)

SUE JACK. Hi.

CASSIDY. Hi.

SUE JACK. Is this a dance hall?

CASSIDY. It is.

SUE JACK. Y'all opening tonight?

CASSIDY. We is.

SUE JACK. Oh. Well, good. Good. I—um, is Reed Hooker, is he around here anywhere?

CASSIDY. He's gone out.

SUE JACK. Oh. Well, how long do you think he'll be gone?

CASSIDY. Don't know. What d'ya want with him?

SUE JACK. Well . . . I'm his wife, Sue Jack Hooker . . . I've been away . . . awhile.

CASSIDY. Yeah. Yeah, I heard about you. But you don't look the same as I thought.

SUE JACK. No?

CASSIDY. Uh-huh.

SUE JACK. Um.

LACEY. Oh, hello. I'm sure you don't remember me but I worked at the Green Torch Dance Hall years ago when you were at the Glitter Palace down in New Orleans. My name's Lacey Rollins.

SUE JACK. Oh yeah, I remember you. You did cartwheels.

LACEY. Right. She's right.

SUE JACK. But your hair was much darker back then — It was jet black, almost a blue-black.

LACEY. Why, I'm flabbergasted! Who'd ever have thought you'd remember me? Tell me. Don't you think this new color is much more flattering? Doesn't it give me a much more perky look?

SUE JACK. Well, you were always very . . . perky. But I do, ah, like it a lot.

LACEY. Why, thanks, sugar. And your hair, it's all done . . . well, just completely differently.

SUE JACK. That's right. It's all different now. (*Turnip enters with the popcorn.*)

TURNIP. Well, here's the popcorn.

SUE JACK. Turnip.

TURNIP. Sue Jack?

SUE JACK. Yeah, its me.

TURNIP. Gosh, you look — I mean, your face —

SUE JACK. I know, it looks like forty miles of bad road, all of it rained on. Well, hell, 'least I made it through three years at Angola, that's something.

TURNIP. Oh, sure.

LACEY. Sure.

TURNIP. Boy, I'm glad they set ya free when they did.

SUE JACK. Yeah, I got lucky. They decided to let some of us out early for Christmas. Probably so they could save on turkey dinners.

TURNIP. Well, gosh. Gosh, what was it like stuck in prison? Did y'all have any fun at all? I mean, what did they do on your birthday?

SUE JACK. Well . . . nothing.

TURNIP. Oh.

SUE JACK. Yeah. Nothing special. Just, you know, the same.

TURNIP. What's that like? The same?

SUE JACK. Oh, I can't really afford t'think about all that right now. I wanna try and make a good impression on Reed when he gets here. Tell me, do I really look plain ugly?

LACEY. No!

TURNIP. No it's just . . . different.

LACEY. Different. (*Echoing Turnip.*)

TURNIP. I mean, from before. You don't — got on your gloves. But other than that . . . well, ya don't look ugly.

SUE JACK. Then will ya do me a favor?

TURNIP. What?

SUE JACK. Stop looking at me like that. You're starting t'get me scared.

TURNIP. What? No, there's nothing t'be scared for.

SUE JACK. I know. It's just I gotta see Reed. I haven't seen him in so long. And I'm standing here in these hand-me-down rags, with my hair all cropped off looking like something a cat dragged in.

TURNIP. You look okay.

SUE JACK. Thanks, I'm sorry. I'm just so jumpy today. I swear if somebody said boo t'me I'd cry.

TURNIP. Ain't nobody gonna say boo to ya.

SUE JACK. Sure. I'll be okay. I mean, I was just so surprised that he called for me.

TURNIP. Who called for you?

SUE JACK. Reed. He — he never visited me the whole time, and I thought I'd lost him for sure and here, outta the blue, he calls and leaves a message telling me t'come here for Christmas.

TURNIP. Oh . . . gosh.

SUE JACK. I've got all this hope welling up in me again. I swear my heart's spinning inside me like a runaway top.

TURNIP. Yeah, well, I don't know what t'say here. Umm. Here's the popcorn, Cassidy, if ya wanna start stringing it up.

CASSIDY. Thanks.

SUE JACK. This is a beautiful jukebox. Prettiest one I've ever seen.

TURNIP. It's Hooker's pride and joy. Says it's got all his favorite tunes on it.

SUE JACK. All these tunes are new. I don't recognize any of them.

CASSIDY. Look, there's some things of yours ya might be wanting.

SUE JACK. What things?

CASSIDY. Just belongings. I found 'em in one of the drawers in Hooker's trunk. I put'em in a box for ya.

SUE JACK. Well, thanks.

CASSIDY. I'll go up and get 'em for ya. Ya might be needing 'em on your travels.

SUE JACK. Alright.

LACEY. (*To Turnip.*) Hey, what was it she called you?

TURNIP. Huh?

LACEY. Was it Turnip? Did she call you "Turnip"?

TURNIP. I guess.

LACEY. Turnip. That's hilarious. Whatever does it stand for?

TURNIP. Just stands for Turnip.

LACEY. But what's it short for?

TURNIP. My name, I guess.

LACEY. Well, what's your name?

TURNIP. . . . Turnip. ˙

LACEY. Oh.

TURNIP. . . . Yeah. (*Whitt Carmichael enters through the front door. He doesn't notice Sue Jack who is seated in the window seat.*)

CARMICHAEL. Hello. Is Hooker here?

TURNIP. No.

CARMICHAEL. Look, I just found out that all of your Gold Coast hostesses have run out in fear of the imminent arrival of Hooker's outlaw wife.

SUE JACK. Why, hello, Whitt.

CARMICHAEL. Sue Jack . . . Good Lord—I hardly recognized you.

SUE JACK. Yes, well, I guess I look kind of different without a frame around me.

CARMICHAEL. Well, well, so the never-miss girl has really returned. Tell me, how are those silk hands of yours? She had the prettiest hands. They never let her down.

SUE JACK. 'Least not to your level, anyway.

CARMICHAEL. You got close though. Back on Esplanade Avenue. You got awfully close. Let me see those hands.

SUE JACK. Oh, it's amazing what three years of raising hogs and picking cotton can do to a pair of hands. Feel for yourself. (*Sue Jack reaches up to rub her calloused fingertips across Carmichael's face. He pulls away.*) Oh Whitt, what's the matter? Don't you wanna see if I lost my touch?

CARMICHAEL. Look . . . I didn't come here to dwell on your hard luck or your felony conviction . . . I have a business proposition to discuss with your husband. (*Cassidy comes walking down the staircase carrying a cardboard box.*)

SUE JACK. Tell me. Reed and I are partners.

CARMICHAEL. Well, in the light of the fact that your dancers have departed, I feel it is now painfully apparent that Hooker will not be able to settle his three hundred and fifty-five dollar debt to me by January first. So, as a matter of convenience, I'd appreciate him signing this property over to me straight away. (*Carmichael hands a paper to Sue Jack. As she looks it over.*) Otherwise, I intend to inform all the people in town Hooker owes money to the distressing news that y'all are opening up your taxi dance hall with absolutely no taxi dancers. Believe me, it could make some of them rubes very, very angry.

SUE JACK. (*Handing the paper back to Turnip.*) I don't know where you get your information, Whitt, but someone just about pulled your leg completely off. Why, our only concern is that there will be so many beautiful ladies dancing here this evening that everyone strolling down this road will be made mindlessly drunk inhaling the intoxicating smell of all the sweet perfumes.

CARMICHAEL. Ah, Sue Jack, I do love it when you wax poetic but I saw all of your charity girls pulling out on this morning's train. They claimed they were escaping your villainous presence.

SUE JACK. That's pure sour grapes. They're just distressed because we rejected them for the dance hall. You see, we only want the creme de le creme working at the Lucky Spot. (*Lacey smiles broadly.*) Come by tonight and see for yourself if you don't believe me.

CARMICHAEL. Don't worry, I'll be back. And so will a lot of other folks who have debts to settle.

SUE JACK. Wonderful. We need some big-time spenders. So long now. Merry Christmas.

CARMICHAEL. And a Merry Christmas to you, Miss Sue.

LACEY. Please do come back. (*Carmichael exits out the front door.*)

SUE JACK. My God. Have all the dancers really gone?

LACEY. I'm afraid so. I'm the only one left.

SUE JACK. I can't believe people think I'm so horrible. I mean, maybe back when I drank I was something of a hothead.

LACEY. Well, Lola Dove was getting everyone all riled up, telling them about the time when you hit her with a brick just t'see if she would bleed.

SUE JACK. Oh, yeah, yeah, well, surprisingly enough that cold, heartless bitch bled a whole lot. Reed's gonna hate me for this when he finds out.

TURNIP. He already knows.

SUE JACK. He does?

TURNIP. He went to try and stop the dancers at the train depot. Guess he didn't make it.

SUE JACK. Well, hell's fire, here he invites me for Christmas and I bring in this whole bag of trouble. What a goddamn mess. God, I'd kill for a drink. Haven't had one in three years.

TURNIP. Well, look. I think I better go try and find Hooker.

SUE JACK. Ooh! Just one straight shot of tequila.

TURNIP. See if he's got anything up his sleeve.

SUE JACK. Or gin, a jolt of gin. (*Turnip exits out the front door, slamming it behind him.*) Okay, okay. I'm fine.

CASSIDY. Well, here's your box for ya. (*Cassidy hands Sue Jack the cardboard box packed with belongings from Sue Jack's past.*)

SUE JACK. Thanks. Thanks a lot. (*Sue Jack stares into the box a moment then takes out a hand mirror.*) Ha! Look here, my silver mirror's cracked. Well, now that's seven years bad luck. Hmm. Wonder when I broke it? God, look at me! How'd all of that sadness ever sink so deep into my face?

Well, let's see what we can do to fix her up. (*Sue Jack takes out some melted rouge and smears it across her cheeks. She becomes disheartened by the effect. She tosses the mirror aside.*) Shouldn't be looking in mirrors. My mama, she shot herself while looking in a full-length mirror. 'Course I'm not like my mama. She went insane due to religious troubles. (*Sue Jack takes out an old bottle of hand lotion, opens it up and smells it.*)

LACEY. Well, I don't know how my mother is; she's not speaking t'me. And I really don't even care 'cause when she was speaking t'me, she never got tired of telling me how I was swivel-hipped and I was never gonna be anything more than some poor man's pudding. Well, I've set out t'prove her wrong. (*To Cassidy.*) So how about your mama? What's she like?

CASSIDY. Well, it's hard t'say 'cause, well she's dead. All of 'em are except me.

SUE JACK. How'd they all die?

CASSIDY. Diptheria. Killed every one of 'em. Then they come out and burned our place down t'ashes. Said it was full of contamination.

LACEY. That's tragic. Having your whole family demolished.

CASSIDY. Of course, my paw, well, I don't know about him, 'cause see I never knowed him. He could be some rich lord living in a castle somewhere or maybe he's just some old bum standing in the breadlines. I'm hoping someday I'll meet him and find out.

SUE JACK. Well, I never met my daddy but if I did, I'd like nothing better than t'spit straight at him.

CASSIDY. Well, all men ain't so bad.

SUE JACK. No. How 'bout your husband? What's he like?

CASSIDY. I, well, I ain't exactly quite got no husband, yet.

SUE JACK. Oh.

CASSIDY. But I will. He's gonna marry me real soon.

SUE JACK. Well, that's good news. (*Pause.*) What sort of wedding you planning?

CASSIDY. Oh, nothing much.

LACEY. Gosh, this sure is a stunning tree, and these berries are just gonna make it look so perky! Don't ya'll think?

SUE JACK. Yeah. You know, you oughta do something

special — dress up at least. Let me look through here. Maybe there's some things you can use. (*Sue Jack rummages through the box.*) God, I'll never forget our wedding. It was St. Patrick's day and it was raining and Thumper Bell . . . Lacey, you remember Thumper Bell? . . .

LACEY. Oh yeh, yeh, the crazy drummer from the Palace.

SUE JACK. Why he kept throwing rice all over us on the wet streets in the rain. Reed and I — we couldn't stop laughing . . . Doesn't that look pretty? (*Sue Jack takes off Cassidy's derby and puts on a fancy hat.*)

LACEY. (*In an attempt to change the focus.*) I've never been married. But I did get left at the church once. Well, actually, it was a home wedding. Oh, we had the house all decorated with colorful flowers and garlands and candlelight. I don't think they'll ever invent anything more romantic than candlelight. Anyway, it's a very funny story — all about how he never came by the house. I guess it makes me out t'look a little foolish. Afterwards, everyone remarked how I took it really well, coming down and joining the party like I did.

CASSIDY. But why didn't he come back t'marry you? What made him not come?

LACEY. I guess he just — Well maybe 'cause I . . . Oh, beats me.

SUE JACK. Here, try on this coat.

CASSIDY. I don't think I better be using your things.

SUE JACK. Look, didn't anybody ever tell you, it's better to give than to receive?

CASSIDY. No.

SUE JACK. Well, occasionally, it's true. (*Throwing the coat around Cassidy.*) There. Lacey, doesn't that look elegant?

LACEY. Well, now that does help!

CASSIDY. Really?

LACEY. My yes. It hides a lot! In fact, I have a dress that'll be just the thing with that coat. I'll run and get it! (*Lacey exits out the side door.*)

SUE JACK. Here's some shoes.

CASSIDY. Why, them's red satin shoes. I always been longing t'have me a pair a them red satin shoes.

SUE JACK. Well, try 'em on.

CASSIDY. No, I, well, I got these different sort of feet. Would it be alright if I tried 'em on upstairs?

SUE JACK. Sure.

CASSIDY. Thanks. (*Cassidy takes the shoes and exits upstairs. Sue Jack goes back to the box. She finds an old deck of cards. She takes out a lace glove and puts it on her hand. She then spots an old teddy bear. She picks it up and holds it with a strange sad wonder. Hooker enters through the front door in a huff. He stops in his tracks when he sees Sue Jack. Sue Jack feels his presence, she drops the toy bear back into the box and turns to face him.*)

SUE JACK. Hi. I, well, I was gonna try and fix up.

HOOKER. No need.

SUE JACK. I'm sorry about running off the dancers.

HOOKER. Yeah.

SUE JACK. I'll try and . . . help out.

HOOKER. I don't think so.

SUE JACK. Well . . . whatever you'd like.

HOOKER. I'd like you outta here.

SUE JACK. I see.

HOOKER. You're like a bad luck charm around my neck. I keep trying t'rip you off and you keep burning my hand.

SUE JACK. I don't wanna burn your hand. I don't mean to.

HOOKER. Then just go.

SUE JACK. I'm not the same as I was Reed. Go on and look at me. You see, I'm not the same. I'm not the same one who kept on hurting you by drinking, and brawling and gambling it all away. And I'm not the young, laughing girl you married with the rosy cheeks and pretty hands. I guess I'm not sure who I am. And, I tell you, it's been making me feel so strange. When I was in prison, the only belonging I had was this old photograph of myself that was taken just before I ran off from home. In it I'm wearing this straw hat decorated with violets and my hair's swept back in a braid and my eyes, they're just . . . shining . . . I used to take out that picture and look at it. I kept on pondering over it. I swear it confused me so much, wondering where she was — that girl in the picture. I could not imagine where she'd departed to — so unknowingly, so unexpectedly. (*A pause.*) Look, I won't drink or yell or fight or shoot pool or bet the roosters or —

HOOKER. Yeah, yeah, and I guess I've heard all that till it's frayed at the edges.

SUE JACK. Please, I don't wanna lose any more. I'm through throwing everything away with both fists.

HOOKER. I'm sorry. I just can't let you in on me ever again.

SUE JACK. Then why did you send for me? Why did you call for me t'come t'you?

HOOKER. . . . I didn't. It was somebody else. It was somebody I'm in kinda a mess with.

SUE JACK. What sort of mess? What somebody?

HOOKER. Look, I really can't afford t'have you flying off the handle.

SUE JACK. I'm alright.

HOOKER. It's just something that happened and I think the best thing is if you just disappeared.

SUE JACK. What are you telling me? Just tell me what you're telling me. (*Cassidy enters at the top of the staircase wearing only one red shoe and holding the other one in her hand.*)

HOOKER. Cassidy, get outta here!

CASSIDY. (*A beat.*) You tell her about us?

HOOKER. Move, do you hear me? Move! Move!

SUE JACK. What are you — what did you — This child?! (*Turnip rushes in the front door. He races behind the counter, grabs a shotgun and heads back towards the front door.*)

TURNIP. Hooker, thank God, come quick! Carmichael's got the whole town riled up. Johnny Montgomery and some of the other guys ya owe money to are taking away everything: the Christmas hog, the Santy Claus mailbox, the Chevy car . . . (*Hooker grabs the shotgun from Turnip and leans it against the wall.*)

HOOKER. Look, we don't need t'start killing people. I can handle Johnny Montgomery. He'll listen to reason. (*Hooker and Turnip exit out the front door.*)

CASSIDY. (*Coming down the staircase.*) You want these things back? (*Sue Jack looks at her, then heads for the counter looking for some liquor.*)

SUE JACK. I want a drink. The real world's getting much too potent. I gotta dilute it with some pure grain alcohol. (*Finding the bottle.*) Ah ha! White mule. I knew I could depend on Mr. Hooker. (*Pouring a drink.*) There now. Let me just

zing one back. (*She throws back a triple shot.*) Ah. So good ol'
hooch is legal again. I like that. No more recooking extract,
fermenting mash, drinking hair tonic. Wanna jolt?
CASSIDY. No thanks.
SUE JACK. Down the hatch. (*She throws back another big shot.*)
So . . . the scum bastard made a play for ya? I mean, you're
having his kid, right?
CASSIDY. That's right.
SUE JACK. You know, someone oughta notify the Children's Aid Society or maybe report that s.o.b. to the Morals
court. I could do that. I think I'll do that. (*She has another
drink.*)
CASSIDY. No, don't do that. He didn't do nothing bad.
SUE JACK. Maybe we'll just have to let the judge decide —
like he decided about me. (*She has another drink.*) But person-
ally, I believe that sexual molestation of a young orphan
child by a raving drunken idiot is sufficient grounds for
criminal prosecution.
CASSIDY. But it weren't like that. Please, ya can't send him
off t'no jail!
SUE JACK. Oh, go on and cry all you want. Tears have
never been precious to me. Not my own or anybody else's.
CASSIDY. Lady, I'm just asking ya t'do what's right!
SUE JACK. Yeah and just what do you suggest is right?
CASSIDY. Well, it's a clear thing. He don't like you. He
don't want you here.
SUE JACK. Did he tell you that?
CASSIDY. Yeah.
SUE JACK. Well, sometimes people don't mean — the
things they say.
CASSIDY. I think he means it.
SUE JACK. I wager he doesn't. (*She pours another drink.*)
CASSIDY. Well, I ain't never had a kid by no man before
and he tol' me he'd marry me 'cause I ain't raising no stink-
ing bastard.
SUE JACK. If he told you he'd marry 'ya, then he's a no good
dirt-crawling liar. See 'cause he's never gonna marry you. He
can't. He's married to me.
CASSIDY. Well, he's divorcing you.

SUE JACK. He's what?

CASSIDY. That's right. He's divorcing you and marrying me.

SUE JACK. Oh, he's been dealing you out a very crooked hand.

CASSIDY. Why, you ain't even pretty. They all said how you was so beautiful but you ain't even pretty. I got the bloom of youth and you ain't even pretty.

SUE JACK. Listen to me, you greasy little runt. He's my husband. He loves me. He can't help it. (*Sue Jack picks up the shotgun and aims it in Cassidy's direction.*) And if I were you, I wouldn't go around spreading lies like that. Understand, I'm never gonna get over loving Reed Hooker. 'Cause even when I don't know who in this godless world I am, or was, or ever will be — the one thing I know as sure as the smell of spring rain is that I utterly, hopelessly love that rotten, worthless son of a bitch! (*Throughout the following, Sue Jack fires the shotgun shattering a mirror, light fixtures and the jukebox.*) I want, want, want him like a crazy shrieking, howling dog. I can't live without him! I'll blow out my brains. I'll shoot you to pieces. I'll rip this fucking place t'the ground. But, by God, I gotta have that miserable, lying, double-crossing, one and only love of my broken life! (*Sue Jack stops firing the gun. She looks around a moment then stumbles across the room and gets the whiskey bottle.*) Oh God, look here. I've been misering the bottle. I didn't mean t'do that. (*Lacey runs in with the dress.*)

LACEY. What in the world . . . ? Are y'all alright? Oh, my Lord, look here. (*Lacey trips and falls as Turnip and Hooker come in together. They have been in a fight. Turnip is carrying Hooker; he is a bloody mess.*)

TURNIP. Thank God, Sue Jack. Thank God for those shots. You scared those bastards away. They almost murdered Hooker. (*Turnip sits Hooker down.*)

HOOKER. Yeah, thanks. Thanks a lot. (*Hooker looks up. He sees the damage, He sees the liquor bottle in Sue Jack's hand.*) What's all this? You've shot this place to shit. My jukebox. Look at my jukebox. (*Hooker rises, fury begins to blind him.*) Why you stupid slut — (*What follows is an all-out, lowdown and*

173

rutty brawl. The other characters are all somehow thrust in and out and back in and out of this massive free-for-all battle that leaves the place in total shambles.)

SUE JACK. Don't you ever hit me.

HOOKER. Hit you? Hit you?! I'm gonna kill you! I'm gonna rip your head off your shoulders.

SUE JACK. Stay away. You stay away!

HOOKER. I'm sick of you ruining my life! You're not gonna ruin it any more!

SUE JACK. I'm ruining your life? That's rich. That's damn rich. You're the worthless, two-timing bastard who messed out on me.

HOOKER. And what the hell else was I gonna do when you shut me out with you drinking for weeks on end, staying binged out of your goddamned mind, gambling away every nickel we ever had?!

SUE JACK. Yeah, well, at least I never messed out on you.

HOOKER. That's a damned lie!

SUE JACK. Don't call me a liar!

HOOKER. (*Running on.*) Why, you stayed for five weeks out in that trash can shack getting drunk and screwing your cousin, the undertaker.

SUE JACK. That was different! That was family!

HOOKER. Bullshit!

SUE JACK. You know good and well I never loved him. But I saw all those poems you wrote to Caroline Carmichael.

HOOKER. You read my poems?!

SUE JACK. That one about how she smelled!

HOOKER. I never said you could read my poems! I'm gonna butcher you for that!

SUE JACK. Go ahead! Poke out my red eyes. Tear out my dying hair. I'm a sickening, wretched, worthless glob of pulp. But at least I never crawled so low as t'mercilessly abduct and rape a poor runt of an orphan child!

HOOKER. Let me at her! I'm gonna shred open your face! I'm gonna tear out your decaying heart! (*Hooker catches Sue Jack. They struggle passionately.*) You bitch!

SUE JACK. You bastard!

HOOKER. I'm glad they stuck you in that jail. I pray you go back! I pray you get nothing but bread and water and blood caked rot for the rest of your useless life! (*Hooker slings Sue Jack to the floor. Sue Jack gets to her feet and grabs the rifle. She comes toward him swinging it at him.*)

SUE JACK. I'm glad I threw Caroline Carmichael over that balcony rail. I'm glad she broke both her arms and gashed up her face. Let that serve as fair warning to any other whore I find in your bed! Fair warning to all whores! (*Hooker grabs the rifle away from her. They start to strangle each other.*)

HOOKER. I'm gonna kill you.

SUE JACK. I'm gonna kill you.

HOOKER. I hate your guts.

SUE JACK. I hate your guts.

HOOKER. You bitch.

SUE JACK. You bastard.

HOOKER. You bitch.

SUE JACK. You bastard. You—

HOOKER. You . . .

SUE JACK. You . . . (*They both collapse on the floor. It is a double knockout. Music B comes up as the lights fade to black.*)*

END OF ACT I

---

*See Special Note on copyright page.

ACT II

SCENE 1

The stage is dark. Music A: "I Need A Little Sugar In My Bowl"* — a low down rinky dink blues tune plays on a record player. It is about eight o'clock in the evening on the same day.

HOOKER's VOICE. Okay, try the switch. (*A little toy village is lit up on the dark stage.*) It's working!
TURNIP. Yeah.
HOOKER. The whole village. (*A beat.*) All lit up. All aglow. Turnip?
TURNIP. Huh?
HOOKER. She gone yet?
TURNIP. Not yet.
HOOKER. Get her outta here. I don't wanna lay eyes on her ever again. (*A beat.*) You hear me?
TURNIP. Yeah. Can I get the lights now?
HOOKER. Go ahead. (*We see that Hooker has a bump on his head, a black eye, and his hand is wrapped in gauze. He is dressed in tails. Turnip wears a baggy suit and a skinny tie. The damage from this morning's brawl has basically been repaired or hidden under the decorations that have been put up for this evening's extravaganza. The record player and three or four large stacks of records sit on the counter top along with a huge punch bowl and coffee pot and a plate of cookies. A few empty chairs are lined up against the wall. Throughout the following Hooker and Turnip line the rest of the stacked up chairs up against the wall.*)
TURNIP. Hooker.
HOOKER. Huh?
TURNIP. I don't think this is gonna work.
HOOKER. Well, then we'll toss it. There're plenty more swell ones. We've got stacks of 'em. (*Hooker removes the record and tosses it into a cardboard box.*)

---

*See Special Note on copyright page.

176

TURNIP. I don't just mean these old records. I mean the whole thing. The whole opening of the Lucky Spot.

HOOKER. What about it?

TURNIP. I really think we oughta put off the Grand Opening. I mean we don't have no music or no taxi dancers; our electric sign's all broke. Face it — the cards are stacking up against us.

HOOKER. Look, we can't put off the grand opening. I owe too damn much money. There're people out there who are waiting to break both my legs. I need anything we can make tonight t'help fend off the wolves.

TURNIP. We're gonna be opening ourselves up to all sorts of ridicule.

HOOKER. Be that as it may.

TURNIP. I mean Cassidy can't be out here dancing around for ten cents a ticket. (*Indicating a huge stomach.*) She's out t'here, for Christ sake.

HOOKER. Are you telling me how to run my affairs?!

TURNIP. No, it's just . . . well, ya oughtta think about her feelings sometimes. She does have 'em.

HOOKER. Hey, I'm not a blind man. I know how I've treated her. I know I'm a bilge bag. I hate my own goddamn guts.

TURNIP. I don't mean t'criticize you —

HOOKER. Go ahead! It's clear I'm culpable for the preposterous condition she's in. I should have taken that chestnut mare, but I took Cassidy instead. (*A beat.*) She had such a sad face; a woebegone countenance. I hoped I could change that face. Instead I've made it worse.

TURNIP. The main thing is she doesn't want the kid to be born out a bastard.

HOOKER. Right. Right. So I'm supposed t'marry her.

TURNIP. Yeah. Well, listen, I don't know much about these things; so correct me if I'm mistaken, but from the looks of it you and Sue Jack are kinda on the outs — But even so if you needed someone to, well, — about Cassidy, I mean — I could take — (*Cassidy comes walking down the stairs. She is dressed in the clothes Sue Jack and Lacey helped her put together in Act I. Her hair is fixed in curls under a hat.*) Oh. Hi, Cassidy.

CASSIDY. Hi.

HOOKER. Hi.

CASSIDY. (*A beat.*) I look okay?

TURNIP. Yeah. Nice.

HOOKER. Your hair's kinda sticking out some around the sides. Come here and let me fix it. (*Cassidy goes to Hooker. He starts working with her hair.*) Hold still. (*A beat.*) Does that pull?

CASSIDY. No.

HOOKER. (*Still working on her hair.*) So . . . Uh, you had any ideas about how t'do this wedding?

CASSIDY. (*A beat.*) No; just signing the papers.

HOOKER. You interested in a cake or a white dress or throwing rice or anything?

CASSIDY. I . . . no.

HOOKER. Maybe we could go out t'eat at a restaurant or something afterwards . . . if you wanted to.

CASSIDY. (*Nodding yes.*) Uh huh.

HOOKER. We'll do that then. There. That looks better — don't lose those hairpins. Gotta go out and . . . work on the sign. (*Hooker exits out the front door. Cassidy turns to Turnip. Both of them are white.*)

CASSIDY. You hear that? He's talking about my marriage t'him. He remembered all about it. He's gonna marry me. He's gonna do it.

TURNIP. I reckon so.

CASSIDY. He's gonna keep his promise. Just like you said. Why you're the one that promised me he'd keep his promise. You're the one! Oh, thank you, Turnip! (*Cassidy grabs Turnip and kisses him.*)

TURNIP. Well, don't kiss me about it! He's only marrying ya on the rebound.

CASSIDY. The what?

TURNIP. The rebound, the rebound, from Sue Jack. Ya don't just want him t'marry ya on the rebound, do ya?

CASSIDY. Yeah. I sure do. I sure do.

TURNIP. Yeah, I reckon so. (*Lacey sticks her head in from the kitchen door.*) Oh, Lacey, come on in! Come on in!

LACEY. (*Over her shoulder.*) The coast is clear. (*Lacey enters the room, Sue Jack follows behind her.*)

TURNIP. (*Not noticing Sue Jack.*) We're just having the biggest celebration! Hooker's proposed marriage t'Cassidy. He's made a definite public proposal! Ain't life a boon! (*Turnip and Cassidy see Sue Jack.*) Oh I — (*Cassidy gasps at the sight of her and runs to hide under a table. Sue Jack wears makeup and has restyled her hair. She is dressed in a glamourous tight fitted dress from her past. She has a bruise on her cheek. Lacey is dressed in an old evening gown with dirty hand prints around the waist.*) SUE JACK. It's alright. It's fine. (*To Cassidy.*) Hey, come on out from under there. I'm not gonna hurt ya. Honestly. Come on out now. (*Cassidy slowly crawls out from under the table.*) Look, I'm sorry I shot at ya this morning. Okay? I guess I just — stepped outta line a little bit.

TURNIP. So, any luck with the phone calling?

SUE JACK. Oh, sure. I've got several friends who want me t'spend Christmas with them. I've just got to decide if I'm looking for a real sophisticated kind of Christmas or a big warm family sort of time, or maybe I just want t'spend a quiet, peaceful Christmas with a few intimate friends.

TURNIP. Yeah. Well, it sounds pretty nice.

SUE JACK. I tell ya, I feel refreshed. All that stupid, miserable hope I've let eat at me for so long has finally been beaten t'death. Reed and I are disbanded. We were never quite right for each other. This morning we tried to . . . kill each other. (*A beat.*) I'm renewed. I'm free t'be a globe-trotter once again. T'live by my wits. Ah, how I love a changing panorama.

TURNIP. Yeah — well — you look real beautiful.

SUE JACK. Right. Gotta impress my old acquaintances. Oh, by the way, Turnip, do you have any idea whatever happened to Thumper Bell? I thought I might try and give him a call — make sure someone remembered to invite him up for Christmas.

TURNIP. No, I — Well, Thumper, he died. I'm sorry t'tell ya. Happened last spring. He, ah, stopped in an alleyway t'pick up some change and got hit by a falling flower box.

SUE JACK. Oh. Rotten luck. Poor Thumper. Well, I'll get my things and be heading out.

TURNIP. Yeah. (*Sue Jack exits out the side door to the bungalows.*) She really get any of those folks she was calling?

LACEY. Didn't sound like it to me.

TURNIP. She's been on the phone all afternoon. Seems like somebody would've come through for her.

LACEY. It's so sad. She'll be spending Christmas all alone.

TURNIP. Sometimes life makes me wanna puke. One stroke of really bad luck and people just can't never seem t'recover.

LACEY. You mean about their little boy.

TURNIP. Yeah, after he died things went hateful crazy.

CASSIDY. Sue Jack and Hooker had some child together?

TURNIP. Yeah. His name was Andrew. (*A beat.*) They called him Andy.

CASSIDY. How old was he?

TURNIP. (*Indicating the height of a 2 – 3 year old child.*) 'Bout this old. You know small.

CASSIDY. And he died?

TURNIP. Yeah. Ran out in the road and got hit by some automobile. They say he was chasing after a hummingbird.

LACEY. Oooh! I'd just run and jump straight off a cliff if I didn't have a place t'go to on Christmas Day.

TURNIP. Hell, I might just do it anyway.

CASSIDY. (*A beat.*) Well, why don't she just stay on here for Christmas?

TURNIP. Here?

LACEY. You'd want her here?

CASSIDY. I wouldn't mind.

LACEY. Well, if you don't mind —

TURNIP. Hooker refuses t'ever lay eyes on her again.

CASSIDY. Maybe if we just explain —

LACEY. I mean after all, we certainly could use an extra taxi dancer.

TURNIP. Hooker ain't listening t'reason. He's trying t'open up this dance hall with two dancers and no music. Claims he needs the money. Why, we'd make more money selling apples on a street corner. But he can't see it. Ah, I don't care! What does any of it matter?! All these miserable people butting around. Trying so hard. For what?! Before it's all over everyone of 'em's gonna be stone cold dead! Absolutely everyone of 'em. (*Snapping his fingers.*) Dead! Dead! Dead! So what the hell are they all sweating?! That's what I'd

180

relish t'know! Oooh!! What a low down rutty rotten little game we're all playing. It ain't like checkers. In checkers somebody wins and somebody loses. It's clear-cut. But playing this other — we're all big-time losers; everyone of us. No ringing in the cold deck, no aces up the sleeves, no hold outs. Just stacking up piles and piles of chips, t'give 'em all away. All losers! Everyone of us — Christ, what a racket.

LACEY. (*A beat.*) Now there's conversation for ya. There's genuine, sparkling, earnest conversation.

CASSIDY. Well, it kinda makes me wanna go beat out all my brains.

LACEY. That's what real conversation'll do t'ya.

CASSIDY. Well, I don't like the feeling. Thinking about how this thing's gonna be dead here it ain't even been born yet. Why it all just gives me goose chills straight up my thighs.

LACEY. I, on the other hand, appreciate a man who will converse with a lady. Tell me, Turnip, do you have any further conversation that I may partake in?

TURNIP. I, well, I do have things to say. Just generally I don't say 'em.

CASSIDY. Look, I'm going out front t'talk t'Hooker. I wanna explain t'him about that lady staying on here through Christmas day. (*A beat.*) I'm going on out t'ask him. (*Cassidy looks uneasily at Turnip and Lacey who are staring at each other.*)

TURNIP. Well . . . 'Bye.

LACEY. Bye.

CASSIDY. Yeah. 'Bye. (*Cassidy exits out the front door. Lacey continues to look at Turnip with wet, listening eyes.*)

TURNIP. . . . I'm not stupid. A lot of people think of me as stupid. My brothers they always called me stupid. But I wasn't. I thought a lot. Mostly about things they never even featured. Like don't always go around making fun of people with harelips 'cause it don't do no good and they can't help it no how.

LACEY. (*A pause.*) You know what you've got? Sensitivity. Real sensitivity.

TURNIP. You're probably right. What can I do about it?

LACEY. You're — You're asking me a vital question in a prolonged conversation. Oh my, oh my, oh my. (*Lacey stumbles around and manages to fall to the floor.*) See here! Didn't I tell ya? It's the bird bones in my ankles. (*Turnip helps Lacey to her feet as Sue Jack comes in carrying the dilapidated cardboard box with her belongings. She wears black lace gloves and a black hat with berries.*)

SUE JACK. Hi.

LACEY. Oh hi.

TURNIP. Hi. (*A beat.*) Can you handle that?

SUE JACK. Sure. Look — I — Well, here's some Christmas things. (*Sue Jack sets down the box. She takes out some gifts wrapped in dirty tissue paper from the large handbag.*) They're nothing, really. Just some things I made while I was in — there. I don't know; I thought somebody might want 'em. Turnip. (*Sue Jack hands a package to Turnip.*)

TURNIP. Thanks.

SUE JACK. Here, Lacey.

LACEY. Thanks, Sugar. I love Christmas presents.

TURNIP. Look, that box is falling apart. Let me go out back here and find you a flour sack or something t'make it easier for ya t'carry. (*Turnip picks up the box.*)

SUE JACK. Don't trouble yourself.

TURNIP. Ain't no trouble. Come on. (*Turnip and Sue Jack exit into the kitchen. Lacey quickly unwraps her gift. It is an embroidered Christmas bell.*)

LACEY. A bell. (*A beat.*) Jingle, jingle, jingle. (*Hooker and Cassidy enter from the front door. Hooker carries a toolbox.*)

HOOKER. Look, I'm about on my last leg around here and I refuse t'have her hanging around just t'kick it out from under me.

CASSIDY. But she ain't gonna kick ya. I swear she ain't.

LACEY. It's Christmas Eve. Give her one more chance.

HOOKER. No. (*Sue Jack and Turnip enter from the kitchen. Sue Jack's belongings have been transferred into a burlap flour sack.*) And what's all this crap? Who brought over these dirty Christmas presents?

SUE JACK. I did. (*Hooker turns to see Sue Jack.*)

HOOKER. Oh. (*A beat.*) Well, we don't need 'em. We've got plenty of our own.

SUE JACK. Alright. (*Sue Jack takes the Christmas presents and slowly puts them in the burlap sack. To Hooker.*) Look, I'll write where I'm staying. You can send the divorce papers on and

I'll sign 'em. (*A beat.*) Well, goodbye everybody. Have a good Christmas.

TURNIP. Goodbye, Sue Jack. Merry Christmas.

LACEY. I — I love my bell. You have a real good Christmas now.

SUE JACK. Yeah, you, too. Goodbye now.

CASSIDY. Goodbye. (*Sue Jack exits out the front door. Cassidy, Lacey and Turnip stare sadly after her, then turn and look at Hooker in stony silence.*)

HOOKER. So enough goldbricking. Everyone back t'work. Tonight's our big night! (*Looking at his watch.*) Come on everybody, as of now we're open for business! (*Turnip is opening the present Sue Jack gave him. Lacey and Cassidy gather around him.*)

LACEY. So what'd she give ya?

TURNIP. Mittens with snowmen on 'em.

CASSIDY. Oh look, ain't it sad, one of 'em's melting. (*Hooker comes over to them; he grabs the mittens from Turnip.*)

HOOKER. Let me see those! (*Hooker roughly puts one of the mittens on his hand, then pulls it off. He takes the mittens and throws them out the front door. He yells to Sue Jack, who is headed down the road.*) Hey you got a lot of nerve walking outta here like this! You know damn good and well we only have two dancers for tonight! And it's all 'cause of you showing your face! But don't let it bother ya! Just run off t'your fancy Christmas parties. Forget about us! We'll do just fine all on our own! (*Hooker turns and comes back inside the room, slamming the front door shut. After a moment Sue Jack enters through the front door.*)

SUE JACK. Alright, Hooker. I'll do the Lucky Spot this one favor. After all, it is Christmas.

HOOKER. Fine! But once we get squared — I don't even wanna remember your face. (*Music B — the trumpet solo from "I Must Have That Man"* — comes up. Sue Jack slowly starts to remove her hat and gloves as the lights fade to blackout.*)

END OF SCENE 1

---

*See Special Note on copyright page.

ACT II

Scene 2

The lights fade up. Music B fades into Music C: "Twelfth Street Rag."* It plays on the phonograph. Sue Jack sits in the window seat doing string tricks. Lacey and Cassidy dance awkwardly together. It is two to three hours later on the same evening.

LACEY. *(Instructing Cassidy.)* Don't look down. Up! Up! Smile! Look happy! Come on, be peppy! Get some zing! Bubble! Twirl out! *(Lacey twirls Cassidy out across the room. Cassidy crashes into the bar. Lacey removes the needle from the record.)*

CASSIDY. It ain't much use. I don't know how t'move around t'this music.

LACEY. Don't worry you'll get the hang of it. See 'cause, your main problem's not the dancing — it's simply that you're not used t'being in the limelight.

CASSIDY. Nah, I ain't used t'being in no limelight.

LACEY. Well, being in the limelight's easy. All ya gotta do is learn how t'emphasize your striking features. That way ya won't fade out.

CASSIDY. I don't wanna fade out.

LACEY. Well then, we'll emphasize your eyes. You've got very pretty eyes. Come here, we'll just darken 'em up some. *(Lacey gets an eyeliner pencil from her evening bag and starts darkening Cassidy's eyes.)* Take me. For awhile I wasn't getting the dances; so I moved over and started in corner dancing. A place where I could really shine.

CASSIDY. What's corner dancing?

LACEY. Well, just dancing in a dark corner. You know, where you start allowing neck kissing, ear biting and body pressing.

CASSIDY. Gosh, are they gonna be biting on my ears?

LACEY. Oh no, you've got years before ya have t'get into corner dancing. You've got the bloom of youth.

CASSIDY. That's good. *(From outside the front door we hear*

---

*See Special Note on copyright page.

Hooker's voice calling through a megaphone in the distance.)

HOOKER. (*Offstage.*) Grand opening! Lucky Spot Dance Hall! Come one! Come all!

SUE JACK. Oh God. Look at Reed out there calling to cars through that megaphone. He's making a laughing stock.

HOOKER. Free prizes! Come one! Come all!

LACEY. Well, we do need the business.

HOOKER. (*Offstage.*) Merry Christmas! Ho, ho, ho!

CASSIDY. I sure hope some people come.

SUE JACK. Would you come to a place with a madman standing out front yelling at ya through a megaphone? (*Turnip enters through the front door.*)

TURNIP. Hey, Lacey, Hooker wants ya t'come out front and do your cartwheels.

SUE JACK. Oh good Christ.

TURNIP. He says maybe you can arrest the attention of some of them passing cars.

LACEY. Well, okay. But I better stretch out a little. (*Stretching.*) One and two and— (*She falls to the floor.*) Oops! My wayward ankles again.

TURNIP. Here, let me help ya up.

LACEY. (*To Turnip.*) Why thank you, Turnip. You're such a lamb. I just can't keep my eyes off your eyes. (*Turnip escorts Lacey out the front door. Cassidy looks after them perturbed. Sue Jack goes back to playing with the string. Cassidy hikes her skirt up over her knees.*)

CASSIDY. Look here, my knees got dirt all on 'em. I have real trouble keeping clean. (*She spits on her hand and starts scrubbing her knees.*) Mr. Pete, he used t'call me a godless bag a stench. Mr. Pete's the man I was with before. He's the one Hooker won me offa. And that was a lucky day for me. See 'cause when I was with Mr. Pete practically all he'd ever give me t'eat was cow feed. Why, if fact be known, the man was downright feeble-minded. Look here where he branded me with his holy cross. (*Cassidy hikes up her skirt and reveals a cross branded to her inner thigh.*)

SUE JACK. My God.

CASSIDY. He's always telling me how all fired holy he is. Him being a member of the Church of Innocent Blood— and me being a godless bag a stench. Lord, my life ain't never

185

been no good till now. But here, well, we have supper together every night. It's the most I ever felt like a family.
SUE JACK. Yeah. Some people need that I guess.
CASSIDY. Uh huh. Look, I just wanted t'tell ya—it wasn't like what you was saying this morning. See Hooker, he wasn't all mean and drunk or nothing like that the night when it happened.
SUE JACK. Jesus, I don't care how it happened. It doesn't matter how it happened. (*A beat.*) Okay, so are you gonna tell me how it happened?
CASSIDY. Well, used to be I'd hear him at night yelling out and gasping for air and such. I reckoned him t'be having bad dreams; so I started rushing down t'his room t'wake him up. I'd bring him water t'drink and wet down his forehead with a cool rag. Afterward he'd never go back t'sleep, but he'd send me back on t'bed telling me how I needed t'get my rest. Then one time he just up and says for me t'stop coming in with the water. Says for me just t'stay put and let him be. And I done that for some nights. I sure didn't like listening t'him, but I stood it. Then this one night I hear such crying, like it's coming from some sick, dying animal. Well, I can't find no control for myself, but t'run in with the water. I wake him up and I wash off his face and I hold him so hard and I say, "Don't be scared no more. I can make ya feel better. I know some ways t'make ya feel better." And I did too, from being out on the trail so long with Mr. Pete. Next day though he moves all my things up t'the attic. (*A beat.*) He locks me up there at nights now. Turnip, he'll come by and unlatch the door in the mornings. I'm hoping all that's gonna be changed once we're married. But I don't really know. Only thing I do know is this thing ain't being born out no bastard. See 'cause bastards they don't deserve nothing. Hooker'll be good to it. Once this skinny kid, he fell outta that mossy tree out front and split up his lip real good. Hooker done this trick with a nickel t'make him shut up crying then he let him keep the nickel.
SUE JACK. He did? He did that nickel trick?

---

*See Special Note on copyright page.

186

CASSIDY. I ain't never seen anything like it.

SUE JACK. (*A pause.*) Yeah, well . . . sometimes I wonder . . . I really do wonder. (*A pause.*) The whole world's in trouble. So what's the use? Huh? (*Sue Jack gets up and starts pacing around the room with crazed exuberance.*) I mean, maybe ya gotta just toss in your hand, pay off your debts; stand up and leave the goddamn table.

CASSIDY. Leave the table?

SUE JACK. Yeah. It's worth a go. Gotta go. Letting go! (*Sue Jack puts Music B* on the record player. She starts dancing with a wild crazed passion.*)

CASSIDY. Gosh! Why're ya dancing around?

SUE JACK. (*Still dancing.*) I don't know. I just feel crazy and lighthearted. Like when you're standing on the very edge of a mountain cliff and you're kicking your legs up t'the sky. (*Sue Jack stands on the bar and starts kicking up her legs.*)

CASSIDY. I feel lighthearted too. (*The women dance around the room.*) It's kinda like we're friends or something. (*Turnip enters carrying Lacey who is whining and laughing.*)

LACEY. Ooh. Ooh. Ow

TURNIP. (*To Lacey.*) There, there, now.

LACEY. (*Gaily.*) I fell down again. I'm always falling — (*They stop and watch the women dance.*)

TURNIP. Why are y'all so happy?

CASSIDY. We're dancing on the edge of a cliff. (*Hooker enters. He wears a silk hat and carries a megaphone. He stops the music.*)

HOOKER. An extravaganza! This was supposed to be an extravaganza! Instead it's a farce, it's a flop. A dream so shattered I can't even remember what the pieces were.

CASSIDY. Oh, don't get discouraged. We still got a roof over our heads and tomorrow we're having ham for Christmas dinner. Things ain't so bad.

HOOKER. Right. Right. Sometimes I just have t'stop myself and take time out t'be grateful I'm not a one-eyed paraplegic with severe brain damage dancing in a cardboard hat. (*A beat.*) Damn. I didn't wanna have the Lucky Spot turning out t'be just like any other roadside attraction.

SUE JACK. I don't think you're in any danger of that!

HOOKER. That's right! Make fun! Laugh at me! You've always got all the smart answers.

SUE JACK. I was just joking.

HOOKER. I'm not a joke.

SUE JACK. Come on, Reed, the whole world's a joke. Consider yourself a real sucker when being taken seriously becomes any sort of goal at all.

HOOKER. Well now if this world is such a goddamn hilarious funny little joke, then please, you tell me, why the hell don't I feel like laughing?

CASSIDY. (*Looking out the window.*) Look, somebody's coming!

HOOKER. Hot damn! We're in business!

LACEY. Oh my God. He's coming up the walk.

HOOKER. Quick, get on some music. (*Turnip puts on Music C — "Twelfth Street Rag."*)

CASSIDY. Where's my hat? I need my hat!

LACEY. Look on your head, silly.

HOOKER. Everybody line up over here. Look pretty!

LACEY. Get peppy, girls! Get peppy!

TURNIP. Okay, here're the ties. I've got the ties.

HOOKER. No, you sell the tickets; I'll sell the ties.

TURNIP. Okay.

HOOKER. No, no I'll sell the tickets, you sell the ties.

TURNIP. Okay, right.

CASSIDY. Here he comes! (*Carmichael enters through the front door. He is dressed in evening attire. At the sight of Carmichael everyone's energy drops except for Lacey who is too busy doing her cartwheels.*)

SUE JACK. HOOKER, TURNIP. Shit.

LACEY. Dance? Dance? Wanna dance?

CARMICHAEL. Yes, I'll have a ticket. Just one, thanks. I'll pass on the neckties for now. (*Carmichael buys his ticket from Hooker, then walks over to the line of women. He scrutinizes them as he paces back and forth. He finally hands his ticket to Sue Jack. They start to dance.*) So the place seems to be hopping. It's a

---

*See Special Note on copyright page.

shame about the jukebox. But you know these old race records of Davenport's aren't so bad. (*The record sticks.*) Kinda scratchy. But not so bad. (*A beat as the record continues to repeat itself.*) Not so bad. Not so bad. Not so bad. (*Turnip finally picks the needle up off the record. Sue Jack and Carmichael continue to dance in silence.*) It's always such a pleasure dancing with you. It's like dancing with a dream. (*Hooker rings the bell.*)

HOOKER. Okay, the dance is over. I said it's over. Look, you came by here to gloat; so you've gloated. Now get out.

CARMICHAEL. Listen to me a minute. You're a smart man. Try to keep a clear head. You know this place will never make it. Do yourself a favor, let me take it off your hands.

HOOKER. I don't get you, Carmichael. Just why are you so dead set t'get at this place?

CARMICHAEL. The truth is I promised my father I'd get it for him. As sort of a Christmas gift. (*Indicating Sue Jack.*) He couldn't stand the idea of her being here after that mess with Caroline. I don't blame him much. Here're the papers. If you sign 'em it'll let everyone off the hook.

HOOKER. I don't know. I'm not real keen on the idea.

CARMICHAEL. Believe me, it's a fair price.

SUE JACK. Well, now that worries me. (*Hooker takes the papers down to a table. He motions to Turnip to come with him.*)

HOOKER. (*To Turnip.*) What d'you think?

TURNIP. Gosh, it's hard t'say. After all the badmouthing he's been doing about us around town I really don't know that we have a frank chance a making it here.

CARMICHAEL. You don't have a blind chance.

HOOKER. I don't know. I got a strong feeling this place isn't realizing its full potential. I mean, look at that painted horse over there. Why it's—otherworldly.

CARMICHAEL. I think you're living in a rosy dream world.

SUE JACK. I smell fish.

CARMICHAEL. What?

SUE JACK. I said I smell fish.

CASSIDY. There's somebody out there. Somebody else is coming.

LACEY. A patron! It's a patron. A real live patron.

189

HOOKER. Turnip, music! (*Music D — "King Joe"* — starts to play.*)

CARMICHAEL. Look, this is a fair offer, but you'll have to accept it, right now.

HOOKER. I — No.

LACEY. How're my lips?

SUE JACK. Red, real red!

CARMICHAEL. Be reasonable. One patron's not going to change anything.

HOOKER. Excuse me now, I'm working.

LACEY. Get perky, everybody! Get perky!

CARMICHAEL. This price goes down three hundred dollars an hour.

HOOKER. No deal, Carmichael. No deal!

SUE JACK. That's a damn good tune.

HOOKER. It's a very pretty tune.

CARMICHAEL. Make that five hundred dollars an hour or fraction thereof.

HOOKER. I said, no deal.

SUE JACK. I do like that pretty tune.

LACEY. Dance. Dance. Wanna dance. (*Lacey turns cartwheels. The patron, Sam, enters. He is a thin shy man in his 60's dressed in clean simple clothes. His face and hands are weatherbeaten from years of farming.*)

HOOKER. Welcome, welcome, welcome.

SAM. 'Evening.

HOOKER. Come right in, sir. Come right on in. Now would ya like t'rent a necktie? I'm afraid they are required.

SAM. Alright.

HOOKER. That'll be fifteen cents.

TURNIP. (*Echoing.*) Fifteen cents.

HOOKER. No, that's twenty cents . . .

TURNIP. (*Echoing.*) Twenty cents . . .

SAM. (*After a beat.*) Alright.

HOOKER. How 'bout this red one. It's very festive. It's just your particular style. Turnip, help the gentleman out with his tie. (*Turnip puts the tie on Sam.*) Now how many dance tickets would you like?

---

*See Special Note on copyright page.

190

SAM. How many ya reckon I'll need?

HOOKER. I don't know. Fifty? A hundred maybe?

SAM. How 'bout a dollar's worth. That's about all I got.

HOOKER. Alright. Fine. Here're your tickets. Now you go on and select any one of our beautiful dance teachers t'be your partner.

SAM. I pick?

HOOKER. Yes, you pick.

SAM. Which one do I pick?

HOOKER. Anyone you want. All of our girls make a wonderful partner. They all have very special qualities.

SAM. (*A beat.*) It's sure hard t'pick.

HOOKER. Well, just go on and point t'one of 'em. It's all the same. Go ahead. Point. (*Sam hesitates a moment then points to Cassidy.*)

CASSIDY. He's pointing at me. Hey, mister, you're pointing at me.

SAM. What do I do now?

HOOKER. Give her your ticket and dance. Dance, quick, before the bell rings. (*Sam hands Cassidy his ticket. Cassidy and Sam make an awkward attempt at dancing.*)

SAM. I hope my hands ain't too clammy for ya.

CASSIDY. No, it's okay. (*A beat.*) I —

SAM. What?

CASSIDY. Nothing. I'm just glad I was picked. I ain't never been picked. (*Music D swells up then comes back down. Music E — "Sweet Lorraine" — comes up.* The lights change indicating the passing of time. Sue Jack and Lacey are now dancing together. Hooker watches Sue Jack from the stairs. Cassidy and Sam continue dancing. Turnip stands by the record player. Carmichael goes outside and lights up a cigarette. To Sam.*) Musta been hard on your wife, having t'be blind all her life. Me, I don't even like the dark. I'm afraid of it.

SAM. Well, she used t'tell me, of everything in the world, the two things she most wanted t'see was the face of a person and a tree. But she said she was happy just being here on this earth.

CASSIDY. How long ago was it she died?

---

*See Special Note on copyright page.

191

SAM. Been almost five weeks now.

CASSIDY. You miss her?

SAM. Oh yeah. She loved watermelon. I used t'slice it up for her and pick out all the seed. (*Lacey twirls over to Turnip. Hooker stares at Sue Jack from across the room. She stares back.*)

LACEY. Hi Turnip.

TURNIP. Hi. You, ah, you wanna dance?

LACEY. Sure. You got a ticket?

TURNIP. I—no.

LACEY. Well, I gotta have a ticket.

TURNIP. Oh. Well, I guess I don't have the monty t'buy one.

LACEY. (*A beat.*) Sorry, then. It's the rules.

SAM. (*To Cassidy.*) Is that your fellow?

CASSIDY. Who?

SAM. The young guy putting on the records. The one you've got your eye on.

CASSIDY. (*Indicating Turnip.*) Him? Oh no. He's just some nitwit. (*Indicating Hooker.*) I'm engaged t'the man on the staircase. (*A beat.*) He's in love with me. (*Sue Jack steps into the outdoor area. Carmichael is sitting on a bench smoking.*)

CARMICHAEL. You wanna drink?

SUE JACK. I quit.

CARMICHAEL. You can't stand me, can you?

SUE JACK. Not really.

CARMICHAEL. It's funny but I like you.

SUE JACK. Well, you can afford to.

CARMICHAEL. There're two things I've always wanted to do to you. One of them was beat you in a game of cards.

SUE JACK. You're a slime, Whitt. A real slime.

CARMICHAEL. Come on. Play cards with me. Let's gamble. Come on. I wanna beat you.

SUE JACK. Shit. (*Sue Jack turns to go inside.*)

CARMICHAEL. Don't go inside.

SUE JACK. Screw you. Go buy some tickets if you wanna take up my time. My time is money. Big money. (*Sue Jack goes inside. Carmichael follows her. Hooker watches them both. Turnip is ringing the bell, indicating that Dance E is over. Lacey rushes up to Sam and Cassidy and throws herself between them.*)

LACEY. (*To Sam.*) Oh, dance with me. Next time let me be your partner. Let me be your one.

SAM. I'm getting kinda tuckered. Maybe I'll sit this one out.

LACEY. Fine, sit with me. I'm a sympathetic listener. (*She pulls him over to a table and starts plucking off tickets from his roll.*) I know how t'show ya a good time. (*Carmichael comes up to Hooker who has been staring at Sue Jack.*)

CARMICHAEL. I'd like some more tickets. (*Carmichael takes out a large bill.*)

HOOKER. What're you still doing here?

CARMICHAEL. Waiting for you t'crack.

HOOKER. Forget about it. I'm not gonna crack. This place could be something great. Look at that lonely guy over there. He's having a damn ball. See that? (*Hooker, Carmichael and Turnip all turn and watch Lacey chewing on Sam's red tie.*)

CARMICHAEL. Ah yes, yes. How very picturesque. (*Music F — "Honeysuckle Rose"* — starts to play. Carmichael turns and heads over to Sue Jack. Carmichael offers her a reel of tickets. She takes them. Hooker can't take his eyes off of them. Turnip continues to watch Lacey and Sam. Cassidy looks from Hooker to Turnip and back again.*)

SUE JACK. (*Dancing and laughing.*) Oh that music sends me someplace, someplace — I wish I could tell you where. Take me away! Please, take me away!

HOOKER. Oh sweet Jesus. Holy Jesus.

TURNIP. What?

HOOKER. Look at Sue dancing. I'll never get over her. There's nobody else like her. Nobody else.

TURNIP. What're you saying?

HOOKER. I love her. I want her. Can't help it. Never could.

TURNIP. I don't get you. (*Cassidy walks over to Hooker and Turnip.*)

CASSIDY. (*To Hooker.*) Hi. You wanna dance?

HOOKER. No. I'm going outside. (*Hooker exits out the side door.*)

TURNIP. (*To Cassidy.*) I'll dance with ya.

---

*See Special Note on copyright page.

CASSIDY. Why don't ya go ask Lacey t'dance? She's the one you're so fond of. (*Cassidy turns and walks away.*)

LACEY. (*To Sam.*) You like my hair?

SAM. It's the color of spun gold.

LACEY. It's all natural. You can feel it if ya want to. Go ahead. Run your fingers right through it.

SAM. (*To Lacey as he fondles her hair.*) I like women's hair. Why I washed and rolled and fixed my wife's hair all up when she died.

LACEY. Well, don't look at me. I'm not dead yet. Where're your tickets?

SAM. They're all gone.

LACEY. Well, excuse me but I believe I have t'go and powder my nose. (*Lacey gets up and walks over to Turnip, counting her tickets. To Turnip.*) Ring the bell sugar. I've already bled that fish dry. I gotta go reel in another one. (*Turnip looks at her coldly and then starts ringing the bell. He takes the record off. Music F stops. Cassidy goes over and sits next to Sam. He offers a stick of gum. Lacey runs over to Carmichael and Sue Jack. To Carmichael.*) Dance? Dance? Wanna dance? Wanna be mine?

CARMICHAEL. No thanks. (*He hands more tickets to Sue Jack. Music G — "Cryin' for the Carolines" — starts up.*)*

LACEY. I waltz, I foxtrot, I tango, I polka —

SUE JACK. Go ahead. I'm on break. (*Sue Jack hands a ticket to Lacey. Lacey grabs the ticket and pulls Carmichael tightly into her arms.*)

LACEY. Come on now. Who's your sugar? (*Sue Jack goes over to pour herself some coffee. Turnip comes up to her.*)

TURNIP. Boy oh boy.

SUE JACK. What?

TURNIP. Well, Hooker, he — he's gone and gotten himself back in love with you. Says he just can't help it. Says he never could.

SUE JACK. Look, I don't want him loving me. (*Turnip echoes.*) We're finished.

TURNIP. You're finished. I don't get it.

SUE JACK. Where'd he go?

---

*See Special Note on copyright page.

194

TURNIP. He's out back. (*Turnip motions to the side door. Sue Jack heads outside. As she goes she passes Lacey who is trying to French-kiss Carmichael.*)

LACEY. (*To Carmichael.*) Come on, sugar, it's not like I've got trench mouth. Although once I did transmit the pinkeye to a man. But that was way back in Alabama.

TURNIP. I swear, I pray I never fall in love. It seems like such a terrible thing. (*Sue Jack comes outside. Hooker is there looking at the sky. He turns and looks at her then turns back to stare at the sky.*)

HOOKER. It's pitch-black out. Not a star in the sky. Isn't that an incredible sight. (*A beat.*) Come here to me.

SUE JACK. We're bad luck for each other.

HOOKER. I don't care.

SUE JACK. I'm not right for you.

HOOKER. You are.

SUE JACK. Well, I'm not the one who's gonna have your kid, am I?

HOOKER. No, you're not.

SUE JACK. She is.

HOOKER. That's right. That's how that went down.

SUE JACK. Do the right thing for once in your lousy life.

HOOKER. You're the right thing.

SUE JACK. I'm the wrong thing.

HOOKER. You're the only goddamned thing.

SUE JACK. Listen, Reed, I — I got sick in prison. I can't have another kid. Not ever.

HOOKER. Doesn't matter. It's okay. We'll do okay.

SUE JACK. No, look at me. I've lost it. The bloom of youth. It's gone. It's over. I jazzed it all away. But her, she's good for you, this Cassidy, I want you to have her and the kid and this place —

HOOKER. (*Overlapping.*) This is bullshit, woman. Just bull-shit 'cause I don't want a goddamn thing in this world but for you to come here to me. Not a goddamn thing —

SUE JACK. I can't Reed. I can't ever be with you —

HOOKER. What do you mean?

SUE JACK. It's over, Christ, just let it be. Let it be!

HOOKER. I'm not gonna let it be!

SUE JACK. Alright, you wanna know?! Ya gotta know.

HOOKER. (*Overlapping.*) Yeah, I wanna know! Yeah, I gotta know!

SUE JACK. You wanna know about Andy. You wanna know about our son? Well, it was my fault.

HOOKER. It was a miserable accident. Couldn't be helped. He pulled away to chase a hummingbird—

SUE JACK. Jesus Christ, don't you get it? There was no goddamn hummingbird. I went into a speak t'get a drink. I left him standing there on the proch. He ran off, a car hit him and I was sitting there in the bar, slinging back a shot of whiskey.

HOOKER. You said you held tight. You said he pulled away from you.

SUE JACK. I lied.

HOOKER. God Almighty. (*Sue Jack turns and goes back inside. Inside Turnip starts clanging the bell as Music G ends.*)

SUE JACK. Hey! Yo! Friends! Let's play some cards!

TURNIP. Cards! Well, hot damn! Hot damn!

LACEY. What fun! What fun!

SUE JACK. Whitt, you game?

CARMICHAEL. Why yes, ma'am, I'm plenty game.

SUE JACK. Good. Fortuitously, I seem t'have a deck of playing cards right here in my silver evening bag.

CARMICHAEL. Well, now, as chance would have it I've a round tucked right inside my breast pocket.

SUE JACK. My, my, but good fortune certainly does abound. (*Sue Jack slings off her lace gloves.*)

TURNIP. Well, alright! Alright! Yes, sir! Yes, sir! (*They both sit down at a table and begin to expertly shuffle their decks. The others crowd around them, murmuring with excitement and amazement. Hooker enters.*)

SUE JACK. So what do you say we make this a real quick gamble. Three games of cut. Best two outta three. Working with a his and her deck.

HOOKER. What's going on here?

SUE JACK. A friendly game of cards.

CARMICHAEL. A very friendly game. What're the stakes?

SUE JACK. If I win I want your three hundred and fifty-five dollar stake on the Lucky Spot. If you win, well, then we can finish off what we started over on Esplanade Avenue.

CARMICHAEL. Deal me in. I feel lucky.

HOOKER. What's this now, Miss Sue, you gonna sacrifice yourself t'save my waning, dying ass?

SUE JACK. I'm just paying off some debts. That's all Hooker. Just paying off some debts.

HOOKER. There's no way. You don't have a prayer.

SUE JACK. Look, I lost most of our stinking money playing the horses and dogs and roosters. As I remember, I was always pretty good with cards.

HOOKER. Yeah, well, just look at your goddamn hands. They're all torn up, for Christ's sake.

SUE JACK. (*Angrily.*) Oh leave me alone. Just leave me the fuck alone! Here, cut. (*Sue Jack shoves the cards over to Carmichael.*)

CARMICHAEL. No, no, no. Ladies first.

SUE JACK. Ah, a gentleman's game. (*She cuts the cards.*) Queen of hearts. (*She shoves the cards to Carmichael.*) Cut. (*Carmichael cuts the cards.*)

CARMICHAEL. Jack of spades. (*Cheers from the people watching the game.*)

TURNIP. (*To Carmichael.*)Better luck next time, ol' buddy.

LACEY. She's still got the touch.

CARMICHAEL. And I still feel lucky. Cut. (*Sue Jack cuts the deck.*)

SUE JACK. King of hearts. (*Turnip echoes.*)

CARMICHAEL. And I thought this was a game of chance.

SUE JACK. Cut. (*Carmichael cuts the deck.*)

CARMICHAEL. Hmm. King of spades.

SUE JACK. My, my my, a lot of court cards in this deck.

CARMICHAEL. Cut.

HOOKER. I'm not watching this. I have no part in this. You're on your own. (*Hooker goes and pours himself a drink.*)

SUE JACK. Yeah, that's where I belong. (*To Turnip.*) Here, spit on my hands for luck. (*Turnip spits on her hands. She rubs them together then cuts the cards.*) Five of clubs.

CASSIDY. Oh no.

TURNIP. Damn.

LACEY. Sweet Jesus. (*Carmichael cuts the deck.*)

CARMICHAEL. Ah me. What have we here? Ace of diamonds.

CASSIDY. She lost.

SUE JACK. Let's have another go. What d'ya say t'a round of Mexican Sweat?

CARMICHAEL. But, I've won the pot, haven't I? Don't wanna risk losing that.

SUE JACK. Well, then I guess tonight's just not my night.

CARMICHAEL. Please, my good fortune embarrasses me. Now why don't you get your coat? (*Sue Jack goes and gets her coat and evening bag.*)

CASSIDY. Where ya going?

SUE JACK. Oh, out jazzing around. Keep the party going till I get back. (*Carmichael escorts Sue Jack toward the front door. Hooker comes toward them.*)

HOOKER. Let her go, Carmichael. She stays here.

CARMICHAEL. You may own that one, but this one here's a free woman.

SUE JACK. Come on now, Reed. A bet's a bet.

HOOKER. I said get the hell away from her. (*Hooker jerks Sue Jack away and starts going toward Carmichael. Carmichael draws a pearl-handled pistol and aims it at Hooker. Everyone freezes.*)

CARMICHAEL. I don't think so. Unless maybe you want your face shot off.

SUE JACK. Alright now. Everything's fine. Let's just get outta here. (*Sue Jack and Carmichael head for the door. Carmichael keeps the gun aimed at everybody. They are almost out the door when Hooker grabs a chair to clobber Carmichael.*)

HOOKER. No, goddamnit! (*Carmichael quickly fires two shots. Both of them barely miss Hooker.*)

SUE JACK. Hooker! Jesus Christ!

HOOKER. Oh I'm fine. Just put my nerves a little on edge.

CARMICHAEL. Next time I shoot between the eyes.

HOOKER. Listen, Carmichael, I'll pay ya the three fifty-five she owes ya — we'll call it even.

CARMICHAEL. I don't believe you have it.

HOOKER. I do if I sell this place to you. You want it so damn bad. Here, I'll sign it over.

SUE JACK. Jesus, Hooker, don't be a goddamn idiot! (*Carmichael produces the contract.*)

HOOKER. You pay me three hundred and fifty-five dollars less than this price. How's that?

CARMICHAEL. I said the price would drop five hundred dollars an hour or fraction thereof. That means that this property is now valued at fifteen hundred dollars less than the price quoted on that contract. Add the three hundred fifty-five dollars Sue Jack sold herself for and that only leaves you about two hundred dollars.

SUE JACK. Forget it. Come on, Whitt. Let's go. (*Sue Jack tries to drag Carmichael out the door.*)

HOOKER. (*To Sue Jack.*) You're not going.

SUE JACK. Damn it t'hell! Just 'cause I go and make a fool outta myself doesn't mean you have to follow suit!

HOOKER. Screw it. I just won the place through freak luck. It ain't nothing t'me. (*Carmichael hands a pen to Hooker.*)

SUE JACK. Stop it! Just stop! Christ, two hundred dollars won't even be enough t'pay off your debts!

HOOKER. So what? This place is a joke. I'm sick of fooling with it. Here, Carmichael. Take the damn thing! (*Hooker signs the paper. Sue Jack rushes in and slams the paper down on the table.*)

SUE JACK. Look, this is nothing to me. He's just one guy, one night. Christ, Reed, don't you realize how many men, how many times—

HOOKER. (*Overlapping.*) Stop it! Don't!

SUE JACK. (*Running on.*) . . . How many nights there were just t'survive in that prison.

HOOKER. (*Overlapping.*) No more. Please.

SUE JACK. (*Running on.*) This?! This is nothing! Nothing!!

HOOKER. (*Overlapping.*) Shut up. You. Be still.

SUE JACK. (*Running on.*) Why, there were days I'd do three prison guards for a cup of dirty water. And once for a pair of shoes I was on my knees—I crawled on my knees—

HOOKER. (*Overlapping.*) Stop! No more! Please! Please! Please! (*Hooker grabs her face in his hands and shakes her with a desperate passion.*) I can't have it. No more. Please. (*Hooker holds Sue Jack tightly. She stares at him dumbstruck; tears stream down her face. Cassidy watches Sue Jack and Hooker, feeling the electric passion between the couple. She turns and runs up the stairs.*)

TURNIP. (*Reaching for her.*) Hey! Hey—

CASSIDY. (*Ripping off the rope ring.*) Let me be! Let me be—

(*Hooker grabs Sue Jack to him. She pulls away. Hooker then gets the contract and hands it to Carmichael.*)

HOOKER. There's the papers. Take them.

CARMICHAEL. Thank you.

SUE JACK. Damn, damn, damn! (*Sue Jack exits out the front door.*)

HOOKER. Goddamnit! Come back here. I'm not running after you.

SUE JACK. (*Offstage.*)I can't, Reed. It's no good. Let it go. Please, let it go.

HOOKER. (*Overlapping.*) I'm not running after you! You hear me? Sue Jack! (*A beat. He runs out the front door after her. Offstage.*) Sue Jack! (*Hooker reenters.*) Hell. (*He slams out the kitchen door.*)

CARMICHAEL. (*To Turnip.*) Here's a check. Give it to him, will you?

TURNIP. Yeah.

CARMICHAEL. Oh, and please arrange to be out of here by January one. That's when the drilling crew — oh well, those high finance matters don't really concern you, poor people, now do they? Well, good night, everyone.

LACEY. Look, Mr. Carmichael —

CARMICHAEL. What?

LACEY. Don't go away lonesome. I'll keep ya company for the night.

CARMICHAEL. Well, it's funny. I've always liked blondes but I'm going to make an exception in your case. Good night now. (*Carmichael exits out the front door.*)

LACEY. Well, he certainly is a spoilsport, isn't he? A man like that doesn't do anybody any good. He's too prissy. Thinks just 'cause he's rich nobody but him matters in the whole wide world. (*She falls and trips.*) Oh, my poor ankle. (*To Turnip.*) Help me up, will you, sugar?

TURNIP. Are you sure your ankles are really weak?

LACEY. What?

TURNIP. Maybe you just pretend they're weak. Maybe you just like t'fall down.

LACEY. Don't be stupid. Nobody likes t'fall down.

TURNIP. No, you're wrong. A lot of people like t'fall down. And why not? It's easy. Ya just go right with the pull of things. Right with the flow. Ya don't ever gotta worry about standing on your own two feet. The only tough part is dragging yourself back up again. Getting back up. (*A beat.*) Yeah, that can be a lot of work.

LACEY. Then help me up. Please.

TURNIP. Help your own self up. (*Lacey drags herself to her feet.*)

LACEY. Oooh! (*Hooker walks in from the kitchen carrying a jug of moonshine. He takes a slug. Lacey turns and looks at him.*) Oooh! I just don't understand, people always despise me, no matter where I go! (*Lacey exits out the side door and disappears through the yard.*)

HOOKER. Women. Christ, they're all the same.

TURNIP. Sweet Jesus. Nobody's got any sense in this world; nobody. We just let it all slip right on past us. No wonder why we keep coming up empty-handed. No damn wonder. (*Turnip exits out the kitchen door. Hooker pauses a beat then turns to Sam.*)

HOOKER. Well, looks like I spoiled everybody's Christmas Eve. So, you having a good time?

SAM. Oh yeah.

HOOKER. Good. I'll put on some more music. (*Hooker puts on Music H — "Sweet Lorraine."* The music plays.*) Want some punch? We got cookies.

SAM. I'm, well, I'm outta tickets.

HOOKER. Forget about it. It's all on the house. Everything's all on the house. (*Hooker tosses Sam a cookie. The two men sway to the music a moment.*) Pretty tune. (*The music swells and the lights fade to blackout.*)

END OF SCENE 2

ACT II

Scene 3

The setting is the same. Cassidy sits at a table humming as she makes paper hats out of newspaper. She wears a

---

*See Special Note on copyright page.

simple dress and has a bow in her hair. The coffee pot is
out on the counter. It is sunrise.
Lacey sits on a stump in the outside area. She wears her
tattered robe.
Sue Jack comes in the front door. She wears the same dress
she had on the night before. She carries a branch of holly.

CASSIDY. Good morning.
SUE JACK. 'Morning.
CASSIDY. It's a pretty morning.
SUE JACK. (*Undecided.*) Yeah.
CASSIDY. You alright?
SUE JACK. I—no.
CASSIDY. Well, I reckon I outta tell ya I broken off my marriage t' Hooker. Tore off the engagement ring. It's gone.
SUE JACK. Well, look, ya better forget about all that and make it up with him. It'll be alright. You'll just make it up.
CASSIDY. Ain't nothing t'make up. The thing is I can't never awaken no love in him for me — 'cause, well, he's got you in his blood; you're his partner.
SUE JACK. I sure as hell don't know about that.
CASSIDY. I do. See I ain't stupid. I know people getting married's supposed to be in love with the people they's getting married to. Ya don't want somebody just marrying ya on the rebound. And it's funny but it makes me feel lighthearted, 'cause now I see, well, maybe love ain't a made-up lie like Santa Claus or something. Maybe it can be true. And if it's true, maybe I can find someone I'd shoot off guns for and find someone who'll hold my face and tell me, please, please, please. Or maybe he'll just, I don't know, give me a slice of watermelon and pick out all the seeds. Why, having this child don't even scare me no more. 'Cause if ya have this love inside ya it don't matter if your father was a lord in a castle or a bum on the road or a murderer in a cage. It don't matter. Well, here's a hat for ya. Merry Christmas. (*Cassidy puts a paper hat on Sue Jack's head. Turnip enters from* R. *He carries a branch of mistletoe. He spots Lacey.*)
LACEY. Hi.
TURNIP. Hi. (*Turnip passes her and heads for the side door.*)

202

LACEY. I guess you think I'm just a gold digger. Well, maybe I am. But if I am it's cause I went broke trying t'crash the movies and all my stuff's in pawn and I don't even have a decent rag on my back. Gosh, the main thing I wanted outta life was fame, wealth and adoration. Instead I'm poor and broke and nobody likes me.

TURNIP. I like talking t'ya. Ya seemed interested in what I had t'say.

LACEY. Really?

TURNIP. Yeah.

LACEY. Oh my, my, my! (*Lacey staggers around in a dither. Suddenly she realizes she is about to fall and quickly sits back down on the stump.*) How nice. Thank you very much, Turnip.

TURNIP. Tell me . . .

LACEY. Yes?!

TURNIP. Do you think I should change my name from Turnip t'something else? I mean, so people — so girls would like me better.

LACEY. Hmm. Well, ya know what they say, "A turnip by any other name would smell as sweet."

TURNIP. Never thought of it like that. Wanna go inside?

LACEY. Sure. (*Lacey stands up and they move from the outside area to the ballroom through the side door.*) Merry Christmas, everyone!

SUE JACK & CASSIDY. Merry Christmas.

LACEY. Look, I've brought over my spray bottle of genuine French perfume. As a gift I'm allowing everyone four sprays apiece. (*To Sue Jack.*) Here, sugar, you go first.

SUE JACK. Well, thanks, Lacey.

TURNIP. (*To Cassidy.*) Here, I brought ya some mistletoe.

SUE JACK. Mmm. Smells good.

TURNIP. If ya put it over two people's heads, they gotta kiss underneath it. (*He holds the mistletoe over their heads.*) See, like this. (*He kisses her.*) It's part of Christmas. (*He hands out the mistletoe to her.*)

CASSIDY. (*Taking it from him.*) Thanks. (*Cassidy goes solemnly up to Sue Jack.*) Oh look, you're under mistletoe. Kiss me quick. (*They kiss. Cassidy walks over to Lacey.*) Now you're under mistletoe. Kiss me. It's part of Christmas. (*They kiss. Cassidy turns and says to Turnip.*) What a fun gift. (*She holds the mistletoe over his head and they kiss again. Hooker and Sam enter the outdoor area. Hooker carries a sack of oranges. Sam carries some peppermint candy canes. Hooker still wears his evening clothes.)*

HOOKER. How many sugar candies ya got?

SAM. 'Bout a dozen.

HOOKER. Well, that oughta be plenty. I'll eat one now. *(Hooker takes a candy cane, sits down on the bench and starts eating it.)*

SAM. Ain't we going in?

HOOKER. You go on in. I don't figure I'm gonna get such a heartwarming reception.

SAM. Well, alright. And thanks for having me over for Christmas. I didn't have no other place t'go.

HOOKER. No, me neither. *(Sam knocks on the side door and says "Hello." Everyone welcomes him.)*

LACEY. Well, look who's here!

CASSIDY. Sam, come on in.

TURNIP. Hey, Merry Christmas.

SAM. Thanks. I hope ya don't mind me coming unexpected.

CASSIDY. Oh, no.

SAM. Hooker, he's the one asked me.

SUE JACK. Where is he anyway?

SAM. Just sitting out back. I brought y'all some sugar candies. *(Sam hands out the candy. Sue Jack heads for the side door.)*

LACEY. Oh look! Sweets! Sugar sweets!

CASSIDY. Why, thanks, Sam.

TURNIP. Thanks. *(Sue Jack stands at the side door watching Hooker eat his candy cane on the bench.)*

SUE JACK. Hi.

HOOKER. Hi. You're back.

SUE JACK. Yeah. Just now. I was out walking. And thinking. Did a lot of thinking.

HOOKER. What'd ya think?

SUE JACK. That I miss you. A lot. A real lot.

HOOKER. Yeah, well, sorry t'say — I miss you too.

SUE JACK. Ya do? Well, thanks. I appreciate it. God I — thanks.

HOOKER. Oh don't be so damn grateful. It makes me feel like an idiot.

SUE JACK. Sorry.

HOOKER. Forget it.

SUE JACK. Sure. I guess I don't really know how to be. I mean there's so much water under the bridge. So much muddy, muddy goddamn water.

HOOKER. Yeah, yeah. I know, I know. So do us both a favor and let's not wallow in it.

SUE JACK. We don't wanna wallow in it.

HOOKER. That reminds me. Our hog's gone. The Christmas pig. Somebody stole it. I don't know what t'do. You got any ideas?

SUE JACK. Well . . . let's see now. I passed by a pumpkin patch this morning. I could go borrow three or four and make us up some pumpkin pudding.

HOOKER. That'd be a treat. We haven't had that in, well, years.

SUE JACK. Yeah. It's been years. Hope I remember how t'make it.

HOOKER. Well, don't ya put a nickel in it?

SUE JACK. Right. Whoever finds the nickel in their portion will have a stroke of dumb luck.

HOOKER. Well, we sure could use some dumb luck.

SUE JACK. We sure could.

HOOKER. God Almighty. T'dumb luck. (*He reaches into the air, and a nickel appears in his fingers. He hands the nickel to Sue Jack.*)

SUE JACK. T'dumb luck. (*They both start to laugh.*)

HOOKER. Now, Christ, will ya come here, please! (*They go into each other's arms.*)

SUE JACK. (*After a beat.*) Merry Christmas, Reed.

HOOKER. Merry Christmas to you, sweet Sue. (*They kiss passionately. Inside Cassidy sits on top of a table. She wears a paper hat and waves a candy cane.*)

CASSIDY. Once I had my fortune told and the fortune-teller tol' me I had a future right here in the palm of my hand. Why this could be the beginning of my future. This could be it! (*Music I — "Sunny Side of the Street"* — starts to*

---

*See Special Note on copyright page.

play on the record player. Sue Jack and Hooker enter from the side door.)

HOOKER. Merry Christmas, everyone! Merry Christmas!

ALL. (*To Hooker.*) Merry Christmas!

HOOKER. Here're some oranges for ya. (*Hooker starts throwing oranges to everyone from his sack.*)

TURNIP. Oranges, look! Oranges!

LACEY. I love citrus!

CASSIDY. They're beautiful!

HOOKER. Yeah, they are. Hey, I wanna dance! I wanna dance with every one of ya! It's Christmas morning and I wanna dance with everyone. (*Everyone starts dancing. They all keep changing partners. Men dance with women, men dance with men, women dance with women. People dance alone. Everyone dances with everyone else as the lights slowly fade to blackout and the music continues to play.*)

END OF PLAY

ABUNDANCE

CAST OF CHARACTERS

BESS JOHNSON
MACON HILL
JACK FLAN
WILLIAM CURTIS
PROFESSOR ELMORE CROME

TIME

The play spans twenty-five years, starting in the late 1860's

PLACE

Wyoming Territory and later in St. Louis, Missouri.

ACT I

Scene 1

Late 1860's. Morning. Spring.

Outside a stagecoach ranché in the Wyoming Territory.

Bess Johnson, a young woman, sits on a bench. There is a bag at her feet. She wears a dirty travelling suit that has no buttons.

BESS. *(Singing to herself.)* Roses love sunshine
Violets love dew
Angels in heaven
Know I love you.

Build me a castle forty
   feet high
So I can see him as he
   rides by
(Bess stops singing and speaks softly to herself.) The size of the sky. The size of the sky. *(Macon Hill enters wearing green goggles and a cape. She is covered with road dust and carries a satchel and green biscuits on a platter. She is whistling. She stops when she sees Bess.)*
MACON. Lord Almighty.
BESS. What?
MACON. You're like me.
BESS. Huh?
MACON. Sure. You're like me. Biscuit?
BESS. Please.
MACON. Go ahead. Help yourself. What's mine is yours; what's yours is mine. After all, you're like me. You've come out

west to see the elephant. Hey, true or no?

BESS. Elephant. No.

MACON. To see what's out there; whatever's out there. *(Beat.)* What do you guess is out there?

BESS. Don't know.

MACON. Right. Could be anything. I savor the boundlessness of it all. The wild flavor. I'm drunk with western fever. Have you ever seen a map of the world?

BESS. Uh huh.

MACON. Well, it stopped my heart. There are oceans out there. Oceans aplenty, and I swear to you I'm gonna see one and walk in one and swim in one for sure. I love water, it never stops moving. I want to discover gold and be rich. I want to erect an ice palace and kill an Indian with a hot bullet. I'm ready for some sweeping changes. How about you? We could be friends throughout it all. It's part of our destiny. I can smell destiny. One day I'm gonna write a novel about it all and put you in it. What's your name? *(Macon produces a pad and pencil.)*

BESS. Bess Johnson.

MACON. *(Writing down the name.)* Good. That's a good name for a novel. Bess Johnson. Will you be my friend?

BESS. It'd be a pleasure. A true pleasure. Could I — could I trouble you for another biscuit?

MACON. Why sure. Sure, I hate stinginess. You'll never get anywhere watching every egg, nickel and biscuit. Ya gotta let it go! Let it go! Go! And I don't give a damn if ya never pay me back.

BESS. Thanks kindly. I'm near pined t'death with famine. These green biscuits taste heaven to me.

MACON. Why, how long ya been at the ranché?

BESS. Ten days, I been waiting here. My travel money's all spent. Yesterday I traded French Pete my buttons for an extra night's lodging. I'm at my rope's end if Mr. Flan don't get here real soon; I don't know what.

MACON. Who's Mr. Flan?

BESS. He's the man who's coming t'pick me up. We're to be wed.

210

MACON. Wed? A wedding?

BESS. That's right. It's been arranged.

MACON. Then you're a bride-to-be?

BESS. Yeah.

MACON. Lord Almighty! Angels sing; devils dance! I'm a bride-to-be, too. It's like I said, you're like me. It's true! It's true! Tell me, do ya know your husband or is he a stranger to ya?

BESS. We had ... correspondence.

MACON. Correspondence. Me too. And he sent you the fare?

BESS. Partial.

MACON. Me too! Me too! *(She whistles a few notes.)* Ya know what I hope? I hope our husbands don't turn out t'be just too damn ugly t'stand.

BESS. You think they'll be ugly?

MACON. Maybe. Maybe. But I hear divorce is cheap and easily obtainable out here in the west.

BESS. I'd never get no divorce.

MACON. Honey, I'd rip the wings off an angel if I thought they'd help me fly! You may find this hard to believe, but back home they considered me the runt of the family. See, those folks are all full, large-bodied people, and to them I appeared to be some sort of runt. But out here I can be whoever I want. Nobody knows me. I'm gonna make everything up as I go. It's gonna be a whole new experience. We're dealing with the lure of the unknown. Yeah, we're hunting down the elephant! Bang! Bang! Bang! What's wrong with you? You're looking morose.

BESS. I — I'm just hoping my husband ain't gonna be real terrible ugly.

MACON. Well, Bess, I hope so too.

BESS. It don't mention nothing about his looks in the matrimonial ad.

MACON. Well, now that ain't good news. Folks generally like t'feature their good qualities in them advertisements.

BESS. 'Course I know I'm no prize. I got nice hair, but my eyes are too close together and my nerves are somewhat aggravated. Still, I was hoping we'd be in love like people in

211

them stories. The ones about princesses and chimney sweeps and dragon slayers.

MACON. Oh, them stories ain't true. They ain't factual. Catapult them stories out of your brain. Do it! Do it! Catapult 'em!

BESS. I don't know, I — well, I bet he's gonna like me some.

MACON. Sure. Maybe he'll be cordial at Christmas.

BESS. I promise I'll be a good wife, patient and submissive. If only he'd come. I hope he ain't forgotten. He sent partial fare. Three letters and partial fare. Three letters all about the size of the western sky.

MACON. Damn! What size is it?

BESS. The largest he has witnessed.

MACON. Glory be.

BESS. And he loves singing. I can sing real pretty. Oh, I'm betting we're gonna be a match made in heaven, if only I ain't left stranded. See, 'cause, well, I don't know how I'll get by. I can't do nothing. I don't know nothing. I oughta know something by now. I went t'school. They must have taught me something there. But I can't even recall what my favorite color is. Maybe it's blue, but I'm just guessing.

MACON. Well, the fact is, if ya know too much, it's just gonna limit your thinking. Take me, I got this brown dress and I don't even get upset about it 'cause I got no recollection in my mind that my favorite color is blue. I mean, it may be, but I don't know it. Have another biscuit.

BESS. It's your last one.

MACON. I saved it for you. (*Jack Flan enters. He is handsome, with an air of wild danger.*)

JACK. 'Morning.

MACON. 'Morning.

JACK. I'm looking for — Is one of you Bess Johnson?

BESS. That's me. That's me. I'm here. I'm here. That's me.

JACK. Uh huh.

BESS. Are you Mr. Michael Flan?

JACK. No, I'm Jack Flan, Mike's brother.

BESS. Oh well, well, pleased t'meet you, Mr. Jack Flan. Would you do me the great favor of taking me t'meet Mr. Michael Flan?

JACK. Mike's dead.

BESS. What?

JACK. Got killed in an accident and died.

BESS. Are you saying Mr. Michael Flan is no longer living?

JACK. That's right; he's dead.

BESS. Dead. Oh my. Oh my. Lord, Lord, Lord.

JACK. What's wrong with you? You never laid eyes on him. You're just some stranger.

MACON. Hey, hey, don't be so grim.

BESS. *(Crying with fury.)* I wanna go home. I'll die if I stay here. I don't wanna die in this miserable, filthy territory!

JACK. Look at her crying. She's a woman alright.

BESS. Oh, how can this be? My husband's dead. He's gone. He's dead. I never even got to meet him or shake his hand or say, "I do." "I do, I do." I worked on saying them words the whole way here. Over cliffs, across streams, in the rain, in the dust. "I do, I do." Every dream I ever had I said in them words. "I do, I do, I do, I do..."

JACK. I'm gonna knock her down.

MACON. Don't do that. *(Jack shoves Macon aside, then goes and knocks down Bess. Macon comes at him with a knife. He takes her by the hair and slings her to the ground.)*

JACK. *(To Macon.)* You're out west now. Things are different here. *(To Bess.)* Come on with me. I'm gonna marry you. But I won't have you crying. Never again. You got that clear?

BESS. Yes.

JACK. Let's go. *(They exit. Macon gets to her feet.)*

MACON. That was something. I didn't mind that. That was something. *(Macon whistles to herself. William Curtis enters. He is neatly dressed. He wears a patch over the left eye. There is a scar down the same side of his face.)*

WILL. Hello. Are you Miss Macon Hill?

MACON. Yes, I am.

WILL. I'm Mr. William Curtis. I've come for you. You're to be my wife.

MACON. Well, here I am. I'm ready to ride. *(They exit.)*

End of Scene 1

Scene 2

Later that day.

Jack's cabin. Jack sits in a chair. Bess is pulling filth-covered blankets off the floor.

BESS. This is a beautiful home. Some women get squeamish over fleas and ticks and lice, not me. We'll root 'em out by bathing with plenty of sheep-dip and then we'll add kerosene to the sheep-dip and boil all our clothes and bedding in the sheep-dip and kerosene. That'll root 'em out. Kill 'em all for sure. I'm gonna be happy here. I can feel it coming.

JACK. Don't start messing with things around here. That's not my way.

BESS. Uh huh. Uh huh.

JACK. *(A beat.)* I'm not used to you being here.

BESS. *(A beat.)* I can — I can cook something.

JACK. There's nothing t'cook. Got some dried beef on the shelf.

BESS. I'll fetch it. *(She gets the dried beef and brings it back to the table.)* Here.

JACK. Thanks.

BESS. Welcome. You're welcome. *(They chew on the dried beef in silence.)* Mr. Flan.

JACK. Yeah?

BESS. Do you like singing?

JACK. No. *(A beat.)*

BESS. Your brother said he liked singing.

JACK. You never met my brother.

BESS. He wrote it in his letters.

JACK. That he liked singing?

BESS. Yes.

JACK. Never said nothing to me about it.

BESS. I got his letters, if ya wanna look at 'em. *(Jack nods.)* Here they are. He wrote three of 'em. *(Jack takes the letters and looks at all three of them.)* In each one of 'em he mentions something about singing. Says there's not much music out

214

here, but for the birds. I was hoping to change things for him. See, me, well, I sing — *(Jack tosses down the letters.)* Pretty letters, ain't they?

JACK. I don't read writing.

BESS. Oh, well, I could read 'em for ya. *(Bess picks up one of the letters and starts to read it.)* "Dear Miss Bess Johnson, I was overjoyed to receive your correspondence accepting my humble proposal of marriage. I sincerely believe you will not be disappointed living in the west. The skies out here are the largest I have witnessed. The stars hang so low you feel you could reach up and touch them with your hand — " *(Jack grabs the letter out of her hand. He tears up the letters.)*

JACK. Hey! You don't read t'me! I ain't no baby. You ain't no schoolmarm. You got that clear?! Nobody reads me nothing! Nothing! Nothing at all!

BESS. *(Overlapping.)* Don't tear 'em! Please, don't tear 'em!

JACK. I did! I tore 'em! They're torn! And I don't want you singing. There'll be no singing. I don't tolerate no singing never. You hear me?

BESS. I do.

JACK. Hey, you better not start crying. Remember what I warned you about crying?

BESS. I won't. I won't never be crying. I'm telling ya. I can do things right.

End of Scene 2

Scene 3

Same day.

William's cabin. Will and Macon enter.

WILL. Come on in. Here we are.

MACON. I see.

WILL. What do you mean by that, Miss Hill?

215

MACON. Nothing. I just see — Here we are.

WILL. I lost it in a mining accident.

MACON. What?

WILL. No need playing coy. I see you see it's missing.

MACON. Oh, your eye.

WILL. Yeah.

MACON. Oh, well, I did observe it'd been removed.

WILL. Man knocked it out with a mining pick. It was an honest mistake. There was no violence or malice intended.

MACON. Hmm. Well, I bet you wish it didn't happen.

WILL. I intend to order a glass one just as soon as finances permit. It'll be brown, same color as the one I have left.

MACON. Uh huh.

WILL. You can tell me right now if this makes a difference. I'll send you back if it does.

MACON. I ain't going back.

WILL. Alright. *(Pause.)* Miss Hill?

MACON. Yeah?

WILL. I got something for you.

MACON. What?

WILL. It's a ring. A ruby ring. *(He takes out a ring.)*

MACON. Oh, I cherish rings.

WILL. It was my wife's.

MACON. Your wife's.

WILL. Yes, she died.

MACON. Oh.

WILL. Last winter. It was snowing. *(Pause.)* She once had a photograph taken of her. Would you like to see it?

MACON. Alright.

WILL. *(He hands her a photograph.)* Her name was Barbara Jane.

MACON. What'd she die from?

WILL. No one could say for sure. She took to bed. A long time I stood by her. One night she coughed up both her lungs. There was nothing to be done.

MACON. She looks pretty sickly.

WILL. I thought she was beautiful.

MACON. Well, I don't think I want her ring.

WILL. Why not?

MACON. Could have her sickness on it. I don't want no part of it.

WILL. She never wore the ring when she was sick. She only wore it the first year of our marriage.

MACON. Why's that?

WILL. She lost three fingers in a sheep-shearing accident. One of 'em was the ring finger.

MACON. Well, y'all certainly seem t'be plagued with all sorts of disfiguring misfortunes around here.

WILL. If the ring won't do, I'll get a piece of tin and bend it around for ya. Maybe in time I can get ya another ring with a stone in it.

MACON. I'd appreciate it.

WILL. The Marrying Squire will be here at the end of the month. At that time we'll be wed.

MACON. Uh huh. *(They glance at each other, then turn away in silence.)*

End of Scene 3

Scene 4

Three months later. A summer's night. In a field. Bess is calling out to Macon who has disappeared into the night.

BESS. Macon! Macon, you out there? Where are you? Where'd you go? Indians could be lurking! Come back! Macon! *(Macon runs onstage, breathless with excitement.)*

MACON. I almost touched it!

BESS. I thought you was lost in the dark.

MACON. I almost did.

BESS. Indians might a' captured you.

MACON. From the top of that far-off hill I almost felt it.

BESS. What?

MACON. That little silver star. The one sitting there so low in the sky. See it?

BESS. Uh-huh.

MACON. Stars send off chills. Closer you get, the more chill you feel. Go on try it. Go on, reach up for it. *(Bess reaches up to touch a star.)* There you go! Jump! Jump! Did ya feel the chill?

BESS. Maybe I might a' felt some sort of small chill.

MACON. The thing we gotta look out for is a falling star. You ever seen a falling star?

BESS. No.

MACON. Well, now, when we see one of them, we gotta run for it. I know I can touch one of them. *(Macon whistles.)*

BESS. That's a nice tune. I never heard it.

MACON. It's a good song. You wanna learn it?

BESS. Oh, I don't sing no more. Jack don't like it.

MACON. Jack don't like singing?

BESS. His brother, Michael, liked singing. But Jack don't. *(Macon whistles a moment.)*

MACON. I don't mean t'speak out, but your husband, well, he don't seem t'got a whole lot to recommend him.

BESS. Oh, he suits me fine. Why, I ain't sure we ain't a match made in heaven. Soon as we get the inheritance money Mr. Michael Flan left. Everything'll be rosy.

MACON. Well, I sure hope things work out for you. I got doubts about my own predicament.

BESS. Don't ya get on with your new husband? He seems a good man t'me.

MACON. Well, I hate to criticize Mr. Curtis. I know he does try; but, well, frankly, I'm allergic to him physically.

BESS. Is it 'cause of his eye?

MACON. Could be part of it. But even with one more eye, I might find him repulsive. *(Macon whistles.)*

BESS. Show me how t'do that.

MACON. What? Whistle?

BESS. Yeah.

MACON. Easiest thing in the world. Just watch me. I'll show ya how. *(Macon whistles. Bess tries to imitate her. She fails. Macon*

starts to laugh.)
BESS. I can't get it!
MACON. You will!
BESS. When?
MACON. Soon! *(Running off.)* Come on! I wanna show you the white jasmine. They're in bloom now down by the pond. *(They exit.)*

End of Scene 4

Scene 5

Three months later. Autumn.

Jack is walking down a path near his property. He carries a load of mining equipment. He sees something coming. He hides behind a rock. Macon appears carrying a bundle. She wears a cape and is whistling. Jack takes out his six-shooter, aims it at Macon and fires. Macon screams in horror and throws the bundle up in the air.

MACON. *Aah! (Jack saunters out from behind the rock brandishing the pistol.)* You trying to kill me?!
JACK. If I was, you'd be dead. *(A beat.)* Better watch out. Bullets make me smile. *(Jack shoots off the gun and then exits. Macon stands frozen with fear and fury. Bess enters.)*
BESS. Macon, you alright?
MACON. Yeah. It was Jack. He seen a snake.
BESS. He kill it?
MACON. Scared it away. Here, I got two small items for ya. Coffee and some shoes.
BESS. Thank you, Macon, but I don't need t'take things from you no more. Me and Jack, well, everything has turned around.
MACON. You talking on account of Lockwood's mine?
BESS. That's right. Jack purchased it last night with all the

inheritance money Mr. Michael Flan left. It's sugared with pure gold like a town of fairies been dancing there. *(Macon whistles for a moment, then stops.)*

MACON. Pause a moment, Bess. Use the round thing above your shoulders and tell me why anyone in this world would sell a mine laden with pure gold?

BESS. — Mr. Lockwood's very old. His eyesight's poor.

MACON. Well, his mind is sharp.

BESS. What're you telling?

MACON. I know that mine. It's dry as a parched tongue. Lockwood salted that claim with gold dust just to lead greedy fools astray.

BESS. I hope that ain't so. 'Cause we paid him for it. We paid him all we had. Oh, what's gonna become of us now? Times is already harder than hard.

MACON. I know. I seen it coming. Now's it's arriving at the front door.

BESS. Not at your door. Things are going good for you and Will Curtis.

MACON. Maybe in your eyes you see it that way. But me, I've come to a staunch conclusion. We gotta go. We gotta go now. We could leave here tonight.

BESS. Where'd we go?

MACON. West. We'd be going west.

BESS. Which way west?

MACON. Out past the Jack pine and yellow cedar, off through the grass that grows scarlet red across the plains, and on and on and onward.

BESS. We'd die of thirst and famine.

MACON. We'll drink plentiful before starting out, then chew constantly on small sticks to help prevent parching. Wild fruits grow all in abundance. Ripe plums will cool our fevered lips.

BESS. What about the Indians?

MACON. I got a cup of cayenne pepper and a corn knife t'take care of 'em. Whatever happens. It don't matter. Why limit the limitless. I'll write a novel about it all and put you in it. Go with me.

BESS. I can't go.

MACON. Why not?

BESS. I'm married.

MACON. He don't treat ya no good.

BESS. I'll learn t'make him.

MACON. You can't change his nature.

BESS. I'm here to try. You go on. You go without me. Please. Ya don't need me.

MACON. You're my one friend.

BESS. I ain't special.

MACON. You looked my way.

BESS. I can't go. I gave out my oath.

MACON. *(A beat.)* Here's the coffee. It's from parched corn and sorghum sweetening, but better than the dried carrot variety you been drinking. And take these shoes; those flaps of skin will never get you through the winter.

BESS. I'll pay ya back someday.

MACON. Don't mention it. I like giving gifts. It's who I am.

End of Scene 5

Scene 6

A year later. Fall.

A clearing.

WILL. *(Offstage.)* Hey, let go of that wood! You ain't stealing no more of my wood!

JACK. *(Offstage.)* Stealing? I ain't stealing nothing! *(A crack of wood offstage.)* Ow! *(Jack is thrown onstage.)*

WILL. I'll kill you, you son of a bitch!

JACK. You calling me a thief?

WILL. That's my wood. Pay me for it fair.

JACK. Miser.

WILL. Shiftless.

221

JACK. Blind mouse, one-eyed, scar-faced farmer —

WILL. *(Overlapping.)* Lazy, no-good, fool's gold miner — *(Jack and Will tear into each other. The fight is brutal. Macon enters. She carries a walking stick and wears field glasses around her neck. She dives into the fight, knocking the men apart with her stick.)*

MACON. Hey, hey, what's going on here? Stop it! Please! Hey! We're all neighbors here. Will Curtis, what is wrong?

WILL. He wants to freeload more of our wood. Hasn't paid me for the last five bundles. He ain't getting nothing else for free.

MACON. Will. Please! There's a bobcat caught in the trap line. Better go check on it before it gets loose. I don't want it on our hands.

WILL. *(To Jack.)* You get off my place. *(Will exits.)*

JACK. Good thing he went off. I might a' had t'kill him.

MACON. You come here looking for wood? *(Jack looks away from her.)* You know where the woodpile is. You take some and haul it on home.

JACK. Just so you'll know, I got things in the works; irons in the fire. Nothing worries me.

MACON. You oughta look to salted pork. Last year we put up 1,560 pounds at three-and-a-half cents a pound.

JACK. It don't interest me. I'd rather gamble for the high stakes. 'Afternoon, May Ann.

MACON. What?

JACK. May Ann. It's a prettier name than Macon. Its suits you better. I think I'll call you that.

MACON. Tell Bess she can keep the needle she borrowed. I won't need it back till Monday.

JACK. Uh huh.

MACON. She's had a hard summer, losing that baby. You need t'watch after her.

JACK. Is that what I need? Is that what I need, May Ann?

MACON. That's not my name.

JACK. It is to me. *(Jack exits. Macon pauses a moment, then looks after Jack through the field glasses. Will enters.)*

WILL. Bobcat got loose. Chewed off its paw. *(Macon quickly stops looking through the field glasses.)*

MACON. Will.

WILL. What?

MACON. I told him t'take some wood.

WILL. You what?

MACON. All they got t' burn is green twigs.

WILL. I don't like that, Macon. Why, that man's a freeloading ne'er-do-well. We don't want nothing to do with him.

MACON. Still I gotta look out for Bess. She's a friend of mine.

WILL. I don't understand about her and you. She's not special. Just some joyless creature with sawdust for brains.

MACON. Don't say that.

WILL. Look, I've observed in her strong symptoms of derangement that just ain't healthy. That ain't right.

MACON. Don't you got one drop of human kindness inside your whole bloodstream. It was just last summer she buried her infant child in a soap box under a prickly pear tree and wolves dug it up for supper.

WILL. Things haven't gone her way, that's true. Still, I cannot agree with her strange and gruesome behavior. How she dresses up that prairie dog of hers in a calico bonnet and shawl; sits there rocking it on the porch, talking to it just like it was a somebody.

MACON. People do strange things t'get by.

WILL. That may be. But everybody's got to make their own way. If they drop down, it ain't for you to carry them. *(Macon turns away from him and looks through the field glasses into the distance.)* I just don't like being exploited. I don't like the exploitation. People should earn what they get. What're you looking at?

MACON. Checking the cows.

WILL. How're the cows? Can you see the cows?

MACON. I see 'em.

WILL. Anyway, what's a load of wood? After all, we seem to be prospering. Last year we sold 1,560 pounds of salt pork at three-and-a-half cents a pound. Friday I'll go into town and see if the copper kettle you ordered from St. Louis has been delivered in the mail. After all, they're the ones with problems and burdens. If their luck doesn't change, they won't make it through the winter. They'll starve to death by Christmas. When the copper kettle comes, it will improve the looks of our cabin. You spoke about it before. You said it would add cheerfulness.

End of Scene 6

Scene 7

Christmas, months later. Night.

Jack's cabin. It is snowing. The wind is howling. Jack sits staring. Bess is on the floor, picking shreds of wheat out of the straw mattress.

BESS. You know what, Jack? Jack, you know what? I think it's Christmas. I've been thinking that all day.

JACK. I don't know.

BESS. I could be wrong. But I might be right. There's not much wheat in all this straw. Not much wheat to speak of. Would you agree it could be Christmas?

JACK. Where's the prairie dog?

BESS. Of course, Macon would have been here by now if it'd been Christmas. She was planning to bring us a galore of a spread. I was looking forward to it. Maybe the bad weather's put her off. The blizzards. Blinding blizzards for weeks now. Keeping Christmas from our front door. Jack, something happened to Prairie Dog.

JACK. It did?

BESS. It was when you went out trying to kill us something this morning.

JACK. Yeah.

BESS. This man came by. Some wandering sort of vagabond dressed in rags. Dirt rags. He wanted a handout. Food, you know.

JACK. We don't have anything.

224

BESS. I told him. I sent him on his way. "We don't have anything," I said. "I gotta go through the straw in the bed mattress picking out slivers of wheat so we won't starve here to death. I don't have food to spare some unknown wanderer." He asked me for just a cup of warm water, but I said no. Not because we couldn't spare it, but just because I didn't want him around here on the premises anymore. Something about him. His face was red and dirty. His mouth was like a hole. *(About the wheat.)* This is not gonna be enough for supper, this right here.

JACK. So what happened to the dog?

BESS. As he, as the vagabond was leaving, Prairie Dog followed after him barking. He picked up a stone and grabbed her by the throat and beat her head in with it. With the rock. She's out back in a flour sack. I'd burn her to ashes, if only we could spare the wood.

JACK. This is your fault.

BESS. Yes it it.

JACK. You're so weak. You make me sick. Christ, you're useless. I may just have to kill you.

BESS. You know what? I think it is Christmas. It's Christmas, after all. And you know what? I got something for you. I been saving it for Christmas. A surprise for you. A present. A Christmas gift. I been hoarding it away for you, but the time has come. The day has arrived. Merry Christmas, Jack. *(She produces a sack of cornmeal.)*

JACK. What is that?

BESS. Cornmeal.

JACK. Cornmeal. What're you gonna do with that?

BESS. Make you some cornbread. Cornbread for Christmas. A surprise.

JACK. Yeah. Yeah, a real big surprise. Boo! Surprise! Boo!

BESS. It's special. It's a treat. Hot cornbread. A lot better than that ash-baked bread we used to have.

JACK. Yeah, sure. But I ain't gonna choke t'death on no ash-baked bread. I ain't gonna turn blue and purple and green till I die eating no ash-baked bread.

BESS. You ain't gonna die eating no cornbread neither.

JACK. You tell that to Mike. You tell that to my brother, Mike, who had himself a big hunk of cornbread and choked t'death on it while riding bareback over the swinging bridge.
BESS. I never knew about that. I never knew how he died. I swear it, I didn't.
JACK. You might not have known it. Possibly you never was told it. But I bet you guessed it. I bet you dreamed it up. First Mike, then the baby, next Prairie Dog, now me. You want us all dead, don't you? You like things dead. You want it all for yourself. Well, here, have it. Take it. *(He throws a handful of cornmeal in her face.)*
BESS. No —
JACK. *(He continues throwing the cornmeal at her.)* There. There you go.
BESS. Stop.
JACK. Take it all!
BESS. I wanted this to be good. I wanted to be your true one.

End of Scene 7

Scene 8

Same night.

Will's cabin. Macon and Will are drinking cordials. It is Christmas.

MACON. I don't think so, Mr. Curtis. I don't believe so in the slightest. We're in no agreement, whatsoever.
WILL. Reliance on one crop is too risky. I'll say no more.
MACON. I'm telling you wheat promises the largest cash return and there's nothing comparable to it.
WILL. Besides there're other cautions to attend. We don't wanna expand too rapidly. We oughtn't get ahead of ourselves.
MACON. But there's no way to get ahead of ourselves. Not with the Union Pacific track-laying crew coming through. We

226

gotta look to the future. Did I steer you wrong about the pork prices? No, I did not. We bought up Dan Raymond's east field with the profits from salt pork. Turn that over in your head a minute.

WILL. Listen here —

MACON. Ssh! Ssh. Just turn it over. Churn it around. Let it fester. Here, now, I'll pour both of us another cordial. After all, it's Christmas. *(She pours out two drinks.)*

WILL. You have a nice way of pouring that drink. It looks delicate.

MACON. It's got a pretty color. The liquor.

WILL. Macon.

MACON. Huh?

WILL. There's, there's something for you. St. Nicholas left it, I guess. *(He hands her a gift with a card. She starts to open it.)*

MACON. A present for me.

WILL. Wait, wait. There's a card. Read the card.

MACON. Oh, yeah. "Merry Christmas, Mrs. Curtis. You are sweet as honey. From Brown Spot." Brown Spot?

WILL. *(He laughs.)* Yeah.

MACON. Brown Spot, the cow?

WILL. She's your favorite one, ain't she?

MACON. Not really, I prefer Whitey.

WILL. Oh, oh, well, pretend it was from Whitey. It was supposed to be from Whitey. Alright, now open the gift. But first, tell me, what do you guess it's gonna be?

MACON. I don't know. I'm hoping for a thing.

WILL. I got a feeling it's what you're hoping for. *(She opens the gift.)* Well?

MACON. What is it?

WILL. It's an eye. A glass eye. It's brown, see?

MACON. Oh, yeah.

WILL. I promised you I'd get one and I've kept that promise. Want me to put it in?

MACON. Alright.

WILL. I need a looking glass. *(He goes to put in the eye.)* I tried it on before, right when it arrived. I been saving it five weeks now. It ain't real ... *(He groans.)* ... comfortable, but it makes

227

a difference in my appearance. I think you'll appreciate it. *(He turns to her, wearing the eye.)* Hello.

MACON. Hi.

WILL. What do you think? Looks pretty real, huh?

MACON. Uh-huh.

WILL. If it wasn't for the scar, no one could guess which was real and which was glass.

MACON. Don't it hurt inside there?

WILL. Sure, but that's part of it. I'll adjust. Give me another cordial. That'll help it. *(Macon pours him another drink.)* I like to watch that pouring. Your hands. Delicate. *(She brings him the drink and starts to leave. He gently holds her arm.)* Say here. *(He drinks the drink.)* Macon, I know most times you don't feel like being nice to me. But I thought tonight, since I got this new eye, maybe you would.

MACON. *(A beat.)* Alright. *(Macon unbuttons her top and takes it off.)* Mr. Curtis?

WILL. Yes?

MACON. Have you thought any more about planting wheat in the east field?

WILL. Not much.

MACON. It'd be a good idea.

WILL. Alright, if that's what you think. We'll do it that way. *(There is a loud, desperate knocking at the door.)*

BESS. *(Offstage.)* Macon! Macon, let me in. Please. Let me in. Please, please. *(Macon rushes to the door. Bess enters. She wears a thin coat. She is covered with snow, wheat and cornmeal. Frozen blood is caked to her forehead.)*

MACON. Bess, Bess, come in. Get in. Look at you. You've been hurt.

BESS. You've got to help. My husband Jack — he's in an insane condition.

MACON. She's freezing. Bring a blanket. My God. My God, Bess.

BESS. He took a torch and set our cabin on fire. It's burning hot, hot in the snow.

MACON. Will, we gotta go see to Jack Flan.

WILL. I'll see to him. I'll go. Both of you stay here. I'll

228

handle his derangement. *(Will exits.)*

MACON. Here, get outta these wet boots. How in the world did you get here? How did you cross the gulch in this blizzard and not freeze to death?

BESS. Freeze t'death. Freeze t'death. I like the sound of that prediction. I long for the flutter of angel's wings.

MACON. Calm down. You're in a fit of delirium. Let me wash off your face for you.

BESS. It's all uncoiling. The springs in my mind. In my body. They're all loose and jumping out. Rusted and twisted.

MACON. I should have come to you. I should have braved the storm. I had your Christmas spread all packed up, I just been waiting for a break in the weather.

BESS. I wish you'd come. I been so lonely. I been going outside and hugging icy trees, clinging to them like they was alive and could hold me back. I feel so empty sometimes I eat warm mud, trying to fill up the craving.

MACON. Hush now. You're with me now. Let me brush out your hair. You got straw and sticks in your hair.

BESS. I just wanna say — I just wanna say —

MACON. What?

BESS. Early disappointments are embittering my life.

MACON. I'll draw you a bath of herbs and water. Sleep will fall on you. It'll restore your peace.

BESS. Macon?

MACON. Huh?

BESS. Let's go west.

MACON. West?

BESS. Let's start all over. Let's start from scratch. See, I've tried and I've tried, but I'm starting to believe Jack, he's just not in my stars.

MACON. I have to say — I have to remember — I did, I always thought I'd make much more of myself than this. My husband gave me a Christmas card from our cow. Still, I need to think things out. There's a lot we don't know. Practical knowledge, reality, and facts.

BESS. But we will go?

MACON. Oh yes, we'll go. Soon we'll go.

BESS. I realize now — now that you're brushing my hair, that I love you so much more; so much more than anyone else.

End of Scene 8

Scene 9

Over two years have passed. It is spring.

Outside Will's cabin. Bright sun shines down on Jack who is sitting on a fence eating a large piece of pound cake. He wears dress pants, but is barefoot and bare-chested. His hair is slicked back.

Will enters, barefoot and bare-chested. He carries two freshly pressed dress shirts.

WILL. Here're the shirts.
JACK. Thanks.
WILL. It's gonna be some feast we're having; some celebration. *(Will puts on his shirt. Jack eats cake.)* Can you believe it's been four years since the Marrying Squire came through here and joined us all together in holy matrimony?
JACK. Happy anniversary.
WILL. I don't know. Time travels.
JACK. Well, what else can it do?
WILL. Yeah.... Have you checked into that new land that's opened up for homesteaders?
JACK. I hear there ain't nothing available that ain't worthless.
WILL. Huh. Well, have you given any more thought to re-building on your own property?
JACK. Everything's burnt up over there.
WILL. Then what're ya gonna do?
JACK. About what?
WILL. This is supposed to be the deadline. Our anniversary. We made a deal, remember? You and your wife could stay

here until this anniversary, then your time was up.

JACK. Fine. Our time's up. Fine.

WILL. You have been living here over two years now. I know
you was sick for a time, but we've been more than generous.
That cabin's damn small.

JACK. All right, we'll go.

WILL. When?

JACK. Now. Right now.

WILL. Where're you gonna go?

JACK. Don't know. What do you care?

WILL. Well, don't go tonight. Wait a while more. Tonight's
a celebration. Macon's been preparing all week. We best not
spoil it.

JACK. Have it your way. *(Jack finishes the pound cake.)*

WILL. Was that the pound cake Macon brought out for us
to sample?

JACK. Yeah. Damn good cake. Warm and moist, right outta
the oven. *(Will hunts around for another piece of cake.)*

WILL. Where's my piece?

JACK. It's all gone.

WILL. She said she left a piece for me. She said she left two
pieces.

JACK. Oh, well, I ate both of 'em.

WILL. Both of 'em. You ate both of 'em. But one of 'em was
for me. One of 'em was my piece.

JACK. Sorry, I was hungry.

WILL. Well, damnation, I'm hungry, too! I'm hungry, too!

JACK. Look, you don't wanna ruin your supper. We're having a huge supper. It'd be a shame to spoil it.

WILL. Well, you didn't mind spoiling your supper. It didn't
bother you none. Damn, I wish I had that cake.

JACK. Well, ya don't. It's gone. I hogged it. What can ya do?

WILL. Nothing. Just nothing. Not a damn thing.

JACK. Here, some crumbs. There's some crumbs left.

WILL. Forget it. I don't want it. Forget it. *(Will picks up some
crumbs with his fingers and sticks them into his mouth.)*

End of Scene 9

Scene 10

Same day.

Inside Will's cabin. Bess wears a cape. She is walking around the room whistling and waving a list in the air. Macon sits at a table putting a waterfall hairpiece on her head.

BESS. The list is complete. Completely complete. The day has arrived. The time has come. We have it all here: tallow, rice, tea, chip beef, grease bucket, water barrel, one kettle, one fry pan, powder, lead, shot — Check it out. See for yourself. The list is complete.

MACON. Do we have heavy rope?

BESS. Yes, we do. There it is right there.

MACON. And a tar bucket.

BESS. Tar bucket, tar bucket, right there. Right there. *(A beat.)* We should go tonight.

MACON. On our wedding anniversary?

BESS. Why drag things out?

MACON. It would be a cruel blow to our husbands, leaving them on our marriage day.

BESS. They'll adjust. They have each other.

MACON. I think we should wait a little.

BESS. It's just we've been waiting so long.

MACON. I wanna see what the pumpkin patch produces. I suspect, it's gonna yield a phenomenal crop.

BESS. I don't care about the pumpkins.

MACON. And I got that rainbow-colored petticoat ordered. I can't leave before it arrives. And next month I'm to be the judge of the baking contest. Last year I won first prize. I got t'stay here and judge. It's your duty if ya win first prize.

BESS. I got this feeling that you're putting me off. You swore last time soon as I got the new items on the list we'd go. Please, I can't stay here no longer.

MACON. Things aren't so bad for you now that you and Jack

have moved in here with us. You seem content most of the time.

BESS. I try not to show my hurt. I hide it in different parts of the house. I bury jars of it in the cellar; throw buckets of it down the well; iron streaks of it into the starched clothes and hang them in the closet. I just can't hide it no more. We got t'go now. You promised. You swore.

MACON. Stop pushing at me. I got things here. Out there, I don't know what. (*Jack enters wearing his clean shirt. He is still barefoot.*)

JACK. (*To Macon.*) Hi.

MACON. Hi.

JACK. Good pound cake.

MACON. Thanks.

JACK. Will's out there upset. Says I ate his piece a' cake.

MACON. I told you one was for him.

JACK. I was hungry.

MACON. Shame on you, Jack Flan. I'll go take this bowl out to him. He can lick the batter. (*Macon exits. There is a horrible moment of silence. Bess gets Jack's boots and takes them to him.*)

BESS. I polished your boots, Jack. (*Jack pus on a boot. Bess stands staring at the floor.*)

JACK. I can't see myself in the toe. (*Bess kneels down and slowly starts to shine the boot. Jack gives her a glance filled with cold-blooded disdain.*)

End of Scene 10

Scene 11

That night.

Will's cabin, after the anniversary supper. Will, Macon, Jack and Bess are all gathered.

JACK. Listen to me. I'm asking you. I'm making a point. Why do we have to be hungry? Why do we have to be hot or cold?

233

Why do we have to stink? If someone could find a cure, a potion, an elixir for one of these conditions or possibly all four of 'em, that person could make a whole lot of money. Picture a killing. Picture money to burn. The facts are simple. Nobody wants to stink. Not really. Not if they thought about it. They'd come to me; I'd give them the potion; they'd cross my palm with silver; thank you very much, next customer.

MACON. It sounds like an exciting prospect.

JACK. It's how my mind works.

WILL. Well, he's right about one thing, nobody wants to stink.

BESS. I know I don't. I used to put vanilla behind my ears, but Jack said I smelt like food.

JACK. I'd love another piece of that delicious pound cake. It melts like butter in my mouth. *(Macon takes the last piece of cake and pushes it onto Jack's plate.)*

MACON. Well, I'm delighted nothing's going to waste.

WILL. Was that the last piece?

MACON. *(Nods.)* Uh huh.

JACK. *(Biting into the cake.)* Mmm, mmm. You cook better than anybody I ever knew.

MACON. Thank you, Jack, but Bess helped out a lot.

BESS. Not much really.

JACK. She's good at scrubbing dishes, but all her cakes fall flat as nickels.

MACON. Why, that's not true, Jack Flan. Why, that two-layer strawberry cake she made for my birthday was a sensation.

BESS. Oh, no, Macon, you don't remember. It was a five-layer carrot cake I made for you, but it only rose half an inch high. We all got such a big laugh out of it.

MACON. Oh, that's right. I remember now.

WILL. Your wife sure is good for a laugh, I'll say that. Remember when she asked me, "How'd I get my eye t'grow back?" *(Everyone laughs.)* She thought this glass eye was a real eye that just sprouted back there in the socket like a radish.

JACK. She's a howl alright.

BESS. *(Cheerfully.)* I guess I've just been dreadfully stupid all my life.

234

MACON. Don't listen to them. They're only having fun. It's all foolishness. Why, no one's even noticed the bow in Bess's hair. Turn around, please. Now isn't that a lovely sight?

JACK. Yes, it is. She's got pretty hair. Her eyes are too close together. But she's got pretty hair. *(To Macon.)* What about you? Your hair looks different tonight. What happened to it?

MACON. Waterfall curls. I ordered them from Boston. They're the latest sensation.

JACK. Ain't they something.

WILL. Delicate.

JACK. Lovely, lovely, lovely.

BESS. The ribbon's my favorite color. It's blue. Macon lent it to me. It's her favorite color, too. We're alike, us two. *(Bess points to a bucket of daisies.)* Both of us love daisies. They're our favorite flower.

MACON. Oh, daisies aren't my favorite flower. My favorite flowers are tulips.

BESS. Tulips?

MACON. They grow in this small country called Holland. They're the most beautiful flowers in the world. Daisies don't compare. Why, daisies are really nothing more than common weeds.

BESS. Well, I'm sure, if I ever got to see a tulip, they'd be my favorite flower, too.

MACON. Maybe someday we'll all go over to Holland and pick rows and rows of tulips. That would be a time to remember. Filling our skirts with golden tulips and tossing 'em up in the sky! Ho! Oh, I feel like being boisterous, let's have some celebrating! I wanna dance!

JACK. Alright!

WILL. Go ahead!

BESS. *(Overlapping.)* Me too! Me too! I love to dance!

MACON. I have a step I know. It's from the quadrille. It's the latest dancing fashion.

JACK. Let's see it!

MACON. Everyone's gotta clap! *(Macon, Bess and Will all start clapping.)* Come on, get the rhythm going! That's good! Keep it going! Jack Flan, why aren't you clapping?

235

JACK. I don't do anything to music. I don't dance to it. I don't clap to it. I like to watch it, but I won't join it.

MACON. You are as ridiculous as ever, surely more so. Here, hold my combs for me. Hold them, silly. Hold my combs. *(Macon gives her hair combs to Jack. He holds them for her. To Will and Bess.)* Clap for me now. Louder, please! Louder! *(Macon does some fancy dance steps to the clapping.)*

BESS. Bravo! Bravo!

WILL. She's delicate! Look how delicate!

JACK. Look at her go! Swing them curls.

BESS. Oh, I wanna join in!

MACON. Come on, Bess! Take a turn! *(Bess starts dancing wildly.)* That's it! Go now! Wow! What a dancer!

WILL. Watch out! Watch out! Oh, let it ride! Yes sir, yes sir, let it ride! *(Bess kicks her foot up high and falls on her butt.)*

BESS. Oops!

MACON. Oh, well, that was good! That was good! Give her a hand!

BESS. I fell down. I can't do things right. I think I'm clumsy.

WILL. You took a spill alright. Up in the air you went and down again.

JACK. Try to be more ladylike. Everyone saw all your things under there.

MACON. Come on, take another spin.

BESS. I don't wanna dance anymore.

MACON. Come on. You can do it.

BESS. No, please, let me be.

MACON. Well, I know, why don't you sing for us?

BESS. I don't sing. You know I don't sing.

JACK. That's right. She told me when we got married that she never sang. Didn't you mention that the very first day we met?

BESS. That's right. At one time I did sing, but I don't anymore.

MACON. Well, if you sang once, you can sing again. Why, I believe I've even heard you singing when you wash the clothes.

BESS. Oh, that's not singing; that's more like humming.

MACON. Well, if you can hum, you can sing. Please, sing a

song for us. I'd like to hear it.

BESS. Can I, Jack?

JACK. I don't know, can you?

BESS. Well, I do remember this one tune.

MACON. Good, let's hear it. You're on stage now. The stage is set for your song. The curtain is rising on you. Welcome Bess Flan and her singing! *(Macon claps.)*

BESS. *(Singing.)*
Down in the valley
The valley so low
Hang your head over
Hear the wind blow
Hear the wind blow, dear
Hear the wind blow
Angels in Heaven
I love you so

Roses are blue, dear
Roses are blue
Roses are blue
They're so, so blue
Blue, real, real blue ...

MACON. That was wonderful.

BESS. I — I guess I've forgotten the song. Some of it. How it goes.

WILL. I know that song. I've heard it before. It didn't sound right.

MACON. Do you know another one?

JACK. She didn't know that one.

MACON. She knew most of it and she's got such a lovely voice.

JACK. I don't know a thing about singing, but it seems to me, if you're gonna sing a song, you need to know the words to the song you pick.

BESS. I used to know a lot of songs. I knew 'em all by heart. It's just I haven't sung ever since I come out here. It felt funny opening up my throat to sing. Like it was somebody else who was singing. Somebody else who wasn't me. I think I'm gonna go outside in the moonlight and pick some night-blooming jasmine out by the pond. Their fragrance draws me to 'em. The smell of 'em and the moonlight. *(Bess exits.)*

JACK. For no apparent reason, she seems to have lost her mind.

MACON. I think you hurt her feelings about her singing.

JACK. What? I did not. I didn't say anything against her singing except she should brush up on the words.

MACON. Maybe you should go see to her.

JACK. She don't want me to see to her.

MACON. Why not?

JACK. She's mad at me about her damn singing.

WILL. All the cake's gone, I suppose.

MACON. Yes.

WILL. My eye's burning. I'm ready to take it out for the evening. *(Macon starts for the door.)* Where're you going?

MACON. Out to see to her. *(Macon exits. Offstage.)* Bess ... Bess ... *(etc.)*

WILL. *(A beat.)* Think they'll be alright out there in the dark?

JACK. I don't know.

WILL. There're wild animals out there this time of night. Coyotes for sure. Bears and wolves.

JACK. Indians, maybe.

WILL. Macon! Macon! *(Will exits.)*

MACON. *(Offstage.)* What? Huh?

WILL. *(Offstage.)* Macon, come back in here. I'll get Bess. *(Jack gets up, goes and pours himself a drink. Macon enters. Jack looks at her, then downs the drink.)*

JACK. Whiskey?

MACON. No

JACK. *(Pouring himself another drink.)* Are you sure ... May Ann?

MACON. Don't you call me that. Ever.

JACK. Alright. Here're your combs back. I been holding them for you. Pretty combs. Lucky, too. Lucky to be running all through your hair.

MACON. Don't talk to me. Sit there and don't talk to me.

JACK. *(A beat.)* May Ann; May Ann; May Ann.

MACON. Shut up.

JACK. You been circulating in my head. All through my head. You're more vivid to me than any other thought. I can't get you outta here. Can't knock you out; can't drink you out; can't scream you out. Never, never. You always here.

MACON. Stop it. Don't do this. Stop it.

JACK. Can't you see that I am outta control of my feelings over you?

MACON. Look, I don't want anything to do with you. I got a husband, Will. You got a wife, Bess, who is my dearest friend of mine. I would never, ever imagine betraying her feelings. Never, ever, even if I did care for you, which I do not and never will and never could; 'cause in all honesty, there's absolutely not one thing about you I can bear to stand. You're mean and selfish and a liar and a snake; I spit on your grave, which can't get dug up fast enough and deep enough to suit me just fine.

JACK. *(A beat.)* Well, I just wanna know one thing. You tell me one thing. Why did you ask me to hold your combs for you? You chose me to hold your combs. You placed them in my hand. Why'd you do that? Huh?

MACON. Because I — You were standing there nearest to me, and I realized how I was afraid when I danced the combs would fly out of my hair and get lost in some faraway, far off corner of the room. You must know, I mean it is common knowledge, that you can have somebody hold your combs for you and still believe with your whole being and heart that you hate them and they're worse than bad, but you just need your combs held and they happen to be standing in arm's reach.

JACK. You certainly are talking a lot. Rambling on. Why's that?

MACON. I — I don't know. I'm just talking. I just feel like talking. I got this sensation that keeps on telling me that silence ain't safe.

JACK. Hush now.

MACON. No, I can't allow no silence 'cause then something real terrible's gonna happen. The world might stop moving and that could start the earth shaking and everything'll just fall into cracks and openings and horrible holes —

239

JACK. Just hush a moment.

MACON. No, I won't, I can't, the world will break open; the oceans will disappear; the sky will be gone; I won't; I can't; I won't —

JACK. Hush or I'll have to gag you.

MACON. It won't do no good. I'll still go on mumbling and moaning all under the gag.

JACK. Maybe then, I'll just have to break your neck. *(Jack grabs her and holds his hand to her throat.)* There now. Be very still. *(Macon freezes.)* Hear that? The world's not falling apart. Hear that? *(She nods her head.)* You can handle it, can't you?

MACON. Yes.

JACK. *(He removes his hand from her throat.)* You can handle it just fine. *(He puts his hand on her breast.)* Tell me how you can handle it.

MACON. I can.

JACK. Just fine.

MACON. Yes. *(They embrace with a terrible passion, tearing at each other like beasts. Finally, Macon breaks away. Tears of rage stream down her face.)* Stay away. You viper. You twisted snake. *(Jack looks at her helplessly. He goes to get a drink. Macon straightens her dress and hair, then sits in a chair with her arms folded. Will comes in the door carrying Bess's cape and an arrow. His face is white. He is in a panic.)* Will?

WILL. She's not out there by the pond. She's disappeared.

MACON. That's her cape.

WILL. I found it on the ground. And this. *(Will produces an Indian arrow from under the cape.)*

MACON. Oh my God. Where is she? What's happened?

JACK. Who's is it?

WILL. Looks like Oglala.

JACK. You think Indians got her? *(Macon runs to the door and calls out in the night.)*

MACON. Oh God! Bess! Bess! *(Will grabs Macon in the doorway.)*

WILL. Macon!

MACON. Please, God! Bess! *(Blackout.)*

End of Act I

240

ACT II

Scene 1

Five years later. Will's cabin. A spring night.

Macon is drinking whiskey. Will and Jack are eating huge pieces of cake. Jack has a mustache.

JACK. I love this cake.

WILL. It's got a delicate flavor.

MACON. I know it's both your favorite. Happy anniversary, everyone.

WILL. Happy anniversary.

JACK. Happy anniversary.

MACON. Can you believe how fast time travels? Nine years I been living out here on this plain. Youth isn't really all that fleeting like they say. I mean, it seems solid, like it was there, the time you spend being youthful. The rest here, it just flies by, like everything'll be over before you can breathe.

JACK. I don't like to discuss time. It's not my favorite subject, I'd as soon not hear about it.

MACON. I'm sorry, Jack. I know anniversaries are hard for you. Here, let's hand out the presents.

WILL. They're some major presents this year. Some major surprises. *(Macon hands out two gifts that are wrapped identically.)*

MACON. Here you go. I ordered them from the catalogue. I hope you like 'em.

JACK. Thanks.

WILL. Thanks, Macon. *(After opening the gift.)* Well, that's nice. A fancy cup.

MACON. It's a mustache cup. So you won't get your mustache wet when you drink.

JACK. Well, that's a crafty idea. It oughta come in real handy.

WILL. I ain't got no mustache.

MACON. Oh, well, maybe you'll grow one. Jack's looks real nice on him. I think mustaches are the coming thing.

JACK. Here, pour me some cordial. Let me test mine out.

MACON. Alright, let's see.

WILL. Anyway, I could still use it. I'll just drink out of this other side. *(Macon pours Jack a cordial. He drinks from his mustache cup successfully.)*

MACON. Oh, look!

JACK. Pretty handy. Pretty handy.

WILL. Macon, I know there's concern now that the railroad's being rerouted, but I went on and splurged. I got these for you. I know they're what ya wanted. *(Will presents Macon with two red pillows.)* Scarlet plush sofa pillows. Two of 'em.

MACON. Oh, thank you, Will! Thank you! They're so pretty; aren't they pretty!

WILL. They'll cheer up the place.

MACON. They will. Oh, I appreciate it, thank you. Now, if only I could get a new room built, I'd be satisfied. But perhaps not. Seems like I've always something to wish for.

WILL. You do like the pillows though?

MACON. Uh huh.

JACK. I got a gift for you May Ann.

MACON. You do? Why thank you, Jack.

WILL. *(About the gift.)* It looks kinda small. *(Macon opens the gift.)*

MACON. A ring. It's a ring. I cherish rings.

JACK. It's sapphire blue. The color you like best.

MACON. *(Trying the ring on.)* Look, how it fits.

JACK. Just right.

WILL. I don't like him giving you a ring. I'm your husband. You're supposed t'wear my ring.

MACON. Will, I wore that tin band ya gave me till it tore right off.

WILL. I always figured to get ya another one. And now he comes in with this sapphire ring, knowing blue is your favorite color just like you was his wife or something. *(To Jack.)* It's not right! You set your own house on fire, set it aflame, burn it t'ashes and then move in here with us. Just come t'stay and don't ever leave; start giving out rings. Rings are what you give to your wife and she's not your wife. She's my wife. She don't want this ring. Save it for you own damn wife.

MACON. Will, what's wrong with you? You know he ain't got no wife.

WILL. I wouldn't be so sure about that.

MACON. I don't wanna be sure about it. I sure don't wanna be sure. But we've hunted all over for her for years.

JACK. We sent out searching parties.

MACON. We put articles in broadsides; and made inquiries to U.S. Army officers.

JACK. I never wanted to give up hope, but when that hunter from the trading post brought us that scalp ...

MACON. She had such beautiful hair.

JACK. It's all I got left of her. My darling Bess. How I miss her apple butter cheeks now that they're gone.

WILL. People don't always die when they're scalped. You know that, don't ya?

JACK. Yeah.

WILL. Sometimes, they take the scalping knife and cut just a small tuft off at the crown of the head. People recover. It happens a lot. Happy anniversary, Jack. *(Will hands an official looking letter to Jack.)*

JACK. What's this?

WILL. A letter from the U.S. Army. They got your wife. They're gonna deliver her to ya in an Army ambulance. *(Jack grabs the letter. He realizes he can't read it. Macon grabs the letter.)* A Mexican fur trader tipped off a Captain Patch at Fort Sully. The Captain says they had to threaten the Chief, Ottowa, with a massacre 'fore he'd sell her back. They got her for two horses, three blankets, a box of bullets and a sack of glass beads.

MACON. I don't believe this. She's alive.

JACK. I wonder what she'll look like? How do people look when they've been scalped?

MACON. It says here, she's been tattooed on her arms and on her chin.

JACK. Tattooed?

MACON. It don't matter. She won't have changed that much. She's alive. They're bringing her to us and she's still alive.

End of Scene 1

Scene 2

A few days later. Bess stands rooted in the center of the room. She is barefoot. Her skin is dark and burnt; her hair is thin and sun-bleached; her chin has been tattooed. She wears an enormous dress that was lent to her at the fort. Macon and Will stand around her. Jack stands alone gazing at her from the corner of the room.

MACON. Bess. Bess. Welcome back. Welcome home. We've missed you. We've prayed for your return and here you are back from the vale of death. Fresh from pandemonium.

WILL. I don't think she likes being inside. I bet, you ain't used to having a roof over your head? It agitates ya, don't it?

JACK. No point in pumping her. She don't wanna talk.

MACON. Well, I'm sure it was an awful experience but it's over. Right now you probably could use a bath. Will, go bring a couple of buckets of water for me from the well. Jack, you go fetch the washtub.

JACK. Alright, but I bet she don't remember what a bath is. *(Will and Jack exit.)*

MACON. Everything's gonna be fine. Just fine. Just very fine. In honor of your homecoming we're having a big juicy ham. *(Bess retches.)* What's wrong?

BESS. Thought of hog eaters make me choke.

MACON. What's wrong with hog? It's just pig. It's just pork.

BESS. *(Fiercely.)* Mud and water animal, bad.

MACON. Well, we could have something else. Vegetables. A lot of vegetables and pumpkin pie for dessert. You remember our pumpkin patch? Well, anyway, it's doing real well. People come by at Halloween time and pick out their own jackerlan-

244

handy. It's not like times are flush around here. Wheat prices have dropped and the railroad's been rerouted. We're in bad debt 'cause of purchasing three fields we don't have the resources to work. But like they say, trouble comes in twos. I'm hoping someday things'll be different and we'll have an abundance. Don't you remember me at all? I'm your friend. I taught you how to whistle. *(Macon whistles.)* Don't ya remember? *(Macon whistles again; she stops. Bess looks at her. Macon whistles with a desperate intent. Bess whistles back to her, very softly.)*

MACON. I don't know but somehow, you survived it.

BESS. I picture you.

MACON. What? You pictured me?

BESS. Hunt the elephant.

MACON. The elephant?

BESS. Bang, bang, bang.

MACON. Right. yes. It's gonna be alright. Everything'll be just like it was. Sour milk will help bleach down that dark skin, and we'll get ya a brand-new dress. A blue one.

BESS. Blue.

MACON. Yeah, one that'll fit ya just right. Lord, that captain's wife musta been bigger than a mule. A real mud and water animal, that captain's wife.

BESS. Oh, big. *(They laugh.)*

MACON. And curls, you're gonna need some false curls. And maybe some cornstarch over that chin. Or veils. Sweet little net veils. *(Bess feels her chin.)*

BESS. Ottawa.

MACON. What?

BESS. To be his bride. They mark me.

MACON. You were a bride?

BESS. *(She nods.)* Two ... two children. Chante, Hunke-she. Ottawa. I thought he was true one. He gave me black horse.

MACON. No, no. He was bad. He was an Indian. He was bad.

BESS. Yes, bad. Sold me. Sold me cheap. Two horses, blanket, beads, bullets. Cheap.

MACON. Bess, you can't — don't ever tell Jack.

MACON. Bess, you can't — don't ever tell Jack.

BESS. No.

MACON. No one else. Don't tell anyone else. *(Jack enters with the washtub.)* Jack. Jack, she's talking. She don't like pork, but she's talking.

BESS. Jack.

JACK. Look at her. She's disgusting.

MACON. Jack, don't —

JACK. *(Running on.)* She smells like old cheese.

MACON. Stop it!

JACK. *(Running on.)* I wish they'd never found her.

MACON. Hush up! Hush! *(Jack grabs Macon passionately in his arms, smelling and caressing her. He rams his fingers through her hair, tearing out her combs.)*

JACK. I want you. Not her. Only you. Understand me?

MACON. *(Overlapping.)* Let me go. Let go. Get away. *(Macon pushes him away.)*

JACK. She may be back. But nothing's changed. *(Jack exits. Macon turns to Bess who stares at her with anguished eyes.)*

MACON. Bess, please, he — I'm sorry. I never — You must believe me. I thought you were dead. They brought us your scalp. You were gone so long. So many years.

BESS. No. You. I saw. *(Pointing to Macon's combs.)* Combs. You gave him. He held them. I saw.

MACON. It'll be over now. I promise. I'll make it up to you. I'll make it right, I swear. Everything will be just the same.

End of Scene 2

Scene 3

A week later. A hot summer night.

Will sits outside the barn hammering together a chain. He now has a moustache.

Macon enters.

MACON. Have you finished?

WILL. Not yet.

MACON. It's always hot. Summer's almost over and it hasn't rained once. There's no relief.

WILL. I think you're working the ox too hard. It needs more rest. More water.

MACON. We have to work the fields.

WILL. If the ox gets sick, it'll be over for us.

MACON. What do you want? The bank is breathing down our necks. When will you finish that?

WILL. I don't know.

MACON. I need it by morning. I can't chase her and be in the fields. Not in this heat.

WILL. I don't like the idea of this.

MACON. I don't know how else to stop her from running away. She bites through rope.

WILL. Why not let her go?

MACON. She's my friend, I have to save her. We got to be patient. We got to wean her from her savage ways. She'll come around in time. God, you look —

WILL. What?

MACON. I don't know, old, I guess.

WILL. Maybe it's the moustache.

MACON. Oh yeah. You have a — You grew one. (*Macon exits. Will continues hammering on the chain.*)

End of Scene 3

Scene 4

A month later. A hot day.

Outside Will's cabin. Jack aims his six-shooter at an offstage target. He fires the gun. He misses his target.

JACK. Damn. (*Jacks shoots two more bullets. He keeps missing his offstage target. This puts him in a rage.*) Damn, hell, damn. (*Ma-*

247

con appears from the direction of the barn.)

MACON. What are ya shooting at?

JACK. Playing cards. I used t'could split 'em at thirty paces.

MACON. Stop wasting powder. *(Jack turns around and points the gun at her.)* You don't scare me anymore.

JACK. And you don't make me smile. *(Jack lowers his gun.)*

MACON. Your wife's here for that.

JACK. Uh huh.

MACON. *(Softly, intensely.)* It's all over between us.

JACK. It wasn't over in the barn last night.

MACON. Well, now it is.

JACK. You been telling me that for some time. I'm starting to doubt your word.

MACON. Go clean out the chicken coop. Earn your keep.

JACK. I still smell you. *(Jack embraces Macon. She responds.)*

MACON. *(With loathing.)* I wanna be rid of you. Why can't I be rid of you? *(Bess appears. She wears a blue dress and is barefoot. She has a shackle around her foot and is chained to an offstage stake. Macon and Jack break apart. They stare at her for a brief moment before Jack exits toward the barn.)* Where're your shoes? You have to wear shoes. We all wear shoes around here. And you need to keep that veil on to cover your face. Those tattoos are not proper. People frown on 'em. *(Will enters. He looks very glum.)* Will! Will, you're back. How'd it go? Not good? Not so good? What? Huh? Speak! Will you speak!

WILL. They won't renew the note. They're repossessing the steeltipped plow and the barbwire. They want our horse and mule and hogs, even our ox. Everything we used as security.

MACON. They can't take our livelihood. The last two years, there's been a drought.

WILL. They've heard all about the drought.

MACON. I'll go into town. I'll fix this myself. You can never get anything done. You're incapable. I'll get my hat and gloves. I'll get this settled. *(Macon goes into the cabin.)*

WILL. *(To Bess.)* I understand why you wanna run away. I'd let you go, but she keeps the key. Me, I'm not sure why I stay. I don't know what I expect to get. She used to be nice to me sometimes for very short intervals of time. Not anymore. I

don't know what I expect to get now. I mean, from now on. *(Macon appears from the cabin wearing a hat and gloves. She carries Bess's shoes and veil.)*
MACON. Have you hitched the wagon?
WILL. Not yet.
MACON. Go do it. *(Will exits for the barn. Throughout the following, Macon dresses Bess in the shoes and veil.)* Will Curtis is a very commonplace type man. Really, anyone who would spend money to buy a glass eye makes me laugh. You'll see, I'll go into that bank and come out with a loan for a windmill, a gang plow and twenty cord of barbwire. Great invention, barbwire. Keeps what you want in and all the rest of it out. There, that's better. That blue dress looks good. You look pretty in it. I sacrificed a lot to get it for you. I want to make you happy. I'd take these chains off, if only you would stay. Will you stay? Bess. Bess. *(A beat.)* I wish you'd speak to me. *(A beat.)* No. Alright. I'll bring some daisies back for you, if I see them on the road. *(Macon exits. Bess jerks violently at her chain. She struggles with fierce rage pounding the chain. She moans with unbearable despair and finally sinks to the ground exhausted. Jack and Professor Elmore Crome, a distinguished looking young man, enter from the barn road. Jack holds money in his hand.*
JACK. *(Indicating Bess.)* Here she is. Right there. Go ahead. Look at her. *(Jack removes her veiled hat.)*
ELMORE. Why is she chained up?
JACK. We've had to restrain her to prevent her from returning to the wilds.
ELMORE. I see. Mrs. Flan?
JACK. I didn't say you could talk to her. *(Elmore hands Jack another bill.)* Alright. But she don't talk back.
ELMORE. How do you do, Mrs. Flan. I'm Professor Elmore Crome. It's an honor to make your acquaintance. I read about your brutal capture in a broadside. What an amazing feat to have survived such an ordeal. You're a remarkable woman. I'm in awe of your strength and courage.
JACK. She don't understand nothing you say.
ELMORE. One more word, please. I just — I just wish so much I could hear about your experiences from your own lips.

I was hoping we could write a book together. A book that would help prevent others from falling prey to similar atrocities.

JACK. Write a book. Why she ain't spoke one word since they brought her back. *(Sympathetically.)* She's just a pitiful specimen.

ELMORE. Please, I have a gift for you. I brought a gift. *(He hands her a silver mirror wrapped in a handkerchief. She looks at herself in the mirror. She touches the tattoos on her chin.)* I know people would want to read about you. People all over the world. I'm sure you have so much to tell. So many adventures to impart. You must know a great deal about Indian ways. About their lives; about their treachery.

JACK. That's enough now. *(Bess looks Elmore in the eye. He looks back at her.)* I said time to go.

ELMORE. Good afternoon, Mrs. Flan. In all honesty, I must say, you have the bravest eyes I have ever witnessed. *(Jack and Elmore start to leave.)*

BESS. Don't —

ELMORE. *(Stopping.)* What?

BESS. Go.

ELMORE. Yes.

BESS. I do. I know treachery. I could write book. A big book. All about treachery.

ELMORE. Excellent.

End of Scene 4

Scene 5

Two months later.

The yard in front of Will's cabin. Will rushes onstage. He is breathing hard. His eyes are grief-stricken. He stops, sits down and puts his hands over his face.

Jack appears from the cabin carrying a pitcher of cool punch and two tin cups.

250

JACK. 'Morning, Will. How're things going?

WILL. The wheat's burnt dead. There's no saving it. The ox just collapsed down in the dirt. He's alive, he's struggling but he can't get back up. Could I have a drink? I'm parched.

JACK. I made this beverage for the Professor and Bess. They get real thirsty working on the book.

WILL. I just want a sip.

JACK. Sorry. (*Macon appears from the fields. She hauls a load of wilted corn. She is in a state of mad frenzy.*)

MACON. Christ. Will. The ox. The look in his eyes. God, how he's suffering. Did you get the gun?

WILL. Not yet.

MACON. Go get it. Shoot him! Kill him! Blow out his brains! I can't bear it! He keeps looking at me like I owe him something!!! (*Will goes into the cabin to get a gun.*) Where were you last night?

JACK. I didn't come.

MACON. I waited for you.

JACK. I couldn't get away.

MACON. Why not? (*Bess is heard singing "Down In The Valley."*)

JACK. Because of her.

MACON. Her.

JACK. Yeah.

MACON. Did you stay with her?

JACK. What could I do? She's my wife. (*Bess and Elmore enter. Bess carries a parasol. She wears a cape and new shoes. She doesn't wear her veil. We see her tattoos. Elmore has a pad and pen. He is constantly taking notes.*)

ELMORE. What a voice you have! Like an angel!

BESS. Every time the Oglalas raised scalps on a pole and threatened to slay me, I'd sing for them. They'd fall to their knees and listen to my song, entranced, like charmed wolves. Ottawa, the head man, gave me strings of beads; others gave me acorns, seeds, ground nuts, feathers. Any treasure they possessed so I would favor them with my singing.

ELMORE. Amazing. Quite a provocative tale. Ah! The punch! Please serve Mrs. Flan a glass. I'm sure she must be parched.

(Jack serves punch, then holds Bess's parasol to shade her.)

BESS. Oh, no. Why I often went months without a drop of any drink during my stay in captivity.

ELMORE. Fascinating. How did you survive?

BESS. I'd chew constantly on a small stick to help prevent parching, or I'd hunt for wild fruits that grow all in abundance. *(Bess whistles softly.)*

ELMORE. You are an amazing creation. How anyone could have endured such hardship.

MACON. She pictured me.

ELMORE. What?

MACON. She pictured me. *(Will comes out of the cabin with a gun.)*

WILL. Macon, I have the gun.

MACON. Not now.

WILL. I — I'm going to shoot the ox. It has to be done. He's suffering. *(Will heads toward the field.)* Won't you please come?

MACON. Shoot it by yourself.

WILL. I'll need somebody to help me slaughter it. Jack, would you?

JACK. The Professor pays you for our room and board. I'm no hired hand. *(Will exits.)*

MACON. Bess, tell the Professor how you pictured me when you was captured.

BESS. I thought about ya. I thought about all my loved ones back home.

ELMORE. It must have been unbearable — your sorrow.

BESS. It's true, I've suffered. But I come out here drunk with western fever. I wanted to see the elephant. To hunt down the elephant. Bang! Bang! Bang! I savor the boundlessness of it all! The wild flavor!

ELMORE. You take my breath away. How powerfully you speak in your simple, unadorned language. When your book comes out we must send you on the lyceum lecture circuit. What a sensation you'd make.

BESS. You flatter me, really.

MACON. My Lord, yes. Just imagine Bess on a big stage in front of a whole room full of people. Such a shy little thing.

She'd die of fright. You need somebody who's got a real knack for that sort of thing. Ya know, I once played the Virgin Mary in a Christmas pageant. I had such a saintly face, an unearthly glow. I cried real tears when the Innkeeper told us there was no room for us at his inn.

ELMORE. *(A beat.)* It seems to me, the sun's very bright here. Why don't we go work in the willow grove down by the pond.

BESS. Yes. I'll tell you all about how the horrid hell hounds tattooed my face with sharp sticks dipped in weed juices and the powder from blue mud stones.

ELMORE. Monstrous savages. Godless perpetrators of butchery. *(Elmore and Bess exit.)*

MACON. I wore a blue robe as the Virgin Mary. Blue looks good on me. It's my best color, although I did not know it at the time.

JACK. Something about you's changed. You've lost the stars in your shoes. You used to run everywhere you'd go.

MACON. Well, what about you? Look at you. Serving punch, toting parasols, bowing and scraping.

JACK. I do, what I do.

MACON. You live like a leech.

JACK. Would you give me back the ring I gave you? I want to give it to my wife. *(An offstage gunshot is heard.)*

MACON. Take it. Here, take it.

WILL. *(Offstage.)* God, it's still alive. Macon!

MACON. Good, it's over. Good.

WILL. *(Offstage.)* It's looking at me.

MACON. I'll kill it. I'll blow it dead. I'll do it! *(Macon exits. Jack looks after her. He tosses the ring up in the air and starts offstage. As he goes toward Bess and the Professor, we hear one last shot.)*

End of Scene 5

Scene 6

The following spring.

Will sits alone in the yard. Bess and Elmore are gathered in Will's cabin. Elmore is looking through a portfolio taking out letters, contracts, illustrations, etc. Bess is waving a check through the air.

ELMORE. A phenomenon. Your book is a phenomenon!

BESS. I've hit pay dirt!

ELMORE. *(Looking at a sheet of figures.)* It's astonishing! No one can believe it!

BESS. I must have a pet song bird! We'll sing a duet together!

ELMORE. Over sixty thousand copies sold!

BESS. Oh, and get me a giant harp with gold cherubs and an ice palace to keep it in.

ELMORE. Whatever your heart desires.

BESS. *(Singing.)* Roses are blue, oh, roses are blue ...

ELMORE. *(Overlapping.)* Now I have some correspondence that requires your attention.

BESS. Yes, yes, proceed; proceed.

ELMORE. *(Presenting a letter.)* The President of Indian Affairs wants to dine with you at the White House the day you arrive in Washington.

BESS. Oh, delightful. I'm delighted. How thrilling! I hope they don't serve any pig.

ELMORE. No, of course not. I'll alert them to your wishes. All pig shall be banned. Now here's an inquiry from actor-manager-playwright Dion Boucicault. He wants to adapt your book into a hit play.

BESS. Dion Boucicault? Who's that?

ELMORE. He's very famous.

BESS. Oh, alright then, I consent. *(Jack enters carrying some luggage. He has shaved his moustache.)*

ELMORE. *(Handing her an illustration.)* Now here's the portrait of you that we want to include in the second edition.

254

BESS. Oh, dear.

ELMORE. I find it very sensitive, yet I feel there's a deep sense of inner strength.

BESS. Hmm. My eyes are too close together. I've got beautiful hair, but my eyes are too close together. *(To Jack.)* Don't you agree?

JACK. No.

BESS. But they're closer together than an average person's eyes, wouldn't you say?

JACK. I don't know. No.

BESS. Well, how close together do you think an average person's eyes are?

JACK. I don't know.

BESS. Then stop offering opinions on subjects you're completely stupid on.

JACK. Alright.

BESS. Don't be so agreeable. Finish fetching our bags and move them out to the carriage. We don't want to miss our train. *(Jack exits into another room.)* Do we really have to bother with him?

ELMORE. Of course, it's entirely your decision, but I'm afraid an anguished, adoring husband makes for excellent pathos.

BESS. Yes. Well, then. I'll manage.

ELMORE. Good. Excellent. Now, according to this schedule, you'll be doing up to one hundred and fifty lectures this season. You stand to profit over twenty-five thousand dollars from the lecture circuit alone.

BESS. Angels sing, devils dance.

ELMORE. Mr. William Sutton is the promoter for the tour. He's a very successful land speculator who is deeply devoted to western expansion and the concept of manifest destiny. He'd like for you to sign this contract agreeing to expound certain philosophical beliefs from the podium.

BESS. Philosophical beliefs? I'm not sure I got any of them. Here, let me see the paper. *(Bess takes the contract and reads it thoroughly. Macon enters the area in front of the cabin. She spots Will.)*

MACON. Repossession. Repossession. That one word they

255

clung to like a pack of sick dogs. They're taking our home. There's nothing to be done, unless they get fifty dollars. Fifty dollars. I asked the man with the red beard if he'd accept potatoes as partial payment. He laughed at me like I was a brand-new joke.

WILL. I told you how it come out. Things are finished here. We'll have to go somewhere else. Start fresh.

MACON. I'd rather choke to death right here in the sun. *(Inside the cabin Jack enters with the bags. He starts for the cabin door. Bess stops him.)*

BESS. Jack, don't forget that basket there, I packed us some food for the road.

JACK. Great. What is it?

BESS. Cornbread. *(Jack nods, picks up the basket and leaves the cabin. He goes into the yard. Macon spots him.)*

MACON. Jack, where're you going?

JACK. The Professor's come for us. Bess's book's selling like wildfire. We're going on a lecture circuit. We've become important people.

MACON. You're leaving right now?

JACK. That's right.

MACON. How long will you be gone?

JACK. For good, I hope.

MACON. God. How will I ever stand living in this great wasteland all alone.

JACK. *(Indicating Will.)* Ya still got him.

MACON. Yeah. Listen, Jack, I'm in trouble. I need fifty dollars to save the homestead.

JACK. I ain't got no money.

MACON. Well, would you talk to Bess for me? Would you put in a good word?

JACK. You talk to her. She's your friend.

MACON. That's right. You're right. She's my friend. I done a lot for her. A whole lot. Goodbye, Jack.

JACK. So long, May Ann.

MACON. I'll always remember you as the possessor of a very handsome pair of eyes. *(Jack exits. Will stares ahead, trying to decide why he doesn't care about killing these people. Macon goes into*

256

the cabin. Will exits.) Bess. I need to talk to you. It's concerning a personal situation. Good afternoon, Professor.

ELMORE. Yes, well ... good afternoon, Mrs. Curtis. *(Elmore gets up and goes into the yard.)*

MACON. I heard you're leaving. You're off. You've made it in the big time.

BESS. That's how it appears.

MACON. I don't begrudge you. I saw it coming. People lap up them atrocity stories. They read 'em all the time in them penny dreadfuls. Now you go and give 'em the real factualized version. Ya even got the marks t'prove it. People'll get up outta their homes and come down to them big halls to see them marks. Them tattoos. People thrive on seeing freaks.

BESS. Well, I'm glad you don't begrudge me.

MACON. No. Why would I?

BESS. No reason. I just thought you wanted to write a book, a novel. You spoke about it. But I guess that was more like a pipe dream, a childish fantasy. Nothing to be taken seriously.

MACON. I had a book in mind at one point. I was gonna write about my adventures.

BESS. I guess, you just never had any, did ya?

MACON. I had some. Some things happened to me.

BESS. Not that much, though.

MACON. Well, I never got my face scarred.

BESS. Do you wish you had?

MACON. Why would I?

BESS. Because, maybe you would like to be ... remarkable. But you're not. You look forward to things by decades. You're settled, staid and dreamless. I see it haunts you how ya just can't compare t'me. To Bess Johnson, the woman who survived five adventurous years of Indian captivity. Who returned to write the book of the century and be adored by throngs all over the globe.

MACON. You don't fool me. I know how ya done it all. You pictured me. You stole from me. You stole me. I showed you how to walk and speak and fight and dream. I should have written that book. People should be clamoring t'meet me; t'talk t'me. I'm the real thing; you're just a watered down milktoast version. Them Indians stole the wrong woman.

BESS. Is that a fact?

MACON. Yeah, it is.

BESS. Well, maybe it ain't too late. Maybe you've got one more chance. Here, take this knife. Take this ink. Go ahead. Cut open your face. Pour in the ink. Go be me, if you think you can. If you think you're so brave. I'll let you be me. You can do my tour. People will rise to their feet and clamor for you. Go ahead. The Oglalas rejoice in wounding themselves. They do it for prayer. They do it to celebrate grief. Come on, do it, celebrate, rejoice, do it — all it is is your face.

MACON. Bess, please — I always cared for you. I always did.

BESS. Then do it. Cut it. To shreds; all to shreds.

MACON. I did, you know. I always did.

BESS. Then do it. Cut it; do it. (Macon takes the knife. Holds it to her face, then sets it down.)

MACON. I'm not gonna cut myself up. I don't wanna be scarred for life.

BESS. (A beat.) No. That would cost too much. And you've gotten so measly you watch every egg, nickel, and biscuit. (Bess starts putting on her hat and gloves.)

MACON. I know we don't like each other. We used to be friends. But somehow we drifted apart. Still you have to admit, you have to see, that you owe me something.

BESS. What do I owe you?

MACON. You — well, you owe me — fifty dollars. At least, fifty dollars. I gave you shoes when you had none and food and coffee and clothes and lodging. I even brought you blue ribbons and a blue dress. Whatever your heart desired, I gave to you.

BESS. Maybe it never occurred t'you. Maybe you never realized the fact, but people don't like being beholding. They resent always needing and always owing. And pretty soon they come to resent whoever it is they been taking from.

MACON. I do. I know that. You've resented me all along.

BESS. Yeah, I believe I have and I don't want you resenting me. So why don't we just call it even.

MACON. But I gotta have it. The fifty dollars. I need it to

save my homestead. They're gonna throw me out on the dusty road. You can't do this to me.

BESS.   Honey, I'd rip the wings off an angel if I thought they'd help me fly. *(Bess leaves the cabin and goes out into the yard. Macon follows her.)*

MACON.   You owe me! I'm due! You can't deny me what's mine! I gave you green biscuits; I combed your hair; I taught you to whistle!

ELMORE.   Are you ready?

BESS.   Yeah.

ELMORE.   Did you read the contract?

BESS.   They want me to demand the immediate extermination of all Indian tribes.

ELMORE.   That's correct.

BESS.   I got no problem with that. Just make sure wherever we go I have a basket of golden tulips to greet me. They're my favorite flower, tulips. *(Bess and Elmore exit as Macon screams after them.)*

MACON.   You thief! Robber — thief! Tulips are mine! They belong to me! I seen the picture! You never did! *(Will enters wearing his eye patch and carrying a satchel.)* God, Will. God. She wouldn't give me the money. She wouldn't give me nothing. She owes me, too. She knows she does. I was her friend. God, I'd like to kill her. I'd like to tear off her head and feed her brains to rabid rats. The selfish, back-biting, stuck-up, black-hearted Indian whore!

WILL.   Macon, I'm leaving here. I'm heading west.

MACON.   West? Where west?

WILL.   Don't know.

MACON.   Maybe we'll try Idaho. They got that Turkey red wheat in Idaho. It's a hard-kernelded wheat. You can grow it all spring.

WILL.   I don't want you with me.

MACON.   What?

WILL.   My first wife, Barbara Jane, well, I loved her. And I remember she loved me. But you never loved me and I never loved you. That's all it's been. I don't want it no more.

MACON.   You leaving me here? With nothing?

WILL. This is yours. Catch. *(Will throws her his glass eye. She catches it.)* I bought it for you. It never done me no good. *(Will exits. Macon paces around the yard tossing the glass eye back and forth, from hand to hand.)*
MACON. I got nothing. Nothing. After all this time. *(A beat.)* Nothing.

End of Scene 6

Scene 7

Fifteen years later.

A hotel suite in St. Louis. Bess drinks a glass of whiskey. Elmore holds a copy of the St. Louis Chronicle.

ELMORE. Are you sure you want to hear this?
BESS. Uh huh.
ELMORE. It's not very good.
BESS. That seems to be the trend.
ELMORE. It's appallingly written.
BESS. Go ahead, Elmore, it's the last one I'll ever get.
ELMORE. The St. Louis *Chronicle* says, "Mrs. Bess Johnson delivered her speech with impassioned fervor. However, the story seemed excessive and outdated like a worn-out melodrama one would read in a dime novel. The text lacked all orderly progressions and seemed to ramble and roam incoherently, as though perhaps Mrs. Johnson had had a drop too many."
BESS. A drop too many! They can't actually expect me to deliver those speeches sans intoxication. What a tight-lipped powder puff. What a worm-ridden toad.
ELMORE. *(Folding up the paper.)* Yes, well, let's put it away.
BESS. God. I can't tell you what a relief it will be to never again to have to rhapsodize about writing with fish blood and being scantily-clad in a thin bark skirt.
ELMORE. Yes. I'm well aware we have played ourselves out. People are no longer interested in hearing about the untamed

savages. Times have changed. Indians today are beloved circus performers. Yesterday, I read in a broadside that they finally arrested your old friend, Ottowa, down by the Pecos River. They'd been hunting him for years. He was the last holdout. The lone one.

BESS. Ottowa, I didn't know he was still alive.

ELMORE. He's not. He drank a lantern of kerosene the night they captured him.

BESS. Oh.

ELMORE. *(Presenting her with contracts.)* Well, here are the final papers disbanding our long and lucrative union. They're all in order. You'll find everything's as we discussed.

BESS. I'm sure they are. I'll just have my attorneys read it over before I sign it.

ELMORE. I admire your consistency, Bess. All these years and you've never trusted me once.

BESS. Sorry, Elmore. I tried that. It never really worked out for me, *(Jack enters smoking a large black cigar. He is dressed dapperly.)*

JACK. 'Afternoon.

ELMORE. Hello, Jack.

BESS. What's that awful thing?

JACK. A ten cent cigar. I won it betting on the comic mule races down at the tent show.

ELMORE. Ah, yes, how was the tent show?

JACK. Pathetic, small town dredge. The freaks were even third rate: armless boy; electric girl; skeleton dude. Oh, but you'll never guess who I ran into. What's her name? We used to know her back when. Her husband wore an eye patch.

BESS. Macon?

JACK. Yes, I think that was it.

BESS. Macon Hill.

JACK. You should see her. Disgusting. She's got some syphilitic disease. It's broken out all over her face. She was working at a little booth dispensing whiskey and tobacco and raisins. I bought some raisins from her. She didn't recognize me. I had to laugh when I saw she had newspaper stuck in her clothes to stay warm. I remember her always thinking she had it so good.

BESS. Your cigar is foul. Put it out. Get it out. *(Jack puts out the cigar.)* God, you're an imbecile. Coming in here, filling the room with your vile smoke. You've given me a sick head. I'm going out for some air. Clear out this room before I get back. *(Bess exits.)*

JACK. Christ, why am I ever nice to that woman? You're lucky you're getting out from under her. I'm stuck with her for life. Tomorrow we leave for our White Plains estate. We'll retire there together till the end of our days. What will it be like?

ELMORE. She can be difficult. But I think, underneath it all, she has real affection for you.

JACK. You think she does?

ELMORE. It's the sort of thing that's only apparent to an outsider.

JACK. Well, I'll say one thing, she'll never find anyone who'll treat her better than I do. She oughta know that by now. I'm her one true one.

End of Scene 7

Scene 8

A few hours later. Early evening.

Macon's tent. Macon sits alone in the dimly lit tent drinking and playing solitaire. There are sores on her face.

BESS. *(Offstage.)* Hello? Anybody here?
MACON. Yeah. *(Bess enters.)*
BESS. Macon?
MACON. Bess?
BESS. I heard you were here.
MACON. Jack tell you?
BESS. Yeah.
MACON. I seen him this afternoon. He bought some raisins.

262

He wouldn't speak to me though.

BESS. Well, you know him.

MACON. Yeah. Why'd you come?

BESS. I — don't know. I was — remembering ...

MACON. Uh huh.

BESS. So much.

MACON. Well.

BESS. How you been?

MACON. Great. Just great. Yeah, for a time I was raking in the green selling this Indian Remedy. A cure for your opium, morphine, liquor and tobacco habit. Hell of a cure it was, too. Then I got this stuff coming out on my face and people kinda eased off on purchasing the cure. But for a time there, I was flush. How 'bout you?

BESS. I don't know. Maybe other people's lives have made more sense than mine.

MACON. It's always a possibility.

BESS. Oh, well. There it is, I guess.

MACON. Yeah, laid right out behind you like a lizard's tail.

BESS. Today I — Well, today I heard that Ottowa, the head man — my husband, was captured. He, ah, poisoned himself on a lantern of kerosene. I don't know why, but it's hard. I'd always thought I might — but now I won't — ever see him once more.

MACON. It's a shame how things turn out. I swear to God, I wish I knew how it could be different.

BESS. Uh huh. Me too.

MACON. 'Least ya got out there and saw the elephant.

BESS. Yeah. Yeah, the Oglalas knew such beautiful places. I saw rivers that were so clear you could see every pebble and fish. And the water was any color you could dream: pink and turquoise; gold and white; lime green.

MACON. Hell of a time you had with the Oglalas.

BESS. Beautiful time I had. Hey, you ever hear from Will Curtis?

MACON. Nah. Will got caught in a threshing machine back in '87. Got his leg cut off in the blade. Bled t'death in a field. Funny, I always figured he'd go piecemeal.

263

BESS. Yeah.

MACON. You know, when I was younger, I never knew who I was, what I wanted, where I was going or how to get there. Now that I'm older, I don't know none of that either.

BESS. Well, one thing I wanted, one thing I know I wanted was, well, I don't know, I guess you'd call it true love. And when I got them three letters from that man, that man, Michael Flan, who wrote to me about the size of the sky, I thought it was all right there, all within my grasp and all I had t'do was come out west and there it'd be.

MACON. Thought you'd just reach up and touch it like a star.

BESS. Yeah. Thought I might. *(Bess reaches her hand up as if she were grabbing a star.)* Aah!

MACON. Feel a chill?

BESS. Just a small one.

MACON. Bess?

BESS. Huh.

MACON. I, well, I've had a bad pain in my heart all day today. I'm scared and it troubles me, but I expect I'll die soon.

BESS. ... What can I do?

MACON. Nothing t'do. I just wanted somebody t'tell, that's all. Someone to tell.

BESS. Well, you can tell me.

MACON. There ain't much t'tell.

BESS. Maybe not, but I'm glad you looked my way.

MACON. Uh huh. Well. Yeah.

BESS. Hey, do you still whistle?

MACON. Me? I — God — I — *(Then definitely.)* No. *(A long beat, then Macon whistles a tune, Bess whistles back. The women both laugh from deep in the bottom of their hearts. The lights fade to blackout.)*

END OF PLAY